1912

Professor Chris Turney is an Australian and British Earth scientist, and an ARC Laureate Fellow in climate change at the University of New South Wales. He is the author of *Ice, Mud and Blood: Lessons from Climates Past* and *Bones, Rocks and Stars: The Science of When Things Happened*, as well as numerous scientific papers and magazine articles. In 2007 he was awarded the Sir Nicholas Shackleton Medal for outstanding young Quaternary scientists, and in 2009 he received the Geological Society of London's Bigsby Medal for services to geology.

www.christurney.com

CHRIS TURNEY

1912

THE YEAR THE
WORLD DISCOVERED
ANTARCTICA

COUNTERPOINT

BERKELEY, CALIFORNIA

Copyright © Chris Turney 2012
Maps copyright © Elaine Nipper 2012

Photo of British expedition member and dog driver Anton Omelchenko below the Barne Glacier (Mount Erebus, Ross Island), December 1911, by Herbert Ponting, courtesy of the Scott Polar Research Institute (P2005/5/647); photo of king penguin, South Georgia, 2011, by Chris Turney; photo of Chris Turney in 1912 explorer gear © John Murray / Crossing the Line Films

Cover design by WH Chong. Text design by WH Chong & Imogen Stubbs. Typeset by J&M Typesetting.
Printed in the United States of America.

Library of Congress Cataloging-in-Publication Data is available.
ISBN 978-1-58243-789-7

COUNTERPOINT
1919 Fifth Street
Berkeley, CA 94710
www.counterpointpress.com

Distributed by Publishers Group West

1 3 5 7 9 10 8 6 4 2

To my grandparents Jim and Bunty,
whose hard work and tales of adventure
continue to inspire me

CONTENTS

INTRODUCTION 1

CHAPTER 1: Looking Polewards 7
Early Ventures South

CHAPTER 2: An Audacious Plan 35
Ernest Shackleton and the British Antarctic Expedition, 1907–1909

CHAPTER 3: A New Land 71
Robert Scott and the Terra Nova *Expedition, 1910–1913*

CHAPTER 4: Of Reindeer, Ponies and Automobiles 105
Roald Amundsen and the Norwegian Bid
for the South Pole, 1910–1912

CHAPTER 5: The Dash Patrol 143
Nobu Shirase and the Japanese South Polar Expedition, 1910–1912

CHAPTER 6: Locked In 177
Wilhelm Filchner and the Second German
Antarctic Expedition, 1911–1912

CHAPTER 7: Ice-cold in Denison 213
Douglas Mawson and the Australasian Antarctic Expedition, 1911–1913

CHAPTER 8: Martyrs to Gondwanaland 259
The Cost of Scientific Exploration

POSTSCRIPT 295

APPENDIX: Lord Curzon's Notes 303

ACKNOWLEDGEMENTS 309

SOURCES 313

INDEX 345

INTRODUCTION

---

*People, perhaps, still exist who believe that it is of no importance
to explore the unknown polar regions. This, of course, shows
ignorance. It is hardly necessary to mention here of what scientific
importance it is that these regions should be thoroughly explored.*

FRIDTJOF NANSEN (1861–1930)

It's early January 2011 and I'm sitting in a four-engine Iluyshin
transporter plane ten thousand metres above the Southern
Ocean, heading towards one of the Earth's most remote places.
The cabin is packed with fifty-odd passengers, fuel, equipment
and the most eclectic range of clothing I've ever seen—multi-
coloured jackets, salopettes, and gloves and hats of all shapes
and sizes, in anticipation of sub-freezing temperatures. Unlike
most of my fellow travellers, who are heading off for a couple of
weeks of climbing, skiing or kiting over ice and snow, I'm about
to fulfil a lifelong dream: to research the geological and climatic
history of a remarkable part of the world.

A few hours earlier we were standing on an airstrip in the
relatively balmy city of Punta Arenas, in southern Chile, threatening to break out in a sweat. Now we're hurtling along in
what feels like an oversized Soviet coffin and about to land on a
worryingly narrow strip of ice. The pitch of the engine suddenly

changes, and we know we're getting close. We take our seats, necks craned to see the fast-approaching mountains and snow.

A slight bounce and we're down on an ice runway at a frigid 79° South. The engines drop to a low whine and we taxi to two blue containers that mark the Union Glacier airbase, our new home. The rear cargo doors open up: brilliant light and freezing air pour into the hold. There's a collective intake of breath. We're in Antarctica, and all it took was four hours.

———•———

In 1897 an exasperated John Campbell, Duke of Argyll, declared in London, a 'very large area of the surface of our small planet is still almost unknown to us. That it should be so seems almost a reproach to our civilisation.' Atlases at the turn of the century only hinted at what lay at the end of a world populated by one and a half billion people. Almost everything south of 50° was described as an Unexplored Region and the vast space left embarrassingly empty.

The dawn of the modern age saw major advances in science, technology, engineering, social reform and politics. Nations were talking to one another with a new confidence, and the world suddenly seemed smaller. And yet, despite the progress made during the Victorian era, the uncertainty over what lay south grated. When the Edwardian world looked to the other side of the planet, it did not know what was there.

While the likes of David Livingstone, Alexander von Humboldt and John Hanning Speke had blazed a trail through Africa and the New World, reaching ever further inland and becoming household names in the process, few western explorers had ventured to the Antarctic Circle. Little was known about it, beyond hearsay: it was a region of wilderness and extremes, of rough and icy seas that took ships on a mere whim, of wild animals in the depths. Imagination and fancy filled any disagreeable gaps in knowledge, for only a handful of adventurers had penetrated this inhospitable region and returned to tell a plausible tale. The Antarctic remained stubbornly off the map, save for a smattering of islands and disconnected coastlines—many of them considered highly suspect—peppering a swathe of white.

Never has a continent been more misunderstood. Antarctica is on a scale hard to grasp: at over fourteen million square kilometres, it is second only to Russia in coverage of the Earth's surface and bigger than all the countries of Europe combined. It is the world's highest continent, with an average altitude of 2300 metres. It contains more than seventy per cent of the world's freshwater, locked up as thirty million cubic kilometres of snow and ice—which, if melted, would raise the planet's seas by an estimated sixty-five metres, easily flooding the likes of Sydney, London and New York. The bitterly cold air on its upper surface contains virtually no moisture, making the Antarctic interior the world's largest desert, while the rocks that make up the rest of the continent span almost the entire age of the Earth. The wildlife along its fringes is some of the most diverse on the planet.

Yet its human history is short: Antarctica was the last continent to be discovered and explored. We have only ventured there in the past two centuries. Land was sighted for the first time in 1820, landfall was made in 1821 and people stayed for their first winter in 1899. Even the Ellsworth Mountains, where I was working in early 2011, were not explored properly until the 1960s.

In ancient times the Greeks believed there must be a land in the south to counterbalance the Arctic. They coined the word *Antarktikos*, 'Opposite the Bear', referring to the constellation Ursa Major, the Great Bear, which hung over the northern sky.

When Antarctica was finally discovered, explorers commonly made comparisons to the polar north—often with disastrous consequences for their expeditions. Over time, as scientific methods became established, a unique land of ice, snow and rock revealed itself. By the turn of the twentieth century enough information had been pieced together to suggest a continent lay in these polar waters. Reports were made of seemingly endless coastlines, of isolated mountain ranges and volcanoes, of ice shelves and glacier tongues that jutted tens of kilometres into the Southern Ocean. Here was a new frontier, a continent untouched by humankind, waiting to be explored—and claimed.

Disparate groups of would-be explorers, scientists and cartographers were soon dispatched south, to see what else might be down there. The early twentieth century's Heroic Age of Antarctic Exploration was born. But explorers did not battle sub-zero temperatures and ice-scarred landscapes just to conquer land, bag a pole or grow an impressive beard. These expeditionary teams—even those intent on scoring a geographical first—went south to scientifically explore the new continent. The pursuit of glory was not enough: a scientific case had to be made to national academies and societies, to ensure the financial support the expeditions so desperately needed. The explorers wanted to understand what made Antarctica tick, and set off intending to bring back sledge-loads of rocks, plant and animal remains, and measurements of the air, snow and ice.

By 1912 five national teams, representing the old and new worlds, were diligently venturing beyond the edge of the known world. Although the British expedition led by Captain Robert Falcon Scott and Roald Amundsen's Norwegian effort are the best known today, there were others: Nobu Shirase for Japan, Wilhelm Filchner for Germany, and Douglas Mawson for Australia and New Zealand. Their discoveries not only enthralled the world: they changed our understanding of the planet. During this one year, at the height of the Heroic Age of Antarctic Exploration, the door to Antarctica was flung open. A frozen continent shaped by climatic extremes, and inhabited by wildlife and vegetation hitherto unknown to science, was uncovered. Feats of endurance, self-sacrifice and technological innovation laid the foundations for contemporary scientific exploration.

Regaled with tales of derring-do, the public became excited by what was being discovered in Antarctica. The expeditions of 1912 went to great lengths to publicise their findings through books, lecture tours, newspaper articles and interviews, records, radio and films—all were used as widely as possible, with varying degrees of success. The blend of research and exploration was a high point in science communication, as the different Antarctic teams strove to enthral and educate those at home.

Over the following decades, though, the tragic events of the era came to overshadow the amazing work accomplished, and much of this work was forgotten outside the small Antarctic scientific community. By drawing on my own experiences in the south and the rich source material from the time, I hope to illustrate why the centenary of this scientific exploration is worth celebrating, and how 1912 heralded the dawn of a new age in our understanding of the natural world.

CHAPTER 1

LOOKING POLEWARDS

Early Ventures South

No man will be a sailor who had contrivance enough to get himself into a jail; for being in a ship is being in a jail, with the chance of being drowned…A man in a jail has more room, better food, and commonly better company.

SAMUEL JOHNSON (1709–1784)

In 1520 the explorer Ferdinand Magellan was one year into his quest to find a westward route from the Atlantic to the Spice Islands of the western Pacific. The expedition to the Indonesian islands known today as the Moluccas was funded by the Spanish, in an attempt to break Venice's stranglehold on the lucrative European spice trade. Leading a Spanish-financed and -crewed expedition was a major undertaking for the Portuguese captain. Not only had he lost a ship, dashed against the rocks while surveying, but he was constantly staving off the threat of mutiny. Reaching 53°S off the southeast coast of South America, Magellan found a passage that he hoped would allow his four wooden vessels to sail to the other side of the Americas.

Magellan's crew were not thrilled to find themselves beating a path down the 570-kilometre-long strait. Their journey was arduous: wild seas and 'williwaw' winds roared off the land, a ship was lost through desertion, and fire-loving locals came perilously close to attacking. Thirty-eight days later, though, the three surviving ships reached the other side of the Americas having negotiated a passage through the 'Land of Fire', Tierra del Fuego. The strain was almost too much for Magellan, who reputedly broke down and cried: against tremendous odds he had sailed across the Atlantic Ocean and into the relatively peaceful Pacific.

From a survivor's account of the voyage, the world learned that the Strait of Magellan is 'surrounded by very great and high mountains covered with snow'. Magellan's travels appeared to confirm the existence of the mythical continent on the southern side of the strait, *Antarktikos*—or, as it later became known, *Terra Australis Incognita*, the 'Unknown South Land'. However, the great navigator did not live to enjoy the fame his discoveries brought, dying—as did most members of the expedition—on the way back to Spain.

Tales of what lay to the south had fascinated ancient and medieval Europe. Stories were told of Prester John, a Christian king who ruled over a fantastical country surrounded by pagan states in the Far East, and within which four rivers of Paradise flowed from an inaccessible mountain of great height at the centre. For centuries speculation about the south continued, untroubled by evidence.

The sixteenth century saw expeditions geared for trade and territorial expansion ploughing new routes into the Southern Ocean. Magellan provided the first point on the map, and cartographers around the world enthusiastically incorporated his discoveries. *Terra Australis Incognita* was an ideal home for the undiscovered Christian country and, using stories of Prester John and others, mapmakers prepared frighteningly detailed charts of the supercontinent's alleged coastline and vast interior. This fantasy persisted over the next hundred years or so, connecting the southern part of Tierra del Fuego, northern Australia and sometimes even Indonesia.

Half a century after Magellan discovered the strait that bears his name, an English adventurer stumbled on the fact that something was amiss. Sir Francis Drake is best known today for playing bowls when the Spanish Armada sought to invade England during the heady summer of 1588, but a decade earlier he was halfway to emulating Magellan's achievement of circumnavigating the globe, and this time surviving. Drake had steered through the strait in a swift seventeen days, and with a happier crew than his unfortunate predecessor, before a huge northwesterly gale blew up. He was pushed back around the tip of South America, considerably further south than anticipated. Where *Terra Australis Incognita* should have been, there was just sea: the great continent in the south was, it seemed, a lot smaller than most had imagined.

Competition in the Netherlands soon led to a spate of discoveries. With the Dutch East India Company holding a strictly enforced monopoly on the only known trade routes of the time, the Strait of Magellan and the south African Cape of Good Hope, other explorers set out to search for an alternative trade route: a Southwest Passage. In 1599 ships in a small Dutch fleet searching off the South American coast for this fabled path became separated, and the Dutch captain Dirk Gerritsz of the *Blijde Boodschap* reportedly found himself at 64°S, where he saw a land of high mountains covered in snow, 'like Norway'. No one knew what to do with this finding, and it was largely dismissed. However, another expedition, led by Jacob Le Maire and Willem Schouten, was not so easy to ignore. In 1616 the two Dutchmen showed it was possible to sail around Tierra del Fuego, and in doing so discovered a mountainous land in the fog that appeared to be a peninsula. This Staten Land seemed to confirm Drake's discovery, and it pushed the northern coastline of *Terra Australis Incognita* further south.

These discoveries took some time to filter through. Explorers and cartographers were reluctant to give up on the idea of a southern landmass, and they continued to join up small pockets of land across vast areas of the southern hemisphere, desperate to make sense of what lay there. A classic example is the Dutchman Abel Tasman, who in 1642 became the first European to sail along the southern coast of Australia, discovering Tasmania in the process. On reaching what we know as New Zealand, Tasman proclaimed his find Staten Land, believing it was connected to the same landmass his compatriots had seen in 1616. The following year the South Atlantic Staten Land was found to be just a small island with plenty more sea to the south. The supposed southern continent was becoming ever smaller.

With unsubstantiated reports and wild rumour continuing to emanate from the south, one of the greatest explorers came to the fore. Captain James Cook was appointed by the oldest scientific society in the world, the prestigious Royal Society in London, to make a thorough search for *Terra Australis Incognita*. On his first voyage he had sailed around New Zealand and shown there was yet more sea polewards. On his second Pacific expedition, between 1772 and 1775, Cook took the *HMS Resolution* further south, probing for a route through the sea ice and bergs. He was hundreds of kilometres inside the Antarctic Circle—and decades ahead of his time. Cooped up for months on a small wooden vessel dwarfed by towering icebergs that seemed to fill the ocean, Cook and the crew were increasingly on edge. Eventually it was too much: having reached 71°S, Cook turned the *Resolution* and headed for home.

Having worked his way through the icebergs and circumnavigating Antarctica without seeing it, Cook returned to Britain with tales of new islands and large seal colonies, pack ice and freezing conditions in the Southern Ocean. His achievement attracted attention around the world. At most longitudes, Cook's record southern latitude is actually part of the Antarctic continent. Cook had pushed the limits of his craft—and men— as far as possible, but was in the wrong area to see any land; he was desperately unlucky not to discover Antarctica.

In 1777 he wrote: 'I strongly believe that there does exist land close to the Pole, from which must proceed the greater part of the ice which we find spread across this vast southern ocean... It would have been folly on my part to risk all we had achieved on this voyage merely for the sake of discovering and exploring a coast which, once discovered and explored, would have proved useful neither to navigation, nor to geography, nor, in truth, to any other science.' He went on: 'Should anyone possess the reso- lution and fortitude to [push] yet further south...I make bold to declare that the world will derive no benefit from it.'

In Cook's view, even if *Terra Australis Incognita* was there, it was of little significance. But not everyone agreed.

————◆————

Cook's report of abundant marine life in the freezing polar waters of the southern hemisphere whipped sealers and whalers into a frenzy. The world was hungry for fur and oil, and the North Atlantic could not keep up with demand. Soon fleets of vessels rushed south to mine what seemed an inexhaustible resource. In their enthusiasm to head south, the hunters often reached unexplored areas years before scientific expeditions. For most, this was a commercial exercise: many took the view that science had little, if any, role to play in their operations. The locations of rich pickings were jealously guarded; ships' routes were left deliberately vague, for fear of giving away lucrative spots on an otherwise blank map. Fantastic stories, no doubt sometimes embellished to draw competitors away from rich seal colonies, were retailed. Yet with the push south there came a series of discoveries that restored some faith in the idea of a southern continent.

One of the first significant finds was made by a British captain, William Smith, who was exploring the seas around South America in his brig, the *Williams*, in February 1819. Blown off course by the region's now-infamous strong winds, Smith found himself far south of Cape Horn and alongside a small cluster of ice-covered islands, which he called New South Shetland. He returned to the islands that October and, finding a landing place, took possession of the land for his monarch, King George III, before heading to Valparaíso, on the Chilean coast, where stories of what he had found soon circulated among sealers.

The British captain tried to convince the Royal Navy officials in Chile of his discovery but they were suspicious of the claims. Nevertheless, Smith and his ship were put under the command of a young naval officer, Edward Bransfield, and sent back south. By January 1820 they reached the islands Smith had claimed and planted the British flag again, this time officially. At the end of the month they probed further south, and at 64°S spotted land. It was late in the summer and the weather was poor—'the most gloomy that could be imagined,' one of the men aboard reported, 'and the only cheer the sight afforded was in the idea that this might be the long sought Southern Continent...The land [was named] Trinity Land in compliment to the Trinity Board.'

Word of Smith and Bransfield's find got out, and suddenly everyone seemed to be discovering parts of *Terra Australia Incognita*. Americans, Russians, British, Norwegians and Australians began tripping over one another to find new seal colonies in the icy southern Atlantic. A Russian explorer, Fabian Gottlieb von Bellingshausen, recorded a sighting of land at 69°S, laying claim to being the first person to see the Antarctic continent. Then, a year after Smith returned from

Trinity Land, the American sealing captain Nathaniel Palmer reported having seen, independently, the same piece of ground as his British counterpart. Discoveries were a source of national pride as ever more finds were made in this new part of the world. And yet, perversely, the next notable revelation had little to do with land.

In 1823 the British sealer James Weddell was commanding two 'small, insignificant' ships, the *Jane* and *Beaufoy*, in the search for seals to the immediate east of William Smith's route to the south. Others who had been in the region had complained bitterly of impregnable, ice-covered ocean. Like Cook, Weddell was way ahead of his time. Keen to mix science with business, he reported a series of observations while exploring, including the temperature of the ocean, the geology of the islands he visited en route and the wildlife he saw—all with accurate geographical fixes. Pushing as far as his supplies would allow, Weddell reached a latitude of 74°15'S and declared this the Sea of George the Fourth.

Not only was this the furthest south achieved in the South Atlantic—a feat that remained unsurpassed until 1912—it was the furthest south reached anywhere. Most importantly, Weddell had found no land. Realising his discovery might provoke controversy back home, on his return Weddell had his chief officer and seamen swear to the accuracy of the log before naval officials. He believed that sea ice was only formed in the vicinity of land and, as none had been found within 20° of his furthest south, there was most probably an open ocean all the way to the South Geographic Pole. His discovery and its implications constituted a case against an ice-covered *Terra Australis Incognita*. But, with later explorers finding the Sea of George the Fourth choked with ice, and reports of coastline in other parts—albeit not so far south—Weddell's claims were openly questioned. The British captain had been extremely lucky: it was not until the 1960s that the sea he found would be so clear of ice again.

Unfortunately for Weddell, his trip was not as lucrative as his employers had hoped, and once home he was cited for a debt of £245, lent by the Commercial Bank in Edinburgh. This was probably the cost associated with Weddell's scientific equipment, and his ship owners washed their hands of him. He fled just before he was due to collect a prestigious fellowship of the Royal Society of Edinburgh from the illustrious Sir Walter Scott. The British authorities remained sceptical of the explorer, and it was only in 1904 that a German geographer suggested the body of water be named the Weddell Sea in honour of the great pioneer.

———•———

James Weddell championed the idea of sailing directly to the bottom of the world, but it was the search for a different pole that had piqued the interest of most scientists and the public during the seventeenth and eighteenth centuries. Although the geographic poles mark the location on the surface of the Earth around which the axis of our planet rotates, there are many others. There is a pole for the greatest distance from a coast (the Pole of Inaccessibility), one for the most frigid place (Cold) and even one for the spot with the greatest range in atmospheric pressure (Variability). In Weddell's time it was the magnetic version that fascinated. Spurred on by the British Royal Navy's desire to understand how the world's compasses might be better used, science gained equal footing with exploration, and became less dependent on enthusiastic amateurs and haughty employers.

The eleventh-century Chinese discovery that the mineral lodestone would naturally point north–south if freely suspended had led to the development of compasses that enabled naviga-tors to plan and explore routes around the world with increased confidence and safety. But navigating by compass was not fool-proof. Over time compasses subtly changed the direction in which they pointed; and the further you went polewards, the more erratic they seemed to become. For a country such as Britain, dependent on ships for trade and military muscle, the situation was serious: a drifting pole could become a hazard for ships.

New data was needed, to test the scientific community's understanding of the planet's magnetism and exploit it. More accurate hydrographic surveys and maps showing magnetic field irregularities would improve the accuracy of navigation, reducing passage times and preventing disaster—and helping in sovereignty claims. The pressure for this data only increased with the shift from wooden craft to metal shipping, further distorting the magnetic signal.

The first to raise the issue was Robert Norman, who in 1581 published a book called *The New Attractive* after he became frustrated at the way compass needles would incline below the 'plaine of the horizon': no matter how carefully he prepared his needles in London, once they were magnetised the north-facing part would dip without fail. Norman found he had to snip the end off the north-seeking part of his needles, thereby allowing them to balance on the pivot. He went on to measure this effect by setting up a magnetised needle vertically and reading the angle of magnetic dip. His dipping needle showed they always pointed to 72°. Norman felt it was something inherent to the needles themselves.

In 1600 Queen Elizabeth I's physician and scientist, William Gilbert, proposed a different, revolutionary idea. It was not the needles themselves that caused the dip, Gilbert argued. Instead, the phenomenon could best be explained if the planet had some-thing akin to a powerful bar magnet inside it. Gilbert did not understand the cause, but we now know the magnetic field is produced by a solid inner iron core surrounded by fluid iron. It is this outer part that acts like a spinning conductor in a bicycle dynamo. Rather than frantically peddling, though, the Earth's system is run by heat from the decay of radioactive elements left over from our planet's formation. The resulting swirling molten iron in the outer core is electrically charged, creating a continuously changing electromagnetic field.

The upshot of all this is that a freely hanging magnetised needle will align itself to the line of magnetic force. Scatter iron filings on a sheet of paper covering a bar magnet and the filings will rapidly align themselves to the magnetic field, tracing a semicircle of iron around the bar, connecting the poles at either end. Depending where on the Earth's surface you stand, the strength and direction of the horizontal and vertical parts of the magnetic field will vary. In the tropics the horizontal force dominates the magnetic field, so a needle will tend to sit parallel to the surface. But, as Robert Norman found, approaching polar regions the amount of dip increases as the field sweeps around the Earth and returns to the magnetic poles. As a result, a needle in their vicinity will approach a more vertical position. Norman's dipping compass enabled people to measure the vertical part of the field, and it could also be an asset for navigation, providing a measure of latitude and, ultimately, proximity to a magnetic pole.

The magnetic core is tilted at a slight angle off the axis of our planet's rotation, by some 11°. However, although a bar magnet in the Earth is a great concept, it is only an approximation of what is going on under our feet. Swirling molten currents, the magnetism of surrounding rocks and changes in the sun's activity all complicate this notion of a simple magnetic field. The result is one of the more perplexing concepts in Earth science: the presence of two different types of magnetic poles in each hemisphere. The better-known magnetic poles are where the field dips at right angles to the surface, while the geomagnetic poles are the theoretical locations for the axis of the Earth's magnetic field if it did truly work like a bar magnet, as William Gilbert envisaged. In each hemisphere these poles are more than a thousand kilometres apart, and over time change their absolute and relative positions to one another as they move across the surface.

Over the next century it was realised that the lines of equal magnetic force were not evenly distributed around the world. An alliance between the Royal Navy and the Royal Society sought to solve this conundrum. In 1693 grandiose plans were made for a purpose-built vessel, *HMS Paramore*, to investigate these magnetic variations on the world's first scientific voyage. Its leader was to be a civilian, the polymath Edmund Halley, remembered today mainly for the comet whose path he predicted. Since his schooldays Halley had been interested in the Earth's magnetism and, having gathered together the limited observations made around the known world, he proposed that the magnetic field was not stable but in fact slowly drifting westwards. To account for these observations, Halley imagined an Earth made up of four magnetic poles, with two in each hemisphere. The *Paramore* would test these ideas by direct measurement. If he had time, Halley would also look for the coastline of *Terra Australis Incognita*.

Halley left Britain in October 1698, only to have a spectacular falling out with an officer on board who repeatedly criticised his handling of the ship in front of the crew. The *Paramore* ignominiously returned to Britain in June 1699, its mission barely started. Halley set out again, this time without the surly officer, and the expedition reached the edge of the Antarctic region at 52°S in the South Atlantic on 1 February 1700. Halley did not see land but spotted his first 'islands of ice'. Thinking at first it was 'land with chaulky cliffs and the topp all covered with snow', he realised his mistake when the *Paramore* managed to heave to and he

discovered there was a real risk of becoming trapped among the
bergs. Halley beat a hasty retreat north. On his return to Britain,
he published his measurements of the magnetic field, and showed
that in the North Atlantic compasses did not point true north.
The geographic and magnetic poles were not one and the same.

Halley never got close to either of the magnetic poles. If he
had, he would have quickly become aware of huge swings, often
daily, in their locations. This was first remarked upon by the
London scientific watch and compass maker George Graham in
the early eighteenth century. Graham took more than a thousand observations in 1722, reporting to the Royal Society that
he had found a rhythm in the number of times his compass
needles swung back and forth each day, with the greatest change
taking place between noon and four in the afternoon.

Halley's and Graham's results showed there was considerably more to the Earth's magnetism than first thought, and
that the problem could not be solved piecemeal. By the nineteenth century, scientists set out to make a more systematic
study by undertaking simultaneous measurements of the Earth's
magnetic properties. At one of those rare moments when
European nations were not fighting, the German scientist and
mathematician Carl Friedrich Gauss persuaded observatories
across Europe and Asia to collaborate in his Magnetic Union.
By 1834 there were twenty-three stations measuring data on the
strength of the magnetic field, the direction of compass readings and other parameters, all using Gauss's instruments, which
allowed the results to be directly compared. The subsequent
Magnetic Crusade established a network of British-run stations
around the world. Soon an array of global observers was taking
synchronised measurements.

To help make sense of the observations being patiently
collected and to test mathematical models of the planet's
magnetic field, it was critical that the surface locations of the

magnetic poles were known. In 1831 the naval officer James Clark Ross led the British effort north by sledging out from his ice-bound ship, *HMS Victory*; after several weeks travelling with Inuit companions he succeeded in finding his compass needle sitting upright. He had reached the North Magnetic Pole. Impressed by Ross's heroics, the Royal Society in 1839 convinced the Navy to send him with two vessels, *HMS Erebus* and *Terror*, to reach its southern counterpart. These forerunners of battleships, designed to bombard targets on land, were heavily reinforced: ideal, reasoned the Royal Navy, for forcing their way through any offending sea ice.

No one knew whether the pole lay on land or sea. After reading of Weddell's travels, Ross favoured the latter.

As Ross headed polewards two other nations were also seeking to reach the South Magnetic Pole and plant their flags on any Antarctic land they might find. A French expedition of two ships set out in 1837, led by the wonderfully named Jules-Sébastien-César Dumont d'Urville, while an American circumnavigation attempt commanded by Charles Wilkes sallied forth in August 1838 with four vessels. Neither made it to the South Magnetic Pole; but by the time Ross reached Hobart he knew of the French and American expeditions. Determined to take another route to the pole, Ross struck out due south from the Tasmanian capital in November 1840, taking with him the young Joseph Hooker as ship's surgeon and part-time scientist. Ross made good progress and, on reaching the pack ice in the early new year, decided to plough the *Erebus* and *Terror* headlong under sail. The experience prematurely aged him—and no doubt many of his crew—yet his luck held. After only four days, Ross's confidence in his ships' ability to survive the pounding of ice was rewarded when the expedition reached open water.

To find the South Magnetic Pole, Ross had an instrument similar to Norman's dipping compass called a Fox Dip Circle, which allowed the dip and strength of the magnetic field to be measured at sea. Some years earlier the British explorer Matthew Flinders, while surveying the Australian coast, had demonstrated that by 'swinging' the ship through the thirty points of the compass and taking magnetic measurements at anchor, he could account for any interference from iron aboard the vessel. The ever-present icebergs made this a risky business—and yet, as Ross pushed on, the average readings did indeed show the Fox dipping needle was moving ever closer to the vertical; he was tantalisingly close to the magnetic pole. But, just as it seemed the explorer was to be rewarded for his bravery, Ross met a vista of mountains, preventing further progress. He claimed this new panorama for Britain and named it Victoria Land, after his monarch. Ross calculated the South Magnetic Pole lay eight hundred kilometres southwest inland: somewhere not even the *Erebus* or *Terror* could go.

Hoping he might yet find an ocean route to the magnetic pole, Ross followed the mountainous coastline away to the south. After sixteen days he reached 78°10'S, beating Weddell's furthest south, but found the expedition path blocked again, this time by what Hooker described as 'a fine volcano spouting fire and smoke'. They had stumbled upon the southernmost active volcano in the world, Mount Erebus, atop Ross Island. To the west was a relatively sheltered anchorage, McMurdo Sound, named after a lieutenant on the *Terror*—but to the east was something unknown to science. Ross wrote that he had discovered 'a perpendicular cliff of ice between one hundred and fifty and two hundred feet [forty-five and sixty metres] above...the sea, perfectly flat and level on top, and without any fissures or promontories on even its seaward face'. Perhaps

inspired by Matthew Flinders's Great Barrier Reef, Ross named
his discovery the Great Ice Barrier. Now known as the Ross Ice
Shelf, this new find lived up to its original moniker: the ice cliff
extended over 720 kilometres to the east and, save for a small
bay filled with whales, offered no ready features or way through.
Disappointed, Ross could go no further, and he turned his
vessels north for home.

International interest continued in the polar regions, but a
tragedy soon unfolded in the north that would leave the south
largely forgotten. Since the time of Magellan, explorers had
probed the Arctic for a new route to the Pacific from the North
Atlantic, without the trouble of going south to wrestle with the
wild seas surrounding Tierra del Fuego. The so-called Northwest Passage was the hoped-for navigable ocean route from the
Atlantic along the largely unmapped Canadian Arctic coastline,
shaving thousands of kilometres off the journey in the process.

In 1845, a few years after Ross's return to Britain, the polar
veteran Rear-Admiral Sir John Franklin took the newly refurbished *Erebus* and *Terror* to make a new search for the Northwest
Passage. Both vessels had been refitted with steam engines and
reinforced with iron plating; but they were never heard from
again. Over the next two decades some twenty expeditions were
sent out to discover what had happened to Franklin and his 129
men. What had worked for Ross had failed for Franklin: the two
ships had been caught by sea ice, and sank. The survivors tried to
make their way south, only to perish shortly after. Tales among
the local Inuit spoke of the last expedition members committing
cannibalism and eating the leather of their own boots.

The silver lining to these gruesome discoveries was that
much of the Canadian coastline was mapped. With a newly
discovered interest in this region, governments around the
Arctic intensified their exploration efforts—mostly led by Scandinavian and American teams, who pushed ever further north.

At the other end of the world, however, things would become moribund for the next fifty years.

The only major effort in the south took place between 1872 and 1876, as part of *HMS Challenger*'s 130,000-kilometre voyage to explore the world's oceans. It was arguably the crowning achievement of Victorian oceanography. Lavishly funded by the British government, the *Challenger* briefly visited the Southern Ocean as part of its circumnavigation and made one surprising contribution to Antarctic research. Rather than driving into the sea ice and bergs—something for which it was ill-equipped— the expedition dredged the seabed near the Antarctic Circle, pulling up a rich mixture of rocks, the make-up of which suggested a land of continental proportions did indeed lie in the south. Scientists suggested it covered an area of eight million square kilometres. Now all that was needed was for someone to go and explore it.

In 1827 one of the most influential institutions in Antarctic exploration and research began life as the dining group of a London gentleman's club. The Travellers Club in Pall Mall met regularly in the Thatched House, a roomy, high-ceilinged public house in St James. Surrounded by portraits and chande- liers, members would regale each other with stories of the new lands they had visited.

By 1830 the group had decided it needed a new scientific institution, the Geographical Society of London, 'whose sole object should be the promotion and diffusion of that most important and entertaining branch of knowledge, geog- raphy'. Thanks to the excellent connections of its government and industrial members, the society received royal patronage within two months of its founding and was renamed the Royal

Geographic Society, affectionately shortened to RGS. Writing in apparently high spirits, members declared in the new society's prospectus that geography was 'a copious source of rational amusement'.

The RGS soon made a call for observations of foreign lands:

> The routes, for example, which travellers may have pursued through portions of countries hitherto but imperfectly known, or inaccurately described, the objects of Natural History that may have presented themselves, the meteorological and magnetic phenomena that may have been observed, the nature of the soil and its products, of its forests, rivers, plains, mountains and other general features of its surface; but above all, the latitudes and longitudes of particular places which the Resident or Traveller may have had the means of determining to a degree of precision on which he may rely; such notices of detached portions of the Earth's surface, where as regular surveys cannot be held, are of extreme importance, as furnishing the only means by which any thing approaching to correctness in our general maps can be attained.

The RGS would then print 'new, interesting and useful facts and discoveries to its members and the public in cheap form'. Guides on how to make observations were produced for would-be explorers, the best known of which was *Hints to Travellers*. Costing just a few shillings, its hundred pages contain recommendations for 'a person who, for the first time in his life, proposes to explore a wild country'. There is a wonderfully eclectic range of instruments suggested for the budding explorer, including those you might expect, such as thermometers, barometers and sextants, through to the more extreme, like a double-barrelled gun for the 'collection of objects of natural history'. The society was leading the charge in exploration, and its mission chimed with the ambitions of the rapidly expanding Empire. Membership soared into the thousands.

Not everyone was impressed with the society as it became more successful. 'I hate the claptrap and flattery and flummery of the Royal Geographical [Society], with its utter want of Science and craving for popularity and excitement,' grumbled Joseph Hooker in the midst of sensationalised reports about Livingstone's exploration of Africa in 1864. And the criticism was compounded by the view that the society was not keeping up with the times. Towards the end of the nineteenth century the RGS remained a bastion of male membership: hardly in keeping with the dawn of the modern era.

In 1892 the society's council announced it had approved the admission of twenty-two female fellows. Learned societies around the world were doing likewise, yet the decision dismayed many RGS fellows, one of whom observed, 'I should be very sorry to see this Society governed by ladies.' The upset fellows succeeded in overturning the decision the following year. The scandal was widely reported, and letters justifying the decision were published in the press. Lord Curzon, who later became viceroy of India and, perversely, the RGS president who finally admitted female fellows to the society in 1913, wrote: 'We contest *in toto* the general capability of women to contribute to scientific geographic knowledge. Their sex and training render them equally unfitted for exploration; and the genus of professional female globe-trotters with which America has lately familiarized us is one of the horrors of the latter end of the nineteenth century.' Those female fellows who had been elected were allowed to stay, but no more were admitted for two decades.

The ensuing fallout was a turning point in Antarctic exploration. Sir Clements Markham was a seasoned member of the RGS who had earlier served as its secretary for twenty-five years.

A naval veteran of the Arctic, a midshipman on one of the many British quests to find Sir John Franklin, Markham lived and breathed geography. When he was just thirty he had successfully smuggled seeds of the cinchona tree—containing precious quinine, the only known anti-malarial drug at the time—out of South America and over to India. There the British mixed tonic water containing quinine with gin to make it more drinkable, and the gin and tonic was born.

While on a trip in the Mediterranean, Markham found himself elected as an uncontroversial president, someone who would be acceptable to both sides. Ever the pragmatist, the new president set about focusing the attention of RGS members and the public on something that would take their minds off 'the Lady problem'—a project dear to his heart, the exploration of Antarctica. Some years later Markham explained the campaign in a message to Lord Curzon: 'You well remember the trouble about the admission of females...We were on the brink of a great secession...I believed, rightly or wrongly, that the only way to restore the Society's credit was to undertake some great enterprise in the cause of geography. I chose the Antarctic Regions. It was a risk, for failure would leave us worse than before. All depended on the leader of the expedition.'

By 1895 the Royal Geographic Society and the Royal Society had formed a joint committee to campaign for a British Antarctic expedition, and in that year the Sixth International Geographical Congress in London declared 'that the exploration of the Antarctic Regions is the greatest piece of geographical exploration still to be undertaken. That in view of the additions to knowledge in almost every branch of science which would result from such a scientific exploration the Congress recommends that the scientific societies throughout the world should urge in whatever way seems to them most effective, that this work should be undertaken before the close of the century.' Markham devoted his presidency to furthering this cause—which makes you wonder what would have happened to British Antarctic exploration had the society approved the admission of female fellows a few years earlier.

The *HMS Challenger* oceanographer John Murray, a friend of Markham's, was a vigorous proponent of Antarctic exploration: 'We must, if possible, have two ships, with landing parties for stations on shore, and with a recognized scientific leader and staff on board of each ship...The difficulties which at present surround this undertaking are fundamentally those of money.' And therein lay the problem: the estimated cost was £150,000, equivalent to more than US$20 million today. The infamous expedition of 1860 led by Robert O'Hara Burke and William John Wills to cross Australia was still relatively fresh in people's minds. Sponsored by the Royal Society of Victoria, it was the most expensive in Australian history, costing £60,000—and seven lives, including those of its leaders. In spite of nationalistic pride, governments were not keen to bankroll high-risk ventures. Murray's figures put the proposed work in the south at the most expensive end of scientific exploration. Public subscription would be vital.

———◆———

The International Geographical Congress's declaration sparked the Heroic Age, a period of feverish exploration. Norway, Belgium, Germany, Sweden, France and a nationalistically minded Scotland joined Britain in the quest to discover the south. Despite the competition, most countries were supportive of one another. Almost all agreed in advance to have different spheres of operation when exploring the region: before 1912, expeditions rarely saw anyone else when they were operating in the Antarctic.

The earliest attempts were considerably smaller affairs than that envisaged by Murray, and relied largely on private funds. One of the first was the 1897–1899 Belgian Antarctic Expedition, led by the naval officer Adrien de Gerlache in the *Belgica*. De Gerlache ignored Ross's discoveries and set out south from Tierra del Fuego. He had intended to make an attempt on the South Magnetic Pole, but abandoned the plan when time ran out. Instead, his expedition inadvertently became the first to spend a winter in the Antarctic region when the *Belgica* was locked in sea ice at 70°S, west of a landmass that appeared to be a continuation of Trinity and Palmer lands.

The crew endured a winter of darkness for which they were poorly prepared. Fortunately, two characters who would later play significant roles in the events of 1912 were on board: the Norwegian first mate Roald Amundsen and the American expedition doctor Frederick Cook. Crew members started complaining of the symptoms of the dreaded disease of vitamin deficiency, scurvy. Bleeding gums, loose teeth and swollen limbs could easily prove fatal. But, amazingly, only two people died. Cook, with Amundsen's support, probably saved most of de Gerlache's crew by feeding them fresh seal meat—which, with its relatively high vitamin C levels, if not overcooked, restored those who ate it to health. The expedition returned home, and an important lesson about the value of fresh meat in surviving the south had been learned.

The first British attempt following the International Geographical Congress's call was another privately funded affair. When the Norwegian Carsten Borchgrevink laid out his plans to lead an expedition south between 1898 and 1900, Markham and the Royal Geographical Society kept their distance. Borchgrevink had been to Antarctica on a sealing expedition just a couple of years earlier, and had shot to fame when he became one of the first to step foot on the continent.

But a Norwegian schoolmaster and seaman was not to be taken seriously by learned men in London. Still, by October 1897 Borchgrevink had secured £35,000 from Sir George Newnes, a newspaper baron, who insisted the expedition fly under a British flag.

The largely Scandinavian team took with them three British and Australian scientists, and returned to Cape Adare in northern Victoria Land, the site of Borchgrevink's first steps. Relations between the Norwegian and the rest of the men became so bad that at one point the leader produced a notice which declared, 'the following things would be considered mutiny: to oppose C.E.B. [Borchgrevink] or induce others to do so, to speak ill of C.E.B., to ridicule Mr. C.E.B. or his work, to try and force C.E.B. to alter contracts.' Somehow they soldiered on, and in 1899 the expedition became the first to winter on the Antarctic continent. At the end the Australian Louis Bernacchi—in charge of magnetic measurements—said, 'We are not sorry to leave this gelid, desolate spot, our place of abode for so many dreary months!'

The following summer they sailed on towards the Great Ice Barrier and reached what the papers described as 'Furthest South with sledge – record – 78 deg. 58 min.' It had been some time since anyone had spoken publicly of trying for the South Geographic Pole. The race was on, if you were in search of fame and perhaps fortune.

———————•———————

The British were not overly concerned with the geographic pole, although there was no doubting this was a good way of raising public interest. The official aim was to discover more about this new land in the south, not merely to reach what many felt was an arbitrary spot on the ground. By lobbying and cajoling where necessary, Markham and Murray managed to secure enough funds from private benefactors and the government of the day to get an officially sanctioned British expedition. Most of the money came from the industrialist Llewellyn Longstaff, who offered £25,000, with the government offering a further £45,000. Britain's National Antarctic Expedition was born.

Markham had for some years maintained a list of young naval officers with the potential to lead the new initiative. The Royal Navy had led polar exploration since the end of the Napoleonic Wars: young officers, it was believed, could be explorers and serve science at the same time. As Admiral Sir Richard Hamilton, another veteran of the search for Franklin, remarked in 1906: 'It was the belief of all of us, then the rising generation of 1850, that polar exploration was essentially the work of young men in full possession of their physical powers, with, of course, a fair amount of knowledge of various sciences...The most experienced whaling captain cannot foresee the rapid changes in ice-movements. So inexperience is not as heavily handicapped in the ice as elsewhere. The power of instant decision is what is required.'

In 1899, two days after advertising for a leader of the National Antarctic Expedition, Markham ran into Robert Falcon Scott, a 31-year-old torpedo officer on leave in London. Encouraged by Markham, Scott applied for the position and was appointed leader—his enthusiasm trumping his polar inexperience.

The National Antarctic Expedition began to take shape. But the alliance between the Royal Geographic Society and the Royal Society, its co-sponsors, was not an easy one. The RGS wished to concentrate on geographical discovery, while the Royal Society wanted to put more resources into scientific observation. Sir Clements Markham considered dedicated scientists undesirable camp followers, 'mud larkers' who impeded the business of discovery by pottering in the field.

The Royal Society had considered Scott to be the leader of the expedition for the journey to Antarctica, and envisaged a trained scientist being the leader on the ice. After all, this was a scientific expedition—or so the Royal Society thought. Professor John Walter Gregory was appointed scientific director. A geologist, he had worked from the tropics to the Arctic and achieved fame as an explorer, naming Africa's Great Rift Valley during one of his sojourns. In anticipation of the rich scientific rewards to be had in the south, Gregory made a call for research ideas in the journal *Nature*. Unfortunately, the two men were not natural teammates. Gregory complained that Scott had 'no knowledge of expedition equipment...On questions of furs, sledges, ski etc, his ignorance is appalling...he does not seem at all conscious of these facts or inclined to get [the] experience necessary.' Scott seemed likely to resign over who was in charge. Markham weighed in, and instead the Royal Society's candidate fell on his sword. With Gregory gone, Scott was now in sole charge of what threatened to become a 'naval adventure'. The relationship between science and exploration had not got off to a good start.

Nonetheless, Scott tried to recruit as much scientific expertise as possible. One of those he attempted to take south was a rising star in polar research, the Scot William Speirs Bruce. Full of scientific and nationalist zeal, he had experience of polar waters in both hemispheres. Keen to take his own group south, Bruce turned down Scott's approach. Instead, he raised private funds, controversially named his effort the Scottish National Antarctic Expedition and set off in his ship, the *Scotia*, in 1902. Two years later Bruce returned home a hero, and described exploring the seas and weather of the Weddell Sea, including discovering a new coastline he called Coats Land after one of his major sponsors. Finding the pack ice too thick, he could not penetrate as far south as Weddell, and vowed to go back.

Markham described the Scottish effort as 'mischievous rivalry', and never forgave Bruce for it.

Meanwhile, Markham had organised the publication of *The Antarctic Manual* before the official British expedition headed south. Meant as a guide for naval officers and scientists, the *Manual* described the history, scientific questions and methods required in the south. It provides a fascinating insight into what was known of the Antarctic at the beginning of the twentieth century: expedition members were to research the ice within glaciers, investigate the saltiness of seawater and acquire skill in 'ski running'; they were advised which geological samples they should bring home, and that 'a sandwich of frozen bear's blubber and biscuit is palatable enough.'

Magnetic observations were a focus of investigation. Although some had been taken on Borchgrevink's expedition, the location of the South Magnetic Pole remained uncertain, making it difficult to verify calculations of the Earth's magnetic field. To try to avoid the problems Ross had complained of more than half a century before, a specially designed wooden ship capable of making precise magnetic measurements was made. Called the *Discovery*, this vessel was Britain's first purpose-built craft for scientific work since Halley's *Paramore*. Lieutenant Albert Armitage, the expedition's deputy and in charge of the observations at sea, complained about the storage of tinned provisions immediately below the instruments, alongside 'unconsidered trifles such as a parrot-cage, a sporting-gun, and various assortments of enamelled ironware', forcing the vessel to be swung just as Ross had done with his ship to ensure accurate readings. But at least it was designed like a Scottish whaling vessel, providing a heavily reinforced oak hull that made short work of the Ross Sea ice.

By the time the *Discovery* left Britain, in 1901, £92,000 had been raised, the largest sum yet collected for a polar expedition. Establishing a base on the McMurdo Sound side of Ross Island, Scott's team spent the next two years exploring the region. Even today, though, the expedition's success is fiercely debated.

Undoubtedly, there were some tangible results. Exploration by the *Discovery* gave an eastern limit to Ross's Great Ice Barrier with the finding of 'rock patches', which were christened King Edward VII Land. On the barrier itself, the expedition located the bay Ross had described as full of whales and flew a hydrogen balloon above it, taking the first aerial photograph of this new continent over what became known as Balloon Bight. Magnetic measurements were made both on shore and at sea, providing a revised estimate of the location of the South Magnetic Pole, which implied it had moved in an easterly direction since Ross's 1841 visit. A party made the first successful ascent of the mountains of Victoria Land and reached a plateau of ice, some three thousand metres high, which suggested that both the geographic and magnetic poles lay at a considerable altitude. Continuous weather observations, painstakingly taken several times each day, showed the climate was like nowhere else on Earth, with temperatures plummeting at the end of summer to around -30° Celsius and staying there until the start of the following summer. On the other side of Ross Island, at a spot called Cape Crozier, the first colony of emperor penguins was discovered, and to much amazement were found to have well-developed chicks in early summer, indicating they had hatched during the harsh winter. A unique land was finally being revealed to the rest of the world.

Much like the Belgian effort, though, the British had their share of controversy. The expedition suffered for a time from scurvy. And while attempting to reach the South Geographic Pole, Scott, the assistant surgeon Dr Edward Wilson and third lieutenant Ernest Shackleton only reached a disappointing furthest south of 82°11'S, among much later-reported acrimony. Most importantly for the British authorities, the *Discovery* was locked in sea ice for two years, rather than the publicly declared plan of one. There was a justifiable fear of escalating costs. By the end of the second season the authorities' patience snapped and they sent two vessels south to recover the men, with orders to abandon the *Discovery* if it could not be released. At the last moment the expedition ship escaped its icy grip, helped by the judicious application of explosives.

And yet, *Terra Australis Incognita* had been shown to be real and Captain Cook's earlier pessimism unfounded. The National Antarctic Expedition returned home to much fanfare and, notwithstanding some mutterings of discontent, Scott was proclaimed a hero. But there was no rush of expeditions south to build on the British work. To understand why, we have to turn our attention to a member of Scott's team: one of the most inspirational explorers of all time, Ernest Shackleton.

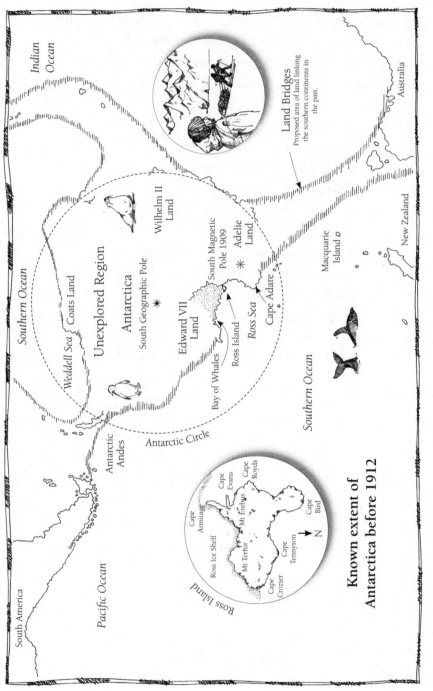

Hypothesised former land bridges from A. E. Ortmann's *Tertiary Invertebrates* (1902).

CHAPTER 2

AN AUDACIOUS PLAN

Ernest Shackleton and the British
Antarctic Expedition, 1907–1909

Yes, they're wanting me, they're haunting me, the awful lonely places;
They're whining and they're whimpering as if each had a soul;
They're calling from the wilderness, the vast and God-like spaces,
The stark and sullen solitudes that sentinel the Pole.

ROBERT W. SERVICE (1874–1958)

In January 1904 a prematurely old-looking middle-aged professor of geology stood up in a packed hall in the New Zealand city of Dunedin and gave one of the most controversial but least reported lectures in the region's history. The Welsh-born Edgeworth David, known affectionately as the Prof, was president of the Australasian Association for the Advancement of Science. David believed science was pitted against a significant foe, one that threatened the antipodean colonies' ability to contribute to the British Empire. To the assembled he calmly proclaimed: 'It should, I think, be one of the aims of this Association to discover and destroy the microbe of sporting mania.'

Not only was sport directing effort away from the advancement of scientific knowledge, he argued—it was also threatening the quality of education. 'When we worship in the cricket or football fields the wood and the leather,' he said, 'we must remember that they are but idols, and must not let them occupy the chief

shrine in our hearts.' Science was suffering. Antarctic exploration promised some answers, but 'geography', he declared, 'like
charity, should begin at home: the real scientific geography of
the interior of Australia is at present almost unknown'. Shortly
afterwards, a flamboyant Anglo-Irishman changed the Prof's
mind about the value of scientific work in the south.

The early Antarctic incursions of de Gerlache, Borchgrevink
and Scott had set the scene for the greatest schoolboy hero
of them all, the most charismatic of Antarctic leaders, Ernest
Shackleton. Born in 1874 in County Kildare, Shackleton moved
with his family to London when he was ten years old. Though
keen for Ernest to pursue a career at sea, the family could not
afford the price of a commission in the Royal Navy. Instead,
Shackleton signed up for the mercantile navy and eventually
joined the Union-Castle Line operating between Southampton
and Cape Town, ferrying passengers, mail and, later, troops
for the Boer War. During one of the crossings he met a young
army officer whose father, Llewellyn Longstaff, was one of
the primary backers of Scott's *Discovery* expedition. With the
bold confidence and good fortune that would define his career,
Shackleton introduced himself to Longstaff senior when next he
was in London. The old man was impressed and insisted Scott
take the young officer south in 1901.

Little love was lost between Shackleton and Scott: both were
strong characters with opposing leadership styles. Nevertheless,
they apparently got on reasonably well at first. So much so that
when Scott made his attempt on the South Geographic Pole, in
1903, he chose Shackleton along with Edward Wilson to accompany him. It is not clear what happened on this trip but Scott's
second-in-command, Albert Armitage, wrote some years later
that 'Wilson and Shackleton were packing their sledges after
breakfast one morning. Suddenly they heard Scott shout to them:
"Come here you BFs." They went to him and Wilson quietly

said: "Were you speaking to me?" "No Bill," said Scott. "Then it must have been me," said Shackleton. He received no answer. He then said: "Right, you are the worst BF of the lot, and every time you dare to speak to me like that you will get it back." Before Shackleton left he told me he meant to return to prove to Scott that he—Shackleton—was a better man than Scott.'

Opinions differ about whether Armitage was telling the truth, so many years after the event and when all the protagonists were dead. But regardless of what was said during the aborted attempt on the South Geographic Pole, Shackleton fell gravely ill and Scott had the young officer invalided home before the end of the expedition. As the relief vessel *Morning* departed a young sub-lieutenant, Edward 'Teddy' Evans, wrote: 'We watched till Scott's men vanished out of sight, when poor Shackleton…broke down altogether and wept.'

Years later Shackleton was asked by a journalist why he was drawn back to the Antarctic when he might have resumed work on a shipping line. 'Men go out into the void spaces of the world for various reasons,' he responded. 'Some are actuated simply by a love of adventure, some have the keen thirst for scientific knowledge, and others again are drawn away from the trodden paths by the "lure of little voices," the mysterious fascination of the unknown. I think that in my case it was a combination of these factors that determined me to try my fortune once again in the frozen south.'

On Shackleton's return to Britain, in 1903, he was feted as a polar hero. At first he seemed content to try different jobs and bask in the glory of his exploits on the ice. He tried to raise expeditionary funds in 1905 but it came to naught, and there the matter seemed to rest. Then Shackleton heard on the Royal Geographical Society grapevine of a future Antarctic expedition. Henryk Arctowski, from Belgium, was proposing to use Ross Island as a base for an attempt on the South Geographical Pole.

This news seems to have spurred Shackleton into action. By February 1907 he had managed to secure support from his then employer, the Scottish industrialist William Beardmore, whose wife appears to have been having an affair with Shackleton at the time. The story has it that, shortly after, Shackleton ran into Arctowski, who told him he intended to announce the Belgian project at the RGS dinner that evening—the venue of choice for aspiring Livingstones to first propose their expeditions. Shackleton managed to get up before Arctowski at the dinner and announce his own plans, much to the Belgian's chagrin. Shackleton was an incredible opportunist, but the strategy worked.

The British announcement was reported in newspapers and came as a bombshell to Scott, who was planning a return to the south himself. If this wasn't enough, the papers suggested Shackleton intended to use the *Discovery*'s old Ross Island base. Since Scott's return, relations between the two men appear to have been largely cordial, even after the 1905 publication of a popular book on the *Discovery* expedition that laid bare Shackleton's illness during their failed attempt on the South Geographic Pole. Scott, though, was horrified at the newspaper reports and sent several letters to Shackleton the next day. 'I needn't tell you that I don't wish to haunt you and your plans but in one way I feel I have a sort of right to my own field of work in the same way as Peary claimed Smith's Sound and many African travellers their particular locality...PS I feel sure with a little discussion we can work in accord rather than in opposition,' he wrote— and, later that day: 'Well goodbye for the present. The subject is very close to my heart so please write openly and freely.'

Scott asked Edward Wilson, as a mutual friend, to negotiate different areas of operation in Antarctica. His preference was for Ross Island, with Shackleton to base himself further east along the Great Ice Barrier—perhaps King Edward VII Land, first spotted from the deck of the *Discovery* just a few years earlier.

In many respects it was an outrageous proposition: Shackleton was well within his rights to work anywhere he pleased, just as Henryk Arctowski was. Shocked, and apparently unaware of his former leader's plans, Shackleton soon found Wilson siding with Scott. A few days later Shackleton telegrammed his old leader at Gibraltar: 'Will meet your wishes regarding base please keep absolutely private at present as certain supporters must be brought round to the new position.'

By March 1907 Shackleton had sufficiently developed his plans to present them to the RGS. He would set about a three-pronged attack on the new continent. While assiduously avoiding naming his base, he stated his intention to send one team south, to strike for the geographic pole; one east, walking across the barrier to King Edward VII Land; and a final team west, for the magnetic pole. The geographic pole was the main target—but 'I do not intend to sacrifice the scientific utility of the expedition to a mere record-breaking journey,' Shackleton wrote. 'I shall in no way neglect to continue the biological, meteorological, geological, and magnetic work of the *Discovery*.' He intended to take scientific observations across all the natural sciences and claim both poles in one fell swoop for the British Empire: an audacious plan.

Press coverage of the funding drive for Shackleton's British Antarctic Expedition reached across the Empire and beyond. Shackleton somehow managed to secure an old wooden sealer, the *Nimrod*; refit it, secure sponsorship, purchase supplies and equipment; and depart for the voyage south—all in less than six months. But he was in trouble. The expedition was massively in debt, and the scientific team was largely a token force. To give themselves the best possible chance, the British Antarctic Expedition dispensed with irksome committees and had no intention of allowing the *Nimrod* to be frozen in the ice. This 'would render the use of a relief ship unnecessary, as the same vessel could come south again the following summer and take us off'. It would save Shackleton money he did not have.

———•———

After reading the newspaper announcements, Edgeworth David wrote to Shackleton requesting to join the *Nimrod* and visit Antarctica on the first leg of the expedition, returning with the vessel at the end of the summer, before the onset of winter darkness. In Antarctica, the new continent, and in Shackleton, the dynamic explorer, David saw a chance for science to compete with sport. Shackleton was delighted, and in typical style wrote back immediately, welcoming David and offering him a berth. David gave the expedition much-needed scientific credibility: until then it had only a geology undergraduate, Raymond Priestley, and a respected, self-taught biologist, James Murray.

Privately, Shackleton was not confident he could get to the South Geographic Pole, writing to Reginald Skelton, a friend from the *Discovery* expedition: 'now with the change of base, to King Edward VII's Land, the future prospects of getting South are somewhat hypothetical.' The finances were not in nearly as good shape as had been made out, and public aims had to be presented bullishly if Shackleton was to secure enough money. When first he approached the RGS, in early 1907, Shackleton claimed he had pledges of £30,000—but this was far from the truth. In fact, shortage of money would be a theme for all of Shackleton's voyages.

Much like other explorers before him, though, Shackleton recognised the lucrative possibilities of offering rich benefactors prospective mineral wealth and a stab at immortality—all they had to do was open their purses. New landmarks would be named after those who had wisely invested in his expedition.

Industrialists and newspaper barons could have their names engraved on the world, alongside those of monarchs.

A friend later remarked of Shackleton that he was 'unique in his love of talking big and his ability to do big things. The two qualities rarely go together.' The wealthy responded. William Beardmore confirmed an earlier offer of £7000, and others soon followed: not so much that the expedition was awash with money, but enough for Shackleton to launch a credible assault on Antarctica.

En route, Shackleton's request in Australia for expedition funding found willing listeners. In the previous two decades there had been calls to scientifically explore the Antarctic region that lay to the immediate south of Australia. Early on the Victorian state government was keen, and offered to jointly fund a British expedition. In Britain the learned societies were strongly supportive. But the British Treasury was wary of the exercise, and quashed the proposal.

Victoria cast around for another partner. By 1889 the state had an offer from Baron Adolf Nordenskjöld, who offered to lead an Australian–Swedish expedition south. Nordenskjöld was something of a catch for the Australians. In 1879 he had become the first to find a route through the Arctic sea ice and bergs to the Pacific—not along the Canadian coast favoured by Franklin and others, but instead via the lesser known Northeast Passage, tracking northern Scandinavia and the Siberian seaboard.

Despite the controversy surrounding its handling of the Burke and Wills expedition, the Royal Society of Victoria was keen to continue expeditionary work and, with Nordenskjöld's offer in hand, established an Antarctic Committee. Sister societies across the pre-Federation colonies were enthusiastically supportive and there seemed a real prospect of an Australian expedition departing in 1890. All that was needed was £5000 to match the money being put up by the Swedes.

Pledges came from the different societies, and appeals were made to the colonial governments and public. In 1889 the Tasmanian deputy surveyor-general, Chas Sprent, published an impassioned plea for Australia to take a lead in exploration, arguing that 'there is more lasting honour to be gained than in fighting the battles of the Old Country against half-armed savages,' and concluding, 'The scientific world is anxious to see a renewal of Antarctic exploration, and nothing would be more gratifying to them, nothing will be more calculated to give the world an earnest [impression] of our desire to help, than for Australia to take up this work.' But by late 1890 the many committees involved had sucked the life out of the enterprise, and the planned expedition fizzled out.

In Australia, Shackleton realised that David was well connected and capable of appealing to the same sentiments that had so nearly ensured an Australian expedition not twenty years earlier. The academic was thrust into the funding spotlight; those on the team, Shackleton reasoned, could use their own contacts. On 10 December 1907 David wrote to the prime minister of Australia, Alfred Deakin, outlining why the recently federated country needed to help finance Shackleton's expedition.

David changed his tune from his 1904 lecture, and waxed lyrical to Deakin on the value of Antarctic research, listing a string of points, including the new continent being Australia's nearest neighbour, its probable control on weather conditions across the country, the changing magnetic conditions that govern navigation in southern seas and the promise of mineral resources. Reaching the South Geographic Pole was point five on the list. Given David's scientific reputation and his having vouched for Shackleton, the federal government awarded £5000. Last-minute appeals in New Zealand secured a further £1000. Shackleton had no British government support, but he had his expedition.

Unaware of just how poorly funded the expedition was, David continued apace with scientific planning, purchasing equipment—often out of his own limited funds—so that the team could make the most of its time in the south. With news of the Australian role in the expedition, the local newspapers trumpeted David's plans. Out of the woodwork came former students of his, chief among them Douglas Mawson, a Yorkshire-born, tall and prematurely balding young geologist who was in the field at the time of the newspaper announcement. On 28 September 1907 Mawson wrote to David: 'I should have dearly loved to have gone myself and shall in any case be with you as far as my imagination can carry me.' Mawson was fascinated by the prospect that Antarctica held the key to one of the great geological unknowns: why living and fossilised plants and animals were commonly found across South America, Africa, Madagascar and Australia.

David had asked in his 1904 Dunedin lecture whether Antarctica was home to the remarkable *Glossopteris*, a fossil plant that dominated the geological record during the Permian period, some 299 to 251 million years ago in Australia, Africa and India. With its distinctive tongue-shaped leaves, and growing up to eight metres in height, it appeared to be a form of tree fern but produced seeds. The most obvious explanation for it being found across the southern continents was an ancient land link to Antarctica, allowing wildlife to freely move between the continents.

Some half-century earlier Joseph Hooker had first remarked upon the similarity of southern flora and asked whether the islands in the Antarctic region were 'the remains of some far more extended body of land'. His friend Charles Darwin was inspired and suggested that the Antarctic region might indeed hold the key to the distribution of many species, speculating that it played a role in the explosion of seed-bearing plants. In

1859, in his world-changing *On the Origin of Species*, Darwin ruminated about the similarities of plants in New Zealand and South America. He suggested that 'this difficulty partially disappears on the view that New Zealand, South America, and the other southern lands have been stocked in part from a nearly intermediate though distant point, namely from the antarctic islands, when they were clothed with vegetation, during a warmer tertiary period, before the commencement of the last Glacial period.'

Darwin wrote to Hooker in 1881 about how his ideas had developed: 'I have been so astonished at the apparently sudden coming in of the higher phanerogams, that I have sometimes fancied that development might have slowly gone on for an immense period in some isolated continent or large island, perhaps near the South Pole.' By the early twentieth century scientists had gathered a wealth of evidence pertaining to this theory. Large-horned tortoises known as *Meiolania* had been discovered in Australian and Patagonian rocks spanning what was thought to be tens of millions of years; living species of South American frogs had closely related cousins living in Madagascar; and marsupials were known to exist in both Australia and South America. The great Austrian scientist Edward Suess was the first to hypothesise that there must have been one large landmass that had united the southern continents. In 1885 Suess called it the lost continent of Gondwanaland.

The Antarctic Manual summed up Suess's evidence succinctly a few years later, stating that the evidence pointed to the possibility that 'communication by land existed between the continental masses of the Southern Hemisphere and the Antarctic continent.' Like Atlantis, these bridges must have sunk below the waves in the past. Antarctica's fossil record offered a means of testing the concept of a land bridge.

This intrigued Mawson, and David approached Shackleton about the young geologist joining the expedition. Reassured by the senior man's recommendation but aware Priestley already filled the role, Shackleton appointed Mawson for the full duration of the expedition as physicist. Around this time, it seems Shackleton also invited David to lead the scientific program, rather than just having the Prof stay for a short visit. Shackleton now had serious scientific clout on his expedition, and it was all largely down to luck.

Setting forth under the banner of the British Antarctic Expedition, the *Nimrod* headed south from the New Zealand port of Lyttleton on 1 January 1908 with a team of twenty-three men. Shackleton was still short by £20,000: everything depended on the success of the expedition and the hope that future funding would eventuate. With Shackleton unable to pay for the coal required to sail the *Nimrod* all the way to Antarctica, the New Zealand government and the Union Steamship Company agreed to help cover some of the costs by towing the expedition ship 2430 kilometres through the stormy South Ocean, to the edge of the sea ice. With the ever-present threat of floundering, the crew were called night and day to station, keeping the pumps going and hoping the ten-centimetre-diameter steel cable between the ships would hold. The journey took fifteen days.

Shackleton was probably the closest thing polar exploration had to a warrior poet, and he relished the challenge. David recalled later that, when conditions were particularly bad, 'Shackleton, in lulls between the fiercer gusts, could be heard reciting Browning—always a danger signal. He knew much of Browning and George Meredith's poetry by heart, and lived in their higher sentiments in moments of extreme danger.'

When the impoverished flotilla finally reached the northern edge of the Ross Sea ice, two weeks later, the lifeline between the two vessels was cut and the tow ship departed for New Zealand. On board were letters from the expedition members for loved ones back home, including an epistle from David to his wife—who was apparently strong-willed and less than pleased about David's presence on the expedition—announcing his decision to stay the full year.

Starting out relatively late from New Zealand did have advantages. Exposed to continuous sunlight, the sea ice that had built up in the Ross Sea over winter was now melting, allowing the *Nimrod* to make quick work of breaking through what remained and reach the Great Ice Barrier just a week after being released from the towline. But it was far from plain sailing. The Great Ice Barrier, at the other end of the Ross Sea, is not a stagnant block. Ice moves towards the sea at a rate of about a metre a day and, at the ocean margins, large pieces can break off to form flat-topped icebergs sometimes many kilometres wide.

Shackleton later recalled fondly in his book of the expedition, *The Heart of Antarctica*: 'About 3 am, we entered an area of tabular bergs, varying from eighty to one hundred and fifty feet in height [around twenty-five to forty-five metres], and all the morning we steamed in beautiful weather with a light northerly wind, through the lanes and streets of a wonderful snowy Venice…A stillness, weird and uncanny, seemed to have fallen upon everything when we entered the silent water streets of this vast unpeopled white city.'

Reaching the Great Ice Barrier, Shackleton pushed east, at pains to stand by the agreement with Scott and establish a base at Balloon Bight. When he brought the *Nimrod* alongside the bay he was shocked to see the coastline had changed drastically; it was no longer recognisable as the one the British had flown above in a balloon. Instead, Shackleton found hundreds of whales inhabiting a markedly different bay, which suggested the area was highly unstable. It was too risky to base his efforts there. Renaming the spot the Bay of Whales, Shackleton probed the Barrier beyond, towards King Edward VII Land, but realised he now risked trapping the ship in the ice—and with it the success of the expedition. To get the ship home that season, he had to establish a base before the short summer ended.

Shackleton resolved to cut his losses and return to McMurdo Sound. There was consternation among those on board, but Shackleton had limited time and funds. It was already the end of January and the *Nimrod* had to head north before the end of February if it was to reach warmer climes safely. One week later the expedition reached Ross Island. Landing at Cape Royds, some forty kilometres north of the old *Discovery* base, and working at a frenzied pace, the expedition members unloaded the supplies from the *Nimrod*, assembled the wooden hut that was to be their home for the next year and waved farewell to the ship before it departed north, three weeks later. The men left behind set about getting ready to hunker down for the two-month winter darkness and prepare for the assault on the poles the following summer.

Never had men been left so far south alone. To the young members of Shackleton's expedition, Antarctica must have seemed otherworldly. The vastness of the landscape, coupled with the extreme swings in light, temperature and sound, could unsettle the strongest of characters. Now they also had to deal with physical isolation from the outside world—and proximity to one another. Antarctic explorers were like the seafarers of the past, forced to rely upon their comrades for company.

The sentiment was captured by Darwin's colleague and friend Thomas Huxley, who wrote: 'how utterly disgusted you get with one another! Little peculiarities which would give a certain charm and variety to social intercourse under any other circumstances, become sources of absolute pain, and almost uncontrollable irritation, when you are shut up with them day and night. One good friend, a messmate of mine, has a peculiar laugh, whose iteration on our last cruise nearly drove me insane.'

The situation would only be exacerbated by continuous darkness. Now known as Seasonal Affective Disorder, the absence of natural sunlight is understood to have a debilitating effect on people. The experiences of de Gerlache and Borchgrevink had shown that, with individuals left to their own devices during the long winter night, depression and listlessness could easily set in. It was critical that everyone be kept busy and a strict routine followed.

To see off any problems, fieldwork was carried out in earnest, the men exploring their immediate surroundings and collecting samples in anticipation of the winter darkness. Shackleton sent David and a small team to make the first successful ascent of nearby Mount Erebus, helping to maintain morale while also allowing him to test the mettle of future sledging-party members. On their return David and Priestley were out all hours during the remaining sunlight, gathering geological samples scattered around the base. Murray collected biological specimens from nearby lakes, while Mawson investigated the structure of the local ice. During the day 'a miscellaneous assortment of cameras, spectroscopes, thermometers, electrometers and the like lay in profusion on the blankets,' Shackleton later wrote; the Prof 'made a pile of glittering tins and coloured wrappers at one end of his bunk, and the heap looked like the nest of the Australian bower bird'. This cornucopia of scientific equipment in and surrounding David's and Mawson's bunks earned that part of the hut the label Pawn Shop.

During winter the team kept weather observations, wrote up the geological samples they had collected, took magnetic measurements, analysed the plant and animal life they had found, and made observations on the 'mysterious Aurora Australis'—the southern equivalent to the Aurora Borealis in the north—that lit up the night sky. It was enough to keep the demons at bay and, during spare time, the men's discussions inevitably wandered to how the news of their base's location was being taken in London. Scott, they decided, was just going to have to live with it.

To prepare for the expedition Shackleton had travelled across Europe and spoken to anyone who would give him the time of day, building on his experiences in the south. Inevitably, much of this advice came from those who had worked in the Arctic. And the most important of them all was Fridtjof Nansen, who lived in the newly independent state of Norway.

Nansen is probably the closest thing to the father of polar exploration. This moustachioed giant was the driving force behind many expeditions, and anyone who was interested in making a serious play in these regions would seek his advice.

Born in 1861 in Norway when it was in political union with Stockholm, Nansen grew up in a small town just outside the capital, Oslo, then called Christiania. By age twenty-seven Nansen had gained a doctorate in zoology for his pioneering work on the central nervous system of lower invertebrates, ideas that later proved to be some of the founding principles of modern nerve theory. But Nansen's passion was skiing, then a little-known pursuit outside Scandinavia. He would frequently go for long-distance trips over the mountains of Norway, competing in national competitions. Sensing this approach might provide a new method of polar exploration, he decided to undertake what would prove to be one of the greatest journeys of all time.

In the late 1880s no one had yet traversed Greenland and it was still thought possible the interior might be ice-free. Taking the brave—possibly foolhardy—decision to land on the ice-strewn east coast, where the only option was to head west, Nansen left for Greenland the day after defending his PhD research to ruffled academics. The skis proved a huge success and, dragging sledges filled with supplies and equipment west, his team made the first crossing of what was found to be an enormous ice sheet.

The success propelled Nansen onto newspaper front pages and he became a national figure, pursued for any number of similar adventures. In 1883 he wrote, 'After my return from the Arctic, I will go to the South Pole and then my life's work will be finished.' Instead, Nansen set about pioneering a fresh approach to reach the North Geographic Pole. Although Ross had reached the North Magnetic Pole in 1831, subsequent expeditions had failed to reach its geographic counterpart. Most had made their attempts by dragging sledges north from the Canadian coastline. Admiral Sir George Richards wrote that sledges 'dragged like ploughs': 'There will never be any more Arctic sledge travelling...I would confirm anyone who proposed such a thing in a Lunatic Asylum.' Nansen took a similar view.

Favouring the idea that the North Geographic Pole was surrounded by sea ice, and recognising the direction that driftwood took across the Arctic, Nansen came up with an imaginative alternative: drive a boat into the sea ice on the Eurasian side of the Arctic and float over the North Geographic Pole. It was inspired thinking, but no vessel was known to be capable of surviving the pressure of being locked up like this for months on end. Nansen had the germ of an idea for a unique ship, and he worked hard to secure financial support from the Christiania Geographical Society in 1890, and later the Norwegian government and king.

No one had attempted to design a ship to be deliberately trapped in ice. Most earlier polar explorers had made do with converted sealing and whaling vessels. Nansen wanted his ship to be 'round and slippery as an eel'. Rather than resisting the ice pressing in from the sides, the ship would lift above it: a rounded hull would avoid the grasp of the ice in 'the way a cherry pip squeezed between thumb and forefinger pops into the air'. It was designed to be prodigiously strong; the living quarters were fully insulated with a combination of natural materials that included reindeer hair, felt and linoleum; there would even be a windmill to run a generator for electric lighting. The ship was christened *Fram*, Norwegian for 'forward', by Nansen's wife, Eva, and launched in late 1892.

This plucky vessel, now housed in a dedicated museum in Oslo, would go on to play a major role in the events of 1912. At thirty-one metres in length, the rounded bilge of the *Fram* is reminiscent of an enormous cockleshell. Individual cabins and communal working spaces bathed in light from triple-glazed skylights make the vessel seem roomier than it really is; indeed, it is not hard to imagine using it for research today.

Though the *Fram*'s design was conceptually brilliant, Nansen could not get his ship far enough along the Siberian coast before it became trapped in the ice. The ship did drift towards Greenland, but not over the North Pole. Realising they would fall short, Nansen, with a colleague, Hjalmar Johansen, decided to ski with sledges and dogs to the pole from the *Fram* at its furthest point north. The two men managed to get within 3° of the North Geographic Pole but were forced to work their way back when it became clear that they did not have enough supplies. Unable to find the *Fram* on their return, the Norwegians pushed on to the northern shore of Franz Josef Land, a collection of islands off the Siberian coast.

Overwintering in the northern darkness, Nansen and

Johansen stumbled across a British expedition based on the southern side of Franz Josef Land the following year. This was a serendipitous meeting, with implications for polar exploration in the south. The Jackson–Harmsworth Expedition was led by an eccentric British adventurer, Frederick George Jackson, who had applied to join Nansen's expedition and been rejected. Jackson then decided to launch his own expedition to the North Pole. Discovering that Franz Josef Land was an archipelago, Jackson realised he could not reach the pole. Instead, he spent his time exploring the islands, making scientific measurements and shooting the local wildlife—including more than one hundred polar bears—south of 81°N.

Before leaving, he had visited Nansen's brother in Norway, taking away with him a package of letters 'soldered up in a zinc case on the chance of seeing something' of Nansen. Just as Stanley met Livingstone, so Jackson greeted Nansen. Once the Norwegian had asked after his wife and whether his country was at war with Sweden, Jackson handed over the letters.

Advice from Nansen and Jackson helped Ernest Shackleton in his preparations, for polar exploration was still far from an exact science. Practical experience was vital in planning, and the same people regularly turned up on different expeditions, sharing experiences and observations—sometimes at a cost. Albert Armitage, who became Robert Scott's second-in-command on the *Discovery* expedition, went north with Jackson. During the exploration of Franz Josef Land, Jackson had dogs and ponies to help transport the sledges of equipment and supplies. Two of the ponies died early on, and the expedition was forced to fall back on the one remaining beast for a large part of their haulage. The final pony later died while the accompanying dogs survived—yet Jackson raved about the use of horses in polar exploration to anyone who would listen, and was dismissive of canine teams. His obsession rubbed off on Armitage, who took the idea south and shared it with Scott and Shackleton in 1901.

Shackleton had intended to use dogs. He had seen them used on the *Discovery* expedition: 'I wish we had had about sixty or seventy,' he later wrote, 'for then I think we could have reached the South Pole.' But Armitage had extolled the virtues of horses after his experiences in the Arctic. On returning to London from the *Discovery* expedition Shackleton had looked Jackson up, and the eccentric British adventurer had suggested the young leader change his plans. Shackleton was swayed by Jackson's arguments and, with characteristic gusto, decided to direct the British Antarctic Expedition's efforts towards horses in the attempt to reach the South Geographic Pole.

While on the ice—with no chance of restocking—the men needed to transport supplies as efficiently as possible and keep weight to a minimum. Nansen's designs for sledges and especially cookers would prove crucial for Shackleton. The 'Nansen cooker' had an inner and outer container that made maximum use of the heat given off by the paraffin-fuelled Primus stove. In a tent it could cook food and melt ice for drinking at the same time, while also giving off valuable warmth. At the base a range of food was available, including tinned food, homemade bread, and local penguins and seals for fresh meat. On sledging journeys it was a different matter. Pemmican—a concentrated mix of protein and fat, made from ground mince and oil, that could be eaten warm or cold—was supplemented by biscuits, cheese, chocolate, cocoa, soluble milk protein, sugar, oats and tea. It was not always enough.

Clothing proved a tougher challenge. While indigenous peoples in the north wore furs and skins, many of the European exploring fraternity were reluctant to don such apparel.

Fur can be restrictive if not used correctly, trapping sweat close to the body, where it can freeze when activity ends—and during heavy work it can be unbearably hot. Instead, Shackleton opted for multiple layers of thin, warm clothing, with a windproof cover. The British and subsequent explorers of 1912 often relied on natural fibres, such as wool and cotton, for the inner layers of their clothing. Nansen favoured tight-fitting pure woollen garments in the Jaeger style, worn close to the skin so the air could be trapped and keep the individual warm—he was renowned for parading this clothing at home as well as in the field, despite it leaving little to the imagination.

For the windproof layer Shackleton used the best available material on the market, a tightly woven gabardine cloth made by Burberry. Jackson had sung the praises of this material, in spite of the apparel having no fixed hood, leaving the neck uncovered in the freezing conditions. To compensate, a scarf had to be wrapped around the neck, ears and head, finished off with a woollen hat—far from perfect, as the neck regularly became exposed, allowing precious warmth to escape. Because of wind gusts, the hat and heavy-duty fur mittens were tied together. Unfortunately, although the mittens helped keep hands warm, they were of no use in working with instruments or doing other work that required some dexterity: inner gloves had to be worn so the mittens could be taken off for short periods.

Accompanying this get-up was the Edwardian equivalent of sunglasses. In the Antarctic there is always the threat of snow blindness, photokeratitis, when the eyes are exposed to extreme levels of ultraviolet light brought about by the high reflectivity of the white surface. The often-blinding light meant Shackleton's men had to wear snow goggles with coloured lenses most of the time outside.

Not all ideas from the northern polar regions were ignored. Finnesko boots, usually made from reindeer stag heads, were stuffed with sennegrass, a type of sedge found in the European Arctic. Borchgrevink wrote enthusiastically on his return from exploration: 'I found that the Lapps' method of never using socks in their Finn boots answered well...if you get wet feet while wearing the grass in the "komager" (Finn boots) you will be warmer than ever, as the fresh grass will, by the moisture and the heat of your feet, in a way start to burn, or produce its own heat by spontaneous combustion.' By night, Shackleton found, the sennegrass could be pulled out and hung up, allowing the trapped moisture to freeze: 'the greater part of it can be shaken away before the grass is replaced on the following morning.'

All this equipment required money from donors. Shackleton needed as many hooks as possible to excite possible supporters, and focused on taking the latest technology to tackle the icy continent. This enabled companies to show off their newest products in the most extreme of environments, and the newspapers loved it, raising the profile of the expedition yet further. Hoping the Great Ice Barrier surface would be solid enough, Shackleton took the first motorcar south, so it could be used to help transport stores on the snow and ice. His patron Beardmore had just taken over the bankrupt Arrol-Johnston manufacturers and was more than happy to provide a new vehicle, showcasing a company that was desperate for publicity. In anticipation of the freezing conditions, the expedition took special low-temperature oil and a cornucopia of wheels, along with wooden skis, that would hopefully be able to cope with the different surfaces.

As if that was not enough, Shackleton also planned to drag a light portable boat, the *Raymond*—named after his son—3200 kilometres to the other side of Antarctica, where he might rendezvous with the *Nimrod*. This ambitious plan was soon dropped.

Just after six o'clock on the morning of 16 January 1909, three men clad in polar gear wearily stepped out from a small green tent on an icy plateau of the eastern Antarctic, and fastened themselves to a laden sledge. For 103 days the men had hauled themselves and their supplies, the tent and a range of scientific equipment across sixteen hundred kilometres of wind-blasted ice, dodging the constant threat of crevasses. Buffeted by snowstorms and blizzards, they had battled hunger and extreme isolation. Now, finally, their objective was within reach. Hooked up, they pushed their aching bodies forward, pulling on the assorted harnesses and straps, and slowly the sledge followed.

Led by Edgeworth David, these three men from Ernest Shackleton's British Antarctic Expedition were proceeding north to the South Magnetic Pole. David's successful assault on Mount Erebus at the end of the past summer had not only provided valuable geological observations of the volcano but also familiarised the men with the equipment and sledging gear. By October 1908 the men had rested after the Antarctic winter and were ready to set out. Making excellent progress, David's team was more than thirteen hundred kilometres from Shackleton's simultaneous assault on the South Geographic Pole by mid-January the next year.

Seen from afar the 51-year-old David cut a diminutive figure. His age was beginning to tell, and he whispered encouraging words to himself while he pulled forward. Accompanying David was his protégé, the tall 26-year-old Douglas Mawson, and Alistair Mackay, a stout Scottish medic, aged thirty. It might sound like the beginning of a bad joke, but this Welshman, Englishman and Scotsman were setting out to do something extraordinary: to complete the journey Ross had started nearly seventy years earlier, and fulfil one of the great hopes of Shackleton's expedition.

The Arrol-Johnston car had promised much but delivered little. Although it looked impressive on the ice, the vehicle proved wholly inadequate for its new climes. As soon as it strayed off the ice the tyres sank. The gleaming metal casing and trappings were stripped off, leaving the driver to sit on the barest of frames above a single engine. The exposed engine had to be regularly defrosted, sometimes by the potentially explosive method of putting a small bowl of petrol under the carburettor and setting it alight; if stuck in the snow, the car would have to be pulled out and a different type of wheel tried.

David later wrote: 'After travelling a little over two miles, just beyond Cape Barne, the snow had become so thick that the coastline was almost entirely hidden from our view. Under these circumstances I did not think it was prudent to take the motorcar further, so Mackay, Mawson, and I bid adieu to our good friends. Strapping on our harness, we toggled on to the sledge rope, and with a "One, two, three" and "away", started on our long journey over the sea ice.' Setting off along the coast, the three men were on their own. They hauled the sledge and spoke little, save for the odd encouraging word amid what David described as 'the wilderness of snow'.

To reach their objective the three men relied on a dipping compass to measure the vertical component of the magnetic field. Mawson was put in charge of the device during the journey and eagerly looked out for the moment when the needle would point vertically. The team was disappointed to realise that the South Magnetic Pole was further inland than the *Discovery* expedition's findings suggested. Stoically, they climbed the mountain chain abutting the Antarctic Plateau; the prospect of searching for rich mineral resources, so important for encouraging investment in their endeavour, would have to wait. Mawson did continue to make geological observations, often making comparisons to the rich mineral seams he had seen back in Australia, at Broken Hill, but this was now secondary to the scientific work. When Mawson fell down a crevasse, swinging on his straps, he collected crystals from the sheer walls of ice, and threw them up for the others to look at; as they travelled over the wind-blown snow and ice, they noted its orientation, giving an insight into the pervasive winds that hurtled off the interior.

Approaching the magnetic pole, Mawson found its location shifted daily, and he had to anticipate its likely movement. To complicate matters further, being close to a pole meant any traditional compass was hopeless for orientation, barely changing over hundreds of kilometres. 'Compass now very sluggish,' David recalled of his time on the plateau, 'in fact the theodolite compass would scarcely work at all. This pleased us a good deal, and at first we all wished more power to it: then amended the sentiment and wished less power to it.'

The instrument for finding the magnetic pole was a Lloyd-Creak dipping circle, a delicate device not designed for the conditions Mawson was operating in: the subfreezing temperatures, buffeting winds and drifting snow all tested the instrument to its limits. Handling a dipping compass and making precise measurements at around -20°C with swirling snow and ice was far from easy. Properly done, the whole process took at least two and a half hours, involving up to three hundred instrument readings, depending on the conditions. 'A back-breaking feat of endurance for the observer and perishing cold for the recorder,' one member of Mawson's 1912 team later wrote. Today, a similar level of precision can be achieved using magnetometers commonly found in smartphones, capable of measuring the dip and strength of the different components of the magnetic field in under a minute—and without the sort of training the Lloyd-Creak circle required.

By 15 January the compass needle was stubbornly holding back from a fully vertical position, but Mawson's calculations—based on a handful of observations—placed the South Magnetic Pole at just seventeen kilometres away. The men were exhausted and their food supplies were dwindling at an alarming rate. They agreed to make a dash for the pole the following day. About three kilometres out from their temporary base, David, Mawson and Mackay resolved to leave most of the gear with their sledge and push on, lighter of foot, allowing them to cover a greater distance.

The danger was that they might not find their way back, with fatal consequences. The compass was hopeless in this regard, and if they lost their bearings the three men would be left with only the clothes they were wearing and the equipment they were carrying. Conditions were good, but Antarctic weather has a habit of closing in rapidly. As a safeguard, the party decided to leave a piece of equipment a further three kilometres on, to act as a guide if the need arose. They walked for three kilometres, stopped for lunch and set up a tripod as another marker. Once more the three men pushed forward in anticipation. The weather remained clear, and their calculations placed the pole eight kilometres away.

A couple of hours later, some 2200 metres above sea level and more than a thousand kilometres from any other human being, they believed they had reached their goal. Disappointingly, the prismatic compass, after some tapping, still pointed to the west. There remained a small element of horizontal force acting on the compass, but it would have to do. The men had been running on less than half-rations for weeks and were exhausted.

It was a clear day with a light wind and only a handful of clouds overhead. The men hoisted the Union Jack at 3.30 pm and congratulated one another. Mawson set up a camera, arranging all three men in frame. Connecting a string to the camera, David declared, 'I hereby take possession of this area now containing the Magnetic Pole for the British Empire,' and pulled the trigger. They gave three cheers for the king. The photo shows three relieved and exhausted figures standing around the flag, bareheaded in a relatively balmy -18°C. The formalities complete, Mawson packed up the camera and, after a heartfelt 'Thank God,' they turned and fled back to the tent they temporarily called home.

With supplies perilously low, the men forced themselves to march back to the coast, hoping they might still be picked up by the *Nimrod*. In such an environment and under such physical strain it was easy to lose your temper, and both younger men became exasperated with David. Mawson's diaries are a catalogue of concerns and irritations. On 31 January: 'Prof's burberry pants are now so much torn as to be falling off. He is apparently half-demented, by his actions—the strain had been too great.' By 2 February, David's boots were frozen on and one foot had gone numb. 'During most of the day the Prof has been walking on his ankles. He was no doubt doing his best this way, and Mac appears to have kicked him several times when in the harness.'

The following day Mackay threatened to declare David insane unless leadership of the team was passed to Mawson. The young geologist was uncomfortable with the plan, writing of David: 'I again said I did not like the business and stated he had better leave matters as they were until the ship failed to turn up.' The next day they made it to what became known as Relief Inlet, on the Victoria Land coast, where Mackay wrote, 'We are now, of course, expecting the ship. The Professor says that Shackleton promised to send her to look for us on the 1st but one can't believe a word he says.'

They had no supplies to speak of and would be forced to live off seal meat; David would be unlikely to survive a journey down the coast to their winter quarters if they were forced to march south, and the inevitable delay in caring for him would almost certainly be fatal for Mackay and Mawson. As Mackay wrote,

'The whole thing is enough to make a man turn religious.'

Indeed, the *Nimrod* miraculously turned up at 3.30 pm the next day. The ship had passed several days earlier, heading north. On board, the first mate, John King Davis, had been uneasy that because of fog he could not see one section of the 320-kilometre coast they were searching. Coal reserves were low, but the ship duly returned south. It was the first of many strokes of luck for Mawson and Shackleton.

In the excitement of reaching the ship Mawson fell down a crevasse and, with the team members too weak to help, Davis had to rescue him. The South Magnetic Pole team had travelled 2030 kilometres, 1180 in relay, on a 122-day journey—with no dogs or ponies, and more than half a tonne of supplies and equipment. It remained the longest unsupported, man-hauling journey in history until the 1980s, and gave the most accurate fix yet on the location of the South Magnetic Pole.

———•———

As David, Mawson and Mackay were heading back to the coast, Shackleton was leading the other team towards its geographic counterpart. Supported by horses, the men dragged their loads over the crevasse-filled Great Ice Barrier, out beyond the record achieved by Shackleton with Scott and Wilson just a few years earlier. Shackleton observed: 'It falls to the lot of few men to view land not previously seen by human eyes, and it was with feelings of keen curiosity, not unmingled with awe, that we watched the new mountains rise from the great unknown that lay ahead of us.'

The mountain range of Victoria Land continued to stretch before them, forming a southwestern limit of the Great Ice Barrier down to 86°S. Realising they would have to climb this formidable obstacle if they were to reach the pole, the four men forged a route up what turned out to be one of the largest glaciers in the world, a formidable fifty kilometres wide and more than 250 kilometres long, tumbling off the eastern Antarctic Plateau. Losing their last pony and a large part of the remaining supplies down a crevasse on what became known as the Beardmore Glacier, the men were forced to relay the remaining stores. For every mile closer to the pole, three had to be covered. As they worked through a maze of crevasses and steep climbs without crampons, sometimes at a snail's pace, supplies disappeared frighteningly quickly.

They still found time to survey this new land: rocks melting out of the ice gave an insight into the bedrock far below their feet; ramparts of rubble deposited when the Beardmore Glacier had been even larger in the past were noted; the ensuing drops in air temperature were diligently recorded. Given the circumstances, it was an impressive scientific achievement.

During Scott's *Discovery* expedition a young Cambridge graduate, Hartley Ferrar, had gone on sledging expeditions to explore the geology of the area surrounding Ross Island and in particular Victoria Land. Ferrar's insight was to recognise that the whole area had the same sequence of rocks: the lowermost levels were a complex series of volcanic deposits that spoke of violent eruptions and later reburial, overlain by more than a kilometre of fine sediments that became known as the Beacon Sandstone, one of the Antarctic's prime geological features. From the fossils it contained, it represented a remarkably stable time from 416 to 245 million years ago, when the area was made up of shallow lakes and rivers that could be readily identified on the ground. Once you saw the Beacon Sandstone, with its distinctive light-brown sands, you knew where you were in time. At the Beardmore Glacier the Beacon Sandstone could be clearly seen, and in it Shackleton found coal seams metres thick with occasional intruded volcanic rocks that showed the sequence had subsequently been buried deep underground.

The findings were all well and good, but Shackleton knew his backers would demand more. He had to get close to the pole if he was to return in glory and pay off his considerable debts. Food supplies were now dangerously low. Non-essential equipment was jettisoned and meals were cut back to eke out a longer trip.

After some 1350 kilometres of backbreaking sledging Shackleton realised they could not make it to the pole. Standing on an ocean of ice more than three thousand metres above sea level, the four men could not take much more. Temperatures averaging -30°C, exhaustion, hunger, altitude sickness and the possibility of scurvy were all taking their toll. By 4 January three of the men were so cold that the clinical thermometer was not even registering a body temperature. They were close to death.

Enough was enough. They decided to make a dash to the furthest possible southerly point and then head home. 'Our last day outwards,' Shackleton later wrote:

> We have shot our bolt and the tale is latitude 88° 23' South, longitude 162° East...At 4 a.m. started south, with the Queen's Union Jack, a brass cylinder containing stamps and documents to place at the furthest south point, camera, glasses and compass. At 9 a.m. we were in 88° 23' South, half running and half walking over a surface much hardened by the recent blizzard. It was strange for us to go along without the nightmare of a sledge dragging behind us. We hoisted her Majesty's flag and the other Union Jack afterwards, and took possession of the Plateau in the name of his Majesty [Edward VII]. While the Union Jack blew out stiffly in the icy gale that cut us to the bone, we looked south with our powerful glasses, but could see nothing but the dead white snow plain.

They could go no further. A mere ninety-seven nautical miles—equivalent to 180 kilometres—short of their goal,

Shackleton turned his small group around and headed back, having set a new furthest-south record. 'Our food lies ahead,' he wrote 'and death stalks us from behind.'

'And thus we went along,' Shackleton later recounted in a recording made of his exploits, 'and thus we returned, having done a work that has resulted with great advantage to science, and for the first time returning without the loss of a single human life.' Their journey back to the *Nimrod* was a close-run thing. Food supplies had been stretched to the limit; the men fell back on Forced March tablets, made from a cocaine base, to sustain them.

Hollow-eyed, with blistered skin and acute frostbite, Shackleton arrived at the Ross Sea base on 28 February 1909. The next day the *Nimrod* returned to search for bodies and instead found the men alive. Shackleton remarked to his long-suffering wife, 'I thought, dear, that you would rather have a live ass than a dead lion.'

———•———

Shackleton's return to Britain in 1909 generated huge excitement. The expedition members were heroes, though the party had not have achieved its main goal of reaching the South Geographic Pole. Shackleton's newspaper sponsor, the *Daily Mail*, heralded the adventurer's achievements. The tales of endurance and near death guaranteed newspaper sales, and Shackleton's fame: he was knighted that same year; learned men courted his opinion; and Madame Tussauds even made a wax model of the explorer, which stayed on display until 1963. 'We could pass the eight Dreadnoughts if we were sure of the eight Shackletons,' the novelist Sir Conan Doyle observed.

Leonard Darwin, Sir Clements Markham's replacement as president of the Royal Geographical Society, hosted a celebratory dinner to honour Shackleton's return to Britain, proclaiming: 'it had been the policy of the RGS not to reward mere record breaking or racing to either Pole; because there was no reason to suppose that any especial scientific interest attached to that particular spot on the earth's surface...The feat performed by Mr. Shackleton would for ever remain notable even if examined in the coldest light of geographical science; for he had succeeded in penetrating for over 400 miles into hitherto absolutely unknown land.'

With Shackleton's discovery that the ranges of Victoria Land continued southeast for hundreds of kilometres, a vast new mountain chain was suddenly added to the world's maps. Coal had been found in the rock faces surrounding the Beardmore Glacier. And, excitingly for scientists, there was what Priestley later described as a 'discovery' of fossils that showed the 'human hazard the Antarctic scientist has to fear'.

Returning to England by ship, Frank Wild—Shackleton's right-hand man—had struck up a conversation with a young woman who enthusiastically listened to his stories of adventure. Keen to give her a keepsake, Wild offered a piece of rock, some limestone collected on the surface of the Beardmore Glacier thrust up from deep below 'with intriguing little marks almost like Egyptian hieroglyphics'. Priestley, evidently not immune to eavesdropping, became concerned. He stopped the exchange and dashed to his cabin, returning with a piece of granite covered in red garnets. 'Give her this, it's much prettier,' Priestley said, 'and you can tell her it came from the furthest south if you like.'

Cross-sections of the original rock were made in Sydney and it was found to be full of tiny fossils of *Archaeocyathus*, an ancestor of sponges and corals. It was the only unambiguous fossil the expedition had collected, and it showed that the Antarctic limestone deep below the ice was Cambrian in age— proof that the new continent held rocks containing evidence of some of the earliest life on Earth, some half a billion years ago. David and Priestley's account of the geology of southern Victoria Land remained the authoritative account for many years afterwards.

Alongside this, Mawson's important magnetic measurements seemed to prove that the South Magnetic Pole was not moving eastward, as Scott's expedition had suggested—it was travelling in a northwesterly direction. David, in particular, was keen to celebrate the young man's achievements: 'Mawson was the real leader who was the soul of our expedition to the Magnetic Pole. We really have in him an Australian Nansen, of infinite resource, splendid physique, astonishing indifference to frost.'

In the first six months of his return, Shackleton lectured 123 times and travelled 32,000 kilometres across two continents. He was a natural speaker, and the latest technology allowed him to bring Antarctica a little bit closer to those who came to listen. Unlike Africa and Asia before it, Antarctica was being explored by westerners when photographs could be taken relatively cheaply and reliably. The public was blitzed with intimate portrayals of the journey into this new world.

Shackleton took camera work in Antarctica—first undertaken on Borchgrevink's expedition at the turn of the century—to the next level. Photography might be the handmaiden of science, as the Victorians had quickly realised, but Shackleton was canny enough to realise that images of Antarctic wildlife would be a hit with ordinary people. Here was the marriage of entertainment and science, in a display of unfamiliar landscapes and creatures. The wildlife shots were so popular that they almost muscled the expedition's exploits out of newspaper reports.

Other team members joined the lecture circuit, desperately trying to raise the funds to cover the expedition's debt. David was not overly keen about charging Australians to hear his talks on Antarctica, but he realised that if his geological work was to be published he would have to do so. He soon ran into a common problem in dealing with Shackleton. In his desire to raise funds Shackleton had sold the film rights in Australia to a distributor, who cried foul when he found out that the Prof was giving talks at the same time. In the end David agreed to delay his appearances until the film had done the rounds.

Others were less happy. Scott seethed over Shackleton's decision to base himself in McMurdo Sound, but kept his views largely to himself and even joined in some of the many celebrations. He wrote a glowing report for the *Daily Mail*, remarking that 'the really brilliant part appears to have been accomplished by the men themselves dragging their loads.' Ultimately, Shackleton had failed to reach the pole, justifying Scott's return south if he could arrange it.

Markham let his feelings get the better of him and was stand-offish. His early enthusiasm for Shackleton disappeared and he would commonly refer to him as 'that ungrateful cad' in conversation. He felt Shackleton had deliberately tried to take what by right was Scott's, using a base he had agreed to avoid. 'I cannot look with any complacency at Shackleton's expedition,' he recorded in his journal. 'Beginning with a breach of faith, his main objects were to forestall his old commander and to reach the pole. He succeeded in the first rather discreditable object, and failed in the second. But the way in which he pushed onwards from 6 Dec to Jan 9 showed extraordinary pluck and resolution, though very poor management... Altogether, while recognizing the remarkable character of his journey, I am not lost in admiration of his character. Disloyal— unfaithful—underhand. While expressing appreciation of his journey, especially of his discovery of coal, I shall not be over-demonstrative.'

Publicly, Markham was more restrained. In *The Lands of Silence*, published after his death, he wrote: 'A noteworthy fact was that both on the outward and the return journey the wind had been very greatly in their favour.' Shackleton was not impressed.

Called 'the undisputed Lion' in British gossip magazines, Shackleton set the Antarctic agenda for years to come—and a challenge for others to surpass his feats. In the summer of 1909 *The Times* remarked on the increasing pace of discovery in the south: 'In 1900 M. Borchgrevink's expedition only penetrated about 50 miles further south than Ross in 1841, but two years later Captain Scott covered a further 200 miles, and seven years later again his then lieutenant has achieved another 400 miles, reaching to within 110 miles of the Pole.' In the *Sphere* newspaper the secretary of the Royal Geographical Society wrote: 'We may surely be left to cherish a hope that the Union Jack will be carried across the hundred miles or so which have been left untrodden by Shackleton and planted at...the South Pole.' The glory of being the first to reach the South Geographic Pole still remained, and more than ninety-seven per cent of the continent awaited discovery.

By the end of 1909 the cost of Shackleton's expedition was put at almost £45,000—half what the *Discovery* exploration had cost, and remarkably cheap for what had been achieved. Shackleton's self-belief was rewarded: the British government granted £20,000 to help pay off outstanding debts. But for anyone else seeking to go the extra 180-odd kilometres in the south, a future expedition would need a far firmer footing than that enjoyed by the optimistic Anglo-Irishman. For Scott to return and finish the job Shackleton had so nearly completed, government support—even from a superpower like Britain—could not be expected.

Prospective expedition leaders and their supporters resorted to cutting exclusive deals with newspapers and book publishers, and undertaking an ambitious, unprecedented series of public talks and private dinners. Shackleton had shown that, even if an expedition was not hugely successful in finding mineral resources, financial backers did have a chance of becoming immortalised in the landscape. Hopeful explorers would travel from one venue to another, often across different countries, lecturing, discussing, being interviewed, pleading with and sometimes cajoling would-be benefactors. Many became exhausted by the race for funding.

Ernest Shackleton had not been the only explorer working towards a pole in 1909. In one heady week during early September, the world learned of two separate American claims to have reached the North Geographic Pole. On 3 September, Dr Frederick Cook, who had been on de Gerlache's expedition south ten years earlier, returned from overwintering in the Arctic and announced he had reached the pole in April the previous year. Opinion was mixed. When the *Manchester Guardian* canvassed whaling captains the feeling was of widespread scepticism, with one exclaiming, 'Keep it out of the papers; it's a complete hoax,' while another who had spent over thirty years of his life in the Arctic said it was 'a really good yarn but obviously of American origin'.

Four days later Commander Robert Peary of the US Navy claimed he too had reached the pole in April of 1909. *The Times* described it as an *'annus mirabilis* in the history of exploration'. Peary was an Arctic veteran in his early fifties who had made several high-profile attempts to reach the Pole—each a failure, and they had cost him dearly, including the loss of his toes to frostbite. Peary's expedition of 1909 was widely thought to be his last realistic chance at success.

On the news of this second claim Cook initially cabled the *New York Herald*: 'Two records are better than one.' Peary cried foul and declared his rival, the seasoned Antarctic explorer, a fraud. When challenged, Cook failed to produce detailed navigational records and fled to Europe. Peary reaped the rewards. Regardless of whether the world believed Peary had achieved his goal or not—and it now seems he had not—the matter was closed. As far as explorers looking for financial backers were concerned, the north had been claimed.

The prospect of glory through scientific exploration encouraged people to risk life and limb, and their reputation, in the pursuit of the unknown at the far ends of the Earth. With the great geographic record apparently secured in the north, eyes turned south. The Americans lost no time in building on their success. By the end of 1909 Peary had declared he would be glad to organise an American Antarctic Expedition in 1911, with the Weddell Sea touted as a possible base for an assault on the South Geographic Pole. In total, seven expeditions were announced. In addition to the American effort, teams from Scotland, Britain, Norway, Japan, Germany, and Australia and New Zealand set out their plans to scientifically explore the Antarctic, most stating they wanted to be the first to reach the South Geographic Pole.

For Robert Falcon Scott, there was only one nation that should finish what Shackleton had started: 'In whatever measure that remaining distance is computed, it is for England to cover it.' The scene was set for 1912.

CHAPTER 3

A NEW LAND

Robert Scott and the *Terra Nova* Expedition, 1910–1913

---

*The highest object that human beings can set before themselves
is not the pursuit of any such chimera as the annihilation of the
unknown: it is simply the unwearied endeavour to remove its
boundaries a little further from our little sphere of action.*

THOMAS HENRY HUXLEY (1825–1895)

Following Shackleton's near miss of the South Geographic Pole
in 1909, Robert Scott started to put his long-held plans for the
south into action. The Antarctic explorer had made private
enquiries to the Royal Geographical Society, wanting to know
whether it would be sympathetic to his ideas. He did not expect
a large amount of money from the RGS, but sought the society's stamp of approval. Leonard Darwin had advised Scott: 'if
you combine new geographical work, and scientific aims, with
an effort to reach higher latitudes, you will have the warm
sympathy of the Council in your efforts.'

His standing was high in many quarters. Remembering
the fiasco over the election of female fellows, Markham wrote
to Lord Curzon in November 1911: 'He secured for our expedition complete success, which to us was so important. For
this we owe him an immense debt of gratitude. It restored our
credit to us, lost by the mismanagement of the female trouble.'

Scott's science program was endorsed with the full backing of the RGS.

Scott held off making a public announcement. He wanted to get as much in place as possible before telling the world he was returning south. But the claim and counter-claim by Cook and Peary in early September 1909 regarding the North Geographic Pole forced his hand.

On 13 September 1909 *The Times* reported Scott's intentions: to claim the South Geographic Pole for Britain alongside a string of scientific aims, including geographic discovery, geology, meteorology, magnetism and biology. The expedition would follow Shackleton's approach of leaving the men south, with the vessel returning north for the southern winter. And the cost? A trifling £40,000—a little less than Shackleton's efforts. Donations could be sent to '36 Victoria Street, London'.

As Scott later explained in the RGS's journal, three teams would set out from a base in the McMurdo Sound, each with a geologist attached: the Southern Party would strike out for the pole; the Western Party would investigate Victoria Land; and six men would make up an Eastern Party, overwintering separately on or near King Edward VII Land, something Shackleton had attempted and failed to do. The pole was a laudable aim, Scott argued, because it was a spot untrodden by human feet. 'Its quest becomes an outward visible sign that we are still a nation able and willing to undertake difficult enterprises, still capable of standing in the van of the army of progress.'

The other areas of exploration offered a greater understanding of the Antarctic. Unlike the McMurdo Sound region, for instance, almost nothing was known of the other side of the Great Ice Barrier. King Edward VII Land remained one of the few known places that no one had set foot on. Was it an archipelago of islands, or connected in some way to Victoria Land? Scott resolved to find out.

But, Scott argued, it was the duty of an explorer to do more than just record his movements—he 'must take every advantage of his unique position and opportunities to study natural phenomena, and to add to the edifice of knowledge those stones which can be quarried only in the regions he visits. Such a result cannot be achieved by a single individual or by a number of individuals trained on similar lines. The occasion calls for special knowledge and special training in many branches.' The naval officer had learned his lesson from the *Discovery* expedition: this time there would be a specialist scientific team.

Charles Royds was Scott's first lieutenant on the previous journey south and, among his many roles, was the expedition's meteorologist. On returning to Britain he had spoken at the Royal Meteorological Society. 'I most sincerely regret that I did not go thoroughly into the work before we left England,' Royds declared with disarming honesty. 'I left with no fixed idea as to how the observations were to be taken, ignorant, I am sorry to say, of the workings of some of the instruments, and entirely ignorant of what was expected to be done by the authorities at home.'

In the report that followed the expedition, the Meteorological Office assumed—quite reasonably—that Royds's undeclared magnetic wind directions were true geographic bearings. A review of the meteorological report in the *Times Literary Supplement* made painful reading: 'How much longer shall we have to wait in England for those entrusted with national affairs to appreciate a little more seriously the requirements of scientific investigation? Probably until the constant leak and loss which we suffer in ignorance are made plainer by one or more exceptional disasters.'

It did not matter that Scott considered the Meteorological Office to be at fault; the damage was done. Other aspects of the *Discovery*'s scientific program had also been criticised. John Walter Gregory, the scientist who had so nearly led the expedition, remarked: 'It is disappointing to learn that we cannot expect any additions to the deep-sea fauna of the Southern ocean,' and, 'More than once during the course of the expedition the observations desired were accidentally noticed, but the conditions are not stated with sufficient precision to be of service.' At the 1908 meeting of the Physical Society of London the organisation's president, Charles Chree, stated that another national Antarctic expedition should have something akin to a 'scientific court martial' to make sure the outputs were of sufficient quality. The message was clear: Scott was on a short leash.

'I have arranged for a scientific staff larger than that which has been carried by any previous expedition, and for a very extensive outfit of scientific instruments and impedimenta,' Scott told the RGS. He enlisted his old friend and colleague from the *Discovery* Edward Wilson, who agreed to be the chief of scientific staff, zoologist and the expedition's doctor. Together they set about choosing the men they needed for the job.

One of the most important questions for scientists of the era was how the Antarctic fitted into the world's climate system. Early on it had been suggested that there was a low-pressure system that sat over the region, with the air flowing southwards until it reached the pole, where it rose, returning at high altitude northwards to descend over the tropics. With the rising air, it was reasoned, there would be ample snowfall over Antarctica, helping to build and maintain the icecap. But in 1898, at a Royal Society discussion in London, John Murray concluded from Ross's observations of southerly winds bringing clear skies to the extreme south that there was a vast high-pressure system—an anticyclone—over the South Geographic Pole. If this opposing view was true, it implied air was descending over the pole, not rising. Snowfall would be considerably less, meaning Antarctica had to be made up of ancient ice that built extraordinarily slowly compared to that in the north.

There were some tantalising clues to which theory was correct. The *Belgica* expedition noted a change in prevailing winds, from westerly in winter to easterly in summer. One interpretation of this was that the hypothesised anticyclone shifted towards the eastern hemisphere in winter as a result of a cold centre developing on that side. This not only meant a high-pressure system was the dominant feature over the ice, but that a major part of the continental mass lay to the east— something now known to be the case. Observations of clouds and smoke spouting from the volcano Mount Erebus also seemed to show there was a poleward flow of the upper air, and that the cold surface layer was probably no more than fifteen hundred metres high.

If this was all correct, how to explain the huge amount of ice seen in Antarctica? After the *Discovery* expedition Scott had remarked, 'I must add that the warm snow-bearing southerly winds which we experienced have not yet been explained. Even in the depth of winter this wind had sometimes a temperature of +10° to +15° [Fahrenheit].' Scott had previously reported that warmer conditions were associated with the greatest amount of snowfall, paradoxically suggesting that during the last ice age conditions were warmer in Antarctica than they were in the present. Evidently no one knew how the new continent worked.

Louis Bernacchi had been responsible for the weather observations on Borchgrevink's Antarctic expedition and later wrote extensively on the subject. Over twelve months Bernacchi had used a cornucopia of scientific equipment to make daily observations, including maximum and minimum tempera- tures, atmospheric pressure and wind speed. Great care had to be taken during these observations; many of the instruments struggled in the conditions. For instance, although spirit thermometers had to be used because mercury froze in the Antarctic winter, the fluid was not entirely accurate for measuring such low temperatures. Cup anemometers were used for wind speed, but these gave questionable readings over time, eventually being destroyed by gusts that exceeded 145 kilometres per hour. On his return Bernacchi made a series of recommendations on how to improve the quality of future measurements. With these, and the experience gained by the unfortunate Royds, Scott's team had essential guidance for the new expedition.

To direct this work Scott and Wilson chose George Simpson, a professional meteorologist who had been working in the Indian Meteorological Service. Simpson enthusiastically raised £500 from his local town to purchase automatic recording thermometers, barometers, anemometers and balloons to capture as much of the Antarctic climate as possible. He diligently followed the recommendations of the Royal Geographical Society's *Hints to Travellers* and had the instruments calibrated at Kew. There would be no question over the quality of the data this time.

———•———

Scott consulted far and wide on other specialists to recruit, including Edgeworth David, who had now largely patched things up with his wife back in Australia. Top of David's list was Douglas Mawson, who was visiting London at the end of the year. Mawson cabled ahead to Scott and asked whether he would be available to meet to discuss Antarctic research. Scott agreed, but was surprised to find the young Australian was not offering to enlist with him.

Instead, Mawson asked Scott if he had 'thought of the coast W. of C. Adare'. Mawson noted in his diary: 'He said that he had not. I expounded the value of it to him and stated that I would join him if he would land me and a party of 3 on that coast. He was much interested in it...I was put down as a member of his expedition to be confirmed by me within 3 weeks. We had talked from noon till 3 pm. He offered me not less than £800 for the 2 years and that I should be one of 3 to form the final pole party provided nothing unforeseen happened before the final dash.'

The offer to go for the pole did not appeal to Mawson, who wanted to lead a largely scientific endeavour. His choice of Cape Adare was significant. During Borchgrevink's first visit to Antarctica he had collected geological specimens, and David's later study of them had suggested a connection to Australia. It was a hint of the landbridge connecting the continents that Mawson had pondered when he wrote to David about joining him in the south with Shackleton.

Later that month Mawson met Scott and Wilson at the expedition headquarters. Scott felt he had his hands full with the expedition plans and, according to Mawson, 'took up a defensive attitude when I told him I would go to the north coast myself. He stated that it had always been his intention to do what he could around the north coast but could promise nothing—In fact he had now set his mind on picking the plums out of the north coast by a boat reconnaissance on the return of the ship.' Mawson might still have joined Scott if he had been made chief scientist, but Wilson already had that position. It seems Mawson was happy to keep his distance: 'I did not like Dr Wilson,' he noted in his diary.

Wilson later wrote to Edgeworth David, telling him that Mawson would not be joining them. 'His reason,' Wilson explained, 'was that there was no work to be done which he considered worth his while, either at King Edward's Land, or from McMurdo Sound, either S. or W. He would have reconsidered his position had Captain Scott seen his way to landing him as one of the party any where on the coast west-ward along from Cape North. But until King Edward's Land is worked out this could not form part of our programme.' In February 1910 Mawson's proposed research agenda was low on the British expedition's list of priorities.

David recommended three young men as alternative geolo-gists: Raymond Priestley, who had been south with Shackleton, Frank Debenham and Griffith Taylor. The last was known for his strong views, which were sometimes forcibly given; Taylor would in later life declare, 'I do not believe that either mental or physical work of a high order is possible for the average Britisher when the wet bulb registers much above 75 degrees,' and would argue the climate of the Australian interior meant it would be best settled by Mongoloids. Still, he was a superb geologist.

Mawson knew him, and expressed his frustration at the British leader's unwillingness to consider Cape Adare: 'I am almost getting up an expedition of my own—Scott will not do certain work that ought to be done—I quite agree that to do much would be to detract from his chances of the Pole and because of that I am not pressing the matter any further. Certainly I think he is missing the main possibilities of scien-tific work in the Antarctic by travelling over Shackleton's old route. However he must beat the Yankees...'

Other men were brought in to support the expedition for logistic or financial reasons. Before Scott's effort, one member of an exploration team would traditionally be assigned the role of photographer. Now they had a professional within the ranks. Herbert Ponting, a 'camera artist', would record the expedition in photographs and on film. The work would help raise much-needed funds, particularly for the second year of the expedition, as Ponting could show a supportive public film and photographs on his return from the first southern summer.

Apsley Cherry-Garrard—Cherry, as he was known on the expedition—and a military man, Captain Lawrence 'Titus' Oates, both paid £1000 and joined. And, learning of a possible competing Welsh Antarctic Expedition to be led by Edward 'Teddy' Evans—one of the officers on the *Morning*, which had brought Shackleton home from Antarctica in 1903—Scott invited the young naval lieutenant to join him as his second-in-command. Evans readily agreed.

Nineteen hundred and nine was not a good year to go knocking on people's doors asking for money. The Liberal chancellor David Lloyd George's People's Budget aimed to eliminate poverty in Britain by redistributing the national wealth through taxes on the better-off. The rich were not feeling—outwardly, at least—flush. And it was the rich who Antarctic explorers traditionally sought help from.

Scott was not the only one to struggle. The Scottish were one of the first to find it too much, and they failed to get their Antarctic venture off the ground. The possibility of American competition aided the British fundraising effort, but across the Atlantic the public battle between Peary and Cook over the North Pole failed to galvanise opinion about joining the race south. Financial support dwindled, ending the prospect of an American expedition to Antarctica.

With the American and Scottish teams seemingly out of the running, Scott was more determined than ever to make his expedition a reality. Travelling across the country he gave public lectures, held private talks, and approached companies and schools to sponsor equipment. For all his efforts, though, Scott was nervous about promising rich mineral reserves, and his approaches to possible backers were lacklustre. 'It would be foolish,' he said to a Manchester audience in February 1910, 'to hold out a great prospect of the discovery of workable minerals. But if there were such minerals in the South Polar region it was

certain we could not get them without going to look for them.'
His deputy, Evans, was not so shy on the subject and used the
promise of riches to great effect, garnering substantial funds for
the coffers.

The trips around the country were not all about acquiring
donations. They were also a chance to meet scientists and engineers to discuss expedition plans. The pioneering Marie Stopes,
an expert in ancient plants, allegedly danced the night away with
Scott in Manchester, and the young scientist extolled the virtues
of finding *Glossopteris* leaves during the expedition. She implored
the naval officer to take her south with him. Scott declined, but
later visited Stopes at the university to learn more about the
fossils she had described so excitedly on the dance floor. Unlike
the lead-up to Scott's previous journey, fundraising was indirectly helping to develop the expedition's research program.

Scott had intended to take the *Discovery* south again, but the
vessel had been sold and its new owners would not release it.
There were not many other choices. Though Shackleton's
Nimrod was available, Scott selected the old whaling vessel that
had been sent south in 1904 to extract him and his men, the
Terra Nova. The ship cost £12,500, more than a quarter of his
original budget, and was in a sorry state. As Evans would later
write, 'Poor little ship, she looked so dirty and uncared for...I
often blushed when admirals came down to see our ship, she was
so very dirty.'

Removing the whale-blubber tanks, with their overpow-
ering stench, workers scrubbed the *Terra Nova* inside and out,
and prepared the vessel in earnest for the expedition's needs.
New living spaces were installed, laboratories were put on the
poop, the hull was reinforced and a large freezer placed on

the upper deck. Because the freezer was free of iron, it was also home to the ship's compass and the Lloyd-Creak dipping circle—meaning the measurements would be taken alongside 150 frozen mutton carcasses.

As early as 1906 Scott was toying with the innovative idea of a motorised sledge for travelling on the ice. The following year he had approached his friend and colleague from the *Discovery* expedition Reginald Skelton, a naval engineering officer, about helping with its design and going south with him. Skelton threw all his spare time into the project. Originally the plan was to have 'an ordinary sledge propelled by a broad drum or wheel with "paddles" or "ridges" on its rim, the wheel to be situated between the sledge runners, like the stern wheel of a river steamer and driven by say an 8–10 HP petrol motor'. With two air-cooled cylinders, this new type of sledge was designed to carry twenty-two times what a man could pull, at a healthy pace of five kilometres an hour. If it worked, it would make a world of difference.

In March 1908 the first prototype was ready for tests in the French Alps. The results were not encouraging: the engine and wheels could not handle the conditions, and the men went home dejected. Skelton went back to the drawing board, returning to a notion he had been playing with for some time. Writing to Scott, Skelton remarked: 'I was trying to think of some arrangement to lay its own track…the same arrangement of engine as before, but the sledge is lengthened and a second broad wheel added and a flexible band with ridges as its outer surface.' This pioneering concept was the forerunner of the tank that would be used in France during World War I.

By March 1910 the redesigned sledge was ready for testing in Norway. Watched on by Nansen, the new motors successfully negotiated slopes and dragged sledges behind, apparently effortlessly. Although there was no steering—a man up front

would pull on a rope attached to the front to alter direction—
the press loved the contraption. With time of the essence, Scott
had to hope that the motorised sledges would be as effective in
the south and transport supplies across the Great Ice Barrier.
He later recorded in his diary: 'A small measure of success [for
the expedition] will be enough to show their possibilities, their
ability to revolutionise Polar transport.'

Scott was fascinated by Shackleton's near miss with the
South Geographic Pole and, remembering Armitage's obsession with horses, decided to try them himself. Cecil Meares, a
mysterious multilingual adventurer with alleged links to British
Intelligence, was dispatched to Siberia to buy dogs, about which
he knew a lot, and ponies, about which he knew nothing. The
quality of the two hundred or so horses available at the market
was not brilliant, from all accounts, and became even less so
with Scott's instructions to buy only white and grey steeds after
Shackleton's observation that the darker horses tended to fare
worst of all on the *Nimrod* expedition. The belief was that white
animals might better resist the cold, and nineteen were bought,
delighting the pony seller who was said to conclude the deal
with a 'plenty big smile'.

Oates, a decorated veteran of the Boer War who would be
responsible for the horses on the expedition, was appalled at
their state and described them as the 'greatest lot of crocks
I have ever seen'. Frank Debenham, one of the geologists,
described it as a 'curious blunder'. Perhaps suspecting the
horses may not be enough, Scott also invited an expert Norwegian skier, Tryggve Gran—who had also been considering
taking his own expedition south—to train members of the
team in the use of skis.

If all this failed, the expedition could always fall back
on man-hauling the sledges. Scott famously wrote of his
Discovery expedition:

Dogs greatly increase the radius of action, but to pretend that they can be worked to this end without pain, suffering, and death is futile. Such sordid necessity robs sledge travelling by dogs of much of its glory. In my mind, no journey ever made with dogs can approach the height of the fine conception which is realized when a party of men go forth to face hardships, dangers, and difficulties with their own unaided efforts, and by days and weeks of hard physical labour succeed in solving some problem of the great unknown. Surely in this case the conquest is more nobly and splendidly won.

⸻

Teddy Evans abhorred the idea of being second-in-command alongside the engineer Skelton, who held a higher rank as commander. Skelton, recognising that this was not a naval operation, said he would be happy to take a civilian title if it would help. The offer was not enough. Evans flatly refused to work with him, and Scott was forced to let Skelton go, despite the three years of work he had done for the expedition. It was not an auspicious start.

And yet, for all the personality clashes, the team was remarkably cosmopolitan. Many of the British members had enlisted from across the Empire, and were accompanied by Gran from Norway, the Australian geologists and two Russian dog drivers who had joined with Meares.

But the Australians, at least, felt there was a general feeling that British was best. Debenham observed: 'the Australian is more or less disliked by the Englishmen I've met. There is a decided "down" on things Australian in the expedition. It is not altogether explained by the acknowledged tendency we have to "bragging" and "swanking". At times it is quite absurd, and these fellows will not believe that Sydney is reasonably up to date or that educational methods in Australia are not hopelessly out of date.'

Scott, though, was open to international expertise furthering research on the poles. Believing the Norwegian Roald Amundsen to be heading for the North Geographic Pole in the *Fram* in 1910, Scott called on the explorer's home during his visit to test the motorised sledges. As Amundsen was a veteran of numerous polar ventures, Scott was keen to discuss the possibility of synchronising their scientific observations in both hemispheres.

When he failed to see Amundsen, Scott attempted to phone him. Both times the master was not in. Disappointed, the British leader returned home to finish his preparations, and sent scientific instruments identical to his own to the errant Norwegian, so that any data collected could be most reliably compared.

In Melbourne, en route to Antarctica, Scott received a telegram from Amundsen that deeply unsettled the British team: 'Beg inform you Fram proceeding Antarctic.' The Norwegians were taking Nansen's ship south.

———•———

The cold blast of the Southern Ocean storm hit the *Terra Nova* as soon as it had left the relatively safe haven of New Zealand. The winds of the Furious Fifties threatened the expedition's survival almost before it had started. Men bailed frantically and animals looked on wild-eyed as fierce waves frequently swamped the deck. Supplies and equipment were thrown from side to side. All hands were called to secure the lashings on the small wooden vessel's deck and to work the pumps as the crew struggled to keep the vessel afloat. The British ship was seriously overloaded and there was a real risk it would flounder. Several days of desperate work by all hands managed to keep the vessel afloat, and the *Terra Nova* was saved, but it was a close call.

Scott had set out far too early from New Zealand. The idea was to quickly break through the sea ice, and lay food and equipment depots across the Great Ice Barrier during the southern summer, in preparation for the assault on the pole the following season. Finding the edge of the pack ice on 9 December 1910, the ship then took three weeks to get through.

Even now it is hard to predict when the ice has weakenened enough for sea travel. In 1912 the best you could do was to look at what others had managed on their journeys. Shackleton had broken through in just two days in 1908, but it had been relatively late in the season and the continuous sunlight over several months had done the hard work of softening the ice.

Reaching Ross Island on 4 January, the British decided to set up their winter headquarters in McMurdo Sound. Opting for a small promontory fourteen kilometres north of Hut Point, the site of the *Discovery* base, Scott named their home Cape Evans after his second-in-command. The *Terra Nova* could not pull alongside, though, because of the remaining sea ice. Instead, over the following eight days, the supplies and equipment needed to support a team of twenty-three men for a minimum of two years were unloaded and hauled two kilometres on to shore. Apart from the loss of one of the three motorised sledges, which fell through the sea ice when being taken off the *Terra Nova*, the operation was completed efficiently. By 18 January the hut was up and the men had moved into their new quarters.

During these early preparations Scott discussed his thoughts on the Great Ice Barrier and its relationship to King Edward VII Land with the leader of the Eastern Party, the naval officer Victor Campbell. Scott was convinced the ice to the west of what he called Balloon Bight was afloat; to the east, he argued, the ice most probably sat on land. Scott saw the bay as effectively a permanent feature that would be available to the *Terra Nova* for dropping off Campbell and his team—implying Shackleton had played fast and loose in his aborted attempt to land there in 1908. The plan was for the Eastern Party to spend the winter in the bay and explore King Edward VII Land the following year.

Reaching their destination on 3 February, Campbell had bad news. 'We were off the place Balloon Bight should have been, but there was no sign of it. Our sights showed we were south of the old Barrier edge in 1902. About midnight we stood looking into a large bay with a great number of whales blowing.' Priestley, the team geologist, felt vindicated on Shackleton's behalf: the bay was unstable. More importantly, the British found the *Fram* anchored there.

Until the British saw the Norwegian ship, it was not clear where Roald Amundsen was heading; some had thought the Weddell Sea. Now it was evident he was in the same region, and it completely threw Campbell's plans. The British party leader, though, was not convinced by where the Norwegian had placed his winter quarters: 'We went over to his hut and had coffee. He has put it up about 2 miles from the ship in what I think not a very good place as it is on the E side of the bay and weak pressure ice extends south of it.'

Over coffee Amundsen offered the British the chance to stay and continue their work. A dejected Campbell felt this would not do and opted to leave. Falling back on Scott's orders— 'Should you be unable to land in the region of King Edward's Land you will be at liberty to go the region of Robertson Bay [the immediate west of Cape Adare] after communicating with Cape Evans'—Campbell returned to base, left word of his discovery and took off north, to Borchgrevink's old base at the tip of Victoria Land. Campbell's eastern team had become the Northern Party.

Meanwhile, Scott was laying depots across the Great Ice Barrier for the attempt on the pole next summer. Tins of food, tea, cocoa, oil, horse fodder, spare sledges and matches were all being cached in a succession of spots across the ice. The plan was to reach as far as 80°S, where the aptly named One Ton Depot would be a major store for the returning parties the following year. However, on the journey south it was clear to Scott that some of the horses were struggling. Oates suggested killing the weakest pony and pushing on. Scott seems to have been a little squeamish and wanted to preserve them for the main effort next season. The overruled cavalry officer responded, 'Sir I'm afraid you'll come to regret not taking my advice.' 'Regret it or not,' Scott supposedly retorted, 'I have taken my decision as a Christian gentleman.' The southernmost depot was laid fifty-seven kilometres short of their target latitude, and the expedition returned to Cape Evans for winter.

Time on the ice had given the men a chance to evaluate their leader. While all recognised his enthusiasm for science, not all were impressed. When out of the room, Scott was commonly referred to as 'the Owner'. Debenham, in a letter to his mother, summed up his thoughts. 'I am afraid I am very disappointed in him, tho' my faith died very hard,' he wrote. 'There's no doubt he can be very nice and the interest he takes in our scientific work is immense, he is also a fine sledger himself and as organiser is splendid. But there I'm afraid one must stop. His temper is very uncertain and leads him to absurd lengths even in simple arguments...What he decides is often enough the right thing I expect, but he loses all control of his tongue and makes us all feel wild...we are, with the exception of the Owner, a very happy family.'

Scientific study continued apace through the winter, even though the new research sometimes made for uncomfortable reading. After working up his field notes from Victoria Land, Debenham wrote: the 'results are not altogether satisfactory. The fact is we trusted too much to the accuracy of the existing maps. Griff [Taylor] got into a mess with The Owner by declaring that the "Discovery" mapping was a disgrace.' But, when they were not pointing out flaws, both geologists also unearthed wild swings in the continent's past climate. Sand-filled cracked mudflats within the Beacon Sandstone testified to hot, dry conditions, while rocks of a different geology to the local bedrock were found scattered on surrounding slopes, transported there by an ice sheet that had been far larger in the past. Alongside these efforts, the other scientists on the expedition worked on a range of projects that tried to capture the essence of Antarctica: the formation of ice, ocean temperatures and saltiness, tidal variations, the biology—including parasites—on land and in the sea, variations in the Earth's magnetism, and, of course, the never-ending changes in the weather.

Edward Wilson kept an eye out and offered friendly counsel.

———•———

On the value of weather observations *Hints to Travellers* counsels earnestly, 'Travellers may make useful meteorological observations for three distinct purposes: 1st, for contouring, or determining elevation above the sea; 2nd, for extending our knowledge of climate; 3rd, for aiding synoptic investigation; while for their own daily knowledge of the weather, they will be useful and interesting.' Ideally, measurements were to be made at 'intervals of 12, 8, 6, or 4 hours, always dividing the 24 hours into equal parts'. Thanks to Simpson's efforts, Scott remarked, there was a 'first class meteorological station' connected by wires to the hut, allowing it to be monitored by 'a profusion of self-recording instruments, electric batteries and switch-boards, whilst the ear caught the ticking of many clocks, the gentle whine of a motor and occasionally the trembling note of an electric bell', all complementing the observations made by expedition members around the base.

These advances greatly reduced the amount of time the poor observer had to spend outside and, in turn, improved the efficiency of a team with limited staff and many observations to make. Simpson, for instance, was also in charge of the magnetic observations and would spend several hours each day at a dedicated hut set up for taking the various different measurements at internationally agreed times.

The conditions in Antarctica often pushed the equipment to its limits, and breakages were common. As Simpson wrote in his diary, 'Every hour or so during a blizzard I have to go out, mount a ladder to the roof of the hut, remove the vane head, clean out the snow, and replace it. With gusts reaching 70 miles an hour and the air full of drift, this is no pleasant matter.' In spite of the risks he faced, Simpson took Antarctic meteorology into the twentieth century.

Since Scott's first expedition it had been noticed that the clouds of volcanic gases given off by Mount Erebus would often drift in a different direction to the wind on the lower slopes. Erebus is effectively an enormous weathervane, pointing out the direction of blow at its 3800-metre summit. The limitation of all weathervanes, though, is their fixed position. If you want to know the conditions at different levels through the atmosphere, Erebus is of little use. And yet these observations were needed to help answer vital questions: why did the continent remain so cold during the long winter, and how did the Antarctic fit into the world's weather systems?

To get around the problem at Cape Evans, Simpson released hydrogen-filled balloons, to which he attached thermometers and barometers that were capable of taking continuous measurements. Balloon runs were only possible in calm weather; when all was ready, a slow-burning match was lit under the hydrogen, supposedly safely. As the balloon rose it was followed by a telescope, providing wind direction. When the match burned

away, the instruments fell to the ground, connected to a thread
held by the operator, so they could be collected later without
too much trouble. At least, that was the idea—in reality it was
rarely easy. Erebus helped a little, offering indications to the
observers. If clouds of smoke were moving quickly, it meant
the balloons would be nigh on impossible to retrieve, and no
attempt to launch was made. But if a balloon did go up, the
subsequent falling equipment would often disappear over the
horizon, invariably leaving Simpson and his assistant with
precious few measurements.

By the end of winter 1911 the system was suitably refined,
and ten balloon runs were successfully recovered. The results
were startling. In contrast to summer, where there was an
expected fall in temperature with height, in winter the temperature rose from the surface up to the first thousand metres, then
fell gradually. As Simpson put it: 'if the base is cooled, a layer of
cold air forms there which has no tendency to rise and warmer
layers rest upon it.' The winter experienced an extreme temperature inversion, and the reason was the brightness of the surface.
'Of the solar energy which falls within the Antarctic Circle,
such a large proportion is lost by direct reflection from the snow
that the remainder is not sufficient to raise the temperature of
the air to the freezing point before the solstice is reached, and
the energy commences to decrease,' Simpson surmised.

Essentially, during the summer the heat from the sun
warms the snow relative to the overlying air, but during the
poorly lit winter the angle of the incoming rays is so low that
most is rapidly lost to space. The result is a counter-intuitive
rise in winter temperature over the Antarctic continent. The
pervasively cold temperatures first described on the *Discovery*
expedition now had a scientific basis.

Evenings would often be taken up by lectures: members of
the expedition would give talks on all manner of subjects, from

hard-rock geology to the Great Ice Barrier, from Antarctic wildlife past and present to the latest thinking on horse keeping. Simpson was the hardest to impress. His demeanour soon earned him the title Sunny Jim—Simpson's 'emphatic way of stating things and his vigorous "You are completely wrong in all you say" always amuses us', Debenham noted, but he was a 'very clear reasoner and one has to be very careful when arguing with him'.

There was good humour as well. After Atkinson gave a lecture on scurvy, 'Ponting summed up the lecture as disappointing from his point of view as it seemed to him that if he didn't eat seal-meat he would get scurvy and if he did he would get rheumatism.' It was 'Universitas Antarctica', inspired by Scott's philosophy 'Science—the rock foundation of all effort.'

———•———

The local wildlife was central to Scott's research program, but the appeal went beyond the scientific. The knee-high Adelie penguins that lived around the base enthralled the men. Cherry later wrote, 'They are extraordinarily like children, these little people of the Antarctic world, either like children or like old men, full of their own importance and late for dinner, in their black tail-coats and white shirt-fronts—and rather portly withal.' Another expedition member was so entranced he wrote a popular book on them, devising a musical score to describe the noises they made.

After the first year of the expedition the film *South with Scott* had top billing for its penguin performances. 'Comic relief is given by the record of an encounter with penguins,' proclaimed the *Manchester Guardian*, 'whose appearance on the screen, scurrying to and fro like nothing in the world but a crowd of frock-coated old gentlemen in a sack-race, is very humorous.'

The film's success vindicated Scott's belief that Ponting's work would help raise public interest, and with it much-needed funds for the expedition.

Part of the fascination was the penguins' inability to comprehend their new neighbours. Scott wrote of the problems they caused due to their 'fatuous conduct':

> From the moment of landing on their feet their whole atti-
> tude expressed devouring curiosity and a pig-headed disregard
> for their own safety. They waddle forward, poking their heads
> to and fro in their usually absurd way, in spite of a string of
> howling dogs straining to get at them. 'Hulloa!' they seem to
> say, 'here's a game—what do all you ridiculous things want?'
> And they come a few steps nearer. The dogs make a rush as
> far as their leashes or harness allow. The penguins are not
> daunted in the least, but their ruffs go up and they squawk
> with semblance of anger, for all the world as though they were
> rebuking a rude stranger—their attitude might be imagined
> to convey 'Oh, that's the sort of animal you are; well, you've
> come to the wrong place—we aren't going to be bluffed and
> bounced by you,' and then the final fatal steps forward are
> taken and they come within reach. There is a spring, a squawk,
> a horrid red patch on the snow, and the incident is closed.

By the early twentieth century penguins had been a focus of scientific research for some years. A German expedition in 1882–1883, one of the first in the region, investigated the king penguins of South Georgia. This work led to some of the first insights into penguins' behaviour and breeding habits, but included the unorthodox method of strapping the birds to posts in leather corsets while in captivity. Unsurprisingly, the British did not continue this practice.

Wilson took charge of much of the biological work, observing the behaviour and characteristics of local wildlife, collecting samples, dissecting and then analysing them under his microscope. In particular, he had developed a passion for the tall, yellow-breasted emperor penguins on the first *Discovery* expedition. Wilson had been transfixed by the discovery of the first colony of these majestic birds on the other side of Ross Island, at Cape Crozier. Visiting the rookery in early summer, during September 1903, he had been disappointed to find the eggs hatched, implying the penguins had mated and the chicks had been born in winter. A later visit suggested the chicks had a mortality rate of around seventy per cent, which seemed remarkably high to the British scientist.

But it was not merely the life cycle of the emperor penguin that fascinated Wilson: the birds were thought to be something of an early evolutionary offshoot. Their full scientific name is *Aptenodytes forsteri*, in honour of Captain Cook's naturalist, Johann Reinhold Forster, who was one of the first to describe these incredible creatures. *Aptenodytes* means 'featherless diver', referring to the birds' remarkable underwater abilities and their four layers of feathers, which look something like scales. To Wilson, these scale-like feathers hinted at something important.

In 1861 a specimen of a small dinosaur was discovered in a Bavarian limestone quarry. Called *Archaeopteryx*, the find was a revelation. Detailed feathers were clearly visible on two slabs of limestone, along with a toothed jaw and a long bony tail. It pointed to birds having evolved from flying reptiles. Despite being a deeply religious man Wilson was not closed to scientific ideas that might question his faith, and he commented in one of his many reports from the *Discovery* expedition: 'The possibility that we have in the emperor penguin the nearest approach to a primitive form not only of a penguin but of a bird, makes the future working out of its embryology a matter of the greatest possible importance.'

The basis of this was a mistaken idea circulating among some academic circles: during early stages of growth, embryos went through different phases of evolutionary history, giving an insight into the origin of a species. If the theory was correct, Wilson needed embryos from various stages of development. Writing on this winter journey, he observed: 'If vestiges of teeth are ever to be found in birds of the present day it will be in the embryos of penguins which are the most primitive birds living now, and the Emperor is quite the most interesting of them all.' Wilson felt the penguins might be descended from dinosaurs, and foetuses would provide the test.

Previous visits had shown that if you wanted to collect eggs it had to be done in the dead of the Antarctic winter. Wilson asked Scott for Cherry and the appropriately named 'Birdie' Bowers—so called because of his astounding beaklike nose— to accompany him in an attempt on Cape Crozier. Scott was probably wary of putting several of his key men at risk but accepted that Wilson had been determined to collect samples since his *Discovery* days. Science aside, there would also be other benefits to the expedition—it would help inform Scott about the equipment and food needed on the Antarctic Plateau the following summer.

Skirting the southern side of Ross Island at the end of June, the three men set off towards the emperor penguin colony. They worked their way there and back over five weeks, much of the time in darkness, battling temperatures as low as -60°C and wind speeds of up to two hundred kilometres per hour. At times it was so cold that the sledge runners failed to melt the surface ice, preventing gliding, and forcing the three men to unclip and carry their load forward by hand. Back at the bases, the others had little idea what Wilson's team was experiencing. Cape Crozier is one of the most exposed places in Antarctica, and even when it is relatively calm in McMurdo Sound the

eastern side of Ross Island can be blowing a gale, or worse. The
men were exposed to the worst of Antarctic weather.

And yet it is this same environment that emperor penguins
call home. The birds gather in winter, during which the males are
presented with an egg that rests precariously on their feet, tucked
under a fold of skin to keep it warm. As many as several thousand birds huddle and shuffle in one great spiral, each individual
taking a turn in the centre. The huddling is thought to reduce
body-weight loss by up to one-half and is remarkably effective at
preserving the rookery as a viable population. When the chicks
hatch during late winter, sometime between late July and early
August, the females take over the care and the males return to
the sea for a well-earned feed. By December the young birds can
fend for themselves. Cherry later wrote, 'I do not believe anybody
on earth has a worse time than an emperor penguin.'

After three weeks of the most trying conditions the three
men somehow reached Cape Crozier, in July. Wilson was
surprised to see not one hundred birds, having observed far
greater numbers on his previous visit. He estimated only one in
four or five of the birds had eggs. During a large storm the men
lost their tent and the canvas cover of a stone shelter they had
built as a temporary base near the rookery. Fortunately the tent
was recovered after the winds temporarily abated, and the men
returned home, much chastened, bearing five eggs—though
two broke on the journey back to the base.

And yet Wilson wished to return and find out why the
number of birds was so low. 'I see no way of deciding this question except by another visit to the rookery—either this year in
September or October or next year by August.'

Cherry does not seem to have been keen on the idea. In his
later account of the harrowing expedition, *The Worst Journey
in the World*, he wrote, 'The horror of the nineteen days it took
us to travel from Cape Evans to Cape Crozier would have to

be appreciated: and anyone would be a fool who went again.'

There had been useful lessons. The rations used on the Cape Crozier trip gave Scott important knowledge about the likely needs of the expedition during its traverse of the plateau, with its anticipated colder temperatures. On the equipment front, the three men had found some of the gear sadly lacking. The woollen layers, due to their absorbent properties, froze easily in the cold and proved difficult to thaw in camp; even hanging the socks in the upper reaches of the tent rarely resulted in them drying for the next day's effort. Scott had a 'sneaking feeling' Inuit fur clothing might be better, but it 'would have been quite impossible to have obtained such articles'.

The reindeer-fur-lined sleeping bags were awful: the fur became moist from the sleeper's breath, which froze solid when the bag was vacated, forcing the men to re-enter an ice-filled bag the next time, a process that sometimes took up to three-quarters of an hour. The ice added hugely to the weight of the bags at the end of the Cape Crozier mission, increasing them from around eight to a staggering twenty-one kilograms (a typical contemporary down-filled polar sleeping bag weighs three to four kilograms). On the plus side, testing of a double-lined tent for added warmth was an 'immense success' and the man-hauling harnesses had a significant fringe benefit. During the Cape Crozier trip Bowers had fallen into a crevasse and found to his relief that he was still connected to the sledge. He was hauled out relatively safely—some comfort to a team facing the rigours of an unknown land.

Towards the end of the 1911 winter Scott laid out his plans for reaching the South Geographic Pole. Drawing on Shackleton's method and travel times, he intended to follow the *Discovery* leader's proven route. Nervous of trusting the ponies, dogs or motor sledges to make it up the Beardmore Glacier, Scott made a series of calculations based on the size of the team—and the time, fuel and food—needed to support an assault on the pole. Scott was all too aware of the severe conditions on the 3000-metre-high plateau and, guided by his past experience, made it clear that the chance of a bad season was high. Conscious of the likely October blasts of cold, Scott intended to start south at the beginning of November. He wanted to reach the upper plateau early in December and ideally reach the South Geographic Pole around 22 December, at the summer solstice. As the men travelled south the sun's daily arc across the sky would flatten, so that by the time the expedition members reached the pole it would be tracking across the sky through the day at a level 23° above the horizon, with virtually no dip in elevation. The team could use a theodolite to fix its location to an accuracy of around 1.5 kilometres, more than sufficient to claim the pole. He estimated a total travel time of 144 days, returning to base sometime around 27 March 1912, at the extreme end of summer.

When Scott had heard that Amundsen was going south, he had reconciled himself to his original timetable. The pole was important, but rushing would jeopardise the broader scientific program. He did not want to race. After all, 'it doesn't appear the sort of thing one is out for.' Writing home, in missives reproduced in the world's newspapers, Scott had reflected dryly, 'If he [Amundsen] gets to the Pole he will be bound to do it rapidly with dogs, and one foresees that success will justify him. Anyway he is taking a big risk and if he gets through he will have deserved his luck. Meanwhile you may be sure that we are doing the best we can do to carry out our plans.' In the end, there was not much Scott could do. He was committed to the horses, and the men could not leave until the temperature was high enough for the creatures to cope with the conditions.

Summing up his plans to the expedition members, Scott said, 'One cannot affect to be blind to the situation, the scientific public as well as the more general public will gauge the result of the scientific work of the Expedition largely in accordance with the success or failure of the main object [reaching the South Geographic Pole]. With success all roads will be made easy, all work will receive its proper consideration. With failure even the most brilliant work may be neglected and forgotten, at least for a time.'

Feeling he had done as much as possible, Scott reviewed the expedition's scientific work to date. Weighing it against the likelihood of Amundsen beating him to the pole, he wrote in his diary, 'It is a really satisfactory state of affairs all round. If the Southern journey comes off, nothing, not even priority at the Pole, can prevent the Expedition ranking as one of the most important that ever entered the Polar regions.'

The *Terra Nova* returned to New Zealand with news of what had happened so far. During a meeting of the Royal Geographical Society in April 1911 the president remarked:

One must remember that it is only in civilized lands where the traveller can reasonably expect to escape all misfortunes; whilst, as for true exploration, its course never does run quite smoothly. These misfortunes are to be regretted, but they do not in the slightest degree dim our confident expectations that Captain Scott will produce splendid scientific results, or shake our hopes of his reaching the Pole. As to the Norwegian expedition, it will be best to say but little about it until we have fuller accounts of their proceedings, both past and future. I am glad, however, to take this opportunity of expressing my own personal opinion that no explorer attains any vested rights merely by exploration, and that we should therefore welcome all foreign scientific competition on the Antarctic continent, wherever it may appear, if information

is given in good time in advance. I hope also that cordial rela-
tionship will always exist between all Norwegian and British
expeditions, as appears in this instance to have been the case.
But I cannot refrain from expressing my regret that Captain
Amundsen did not give us an opportunity of discussing his
Antarctic proposals before he left Europe for the south.

———◆———

What happened during the following Antarctic summer is one
of the great tales of exploration history. Scott has received bad
press in recent years, with some—perhaps fair—criticism of his
planning. But his was also a hugely ambitious scientific program.
Logistically, the British attempt on the pole was complex,
involving sixteen men who peeled off in small groups as the pole
was approached, all supported by ten ponies, two dog teams and
two motorised sledges.

From the outset Scott was frustrated by slow progress. The
weather was ominously changeable: 'One has a horrid feeling
that this is a real bad season,' he wrote on 4 December. Large
swings in temperature, accompanied by high winds and heavy,
wet snowfalls, led to delays.

The motorised sledges found things particularly difficult.
Parts were in short supply, and the men struggled to keep the
technology going in the alien environment. The sledge chains
regularly slipped off and the engines frequently overheated.
The convoy would often have to stop and turn them off. Only
once the motors had cooled could they be restarted—worryingly, warmed by a blowtorch—and the cavalcade continue. But
this intensive nursing was not enough. After several days, with
the cylinders cracked and spare parts exhausted, the machines
were ignobly dumped and the men were forced to continue on
foot, dragging the sledges of supplies and equipment. Scott

must have rued his decision not to bring Skelton, with his intimate knowledge of the motors' inner workings.

The large convoy took fifteen painful days to reach One Ton Depot at 79°29'S. Shackleton, the expedition leader vented in his diary, had been lucky on his expedition—Scott felt it terribly. But his problems were not all down to the conditions. The combination of transport had unintended consequences: the dogs would attack faltering horses and had to be beaten off with sticks. By the time the expedition had reached the base of the Beardmore Glacier the Manchurian ponies had proved a failure. The low temperatures, along with the animals' need for specialised feedstock and their inability to walk on the thin snow crust of the Great Ice Barrier, meant the expedition would often be held up for several days, slowing the British team when they could ill afford it. When the horses did proceed, they often could only drag lighter-than-expected loads.

To make up for lost time, Meares's dogs were ordered to push on. Originally the canine teams were only meant to cross half the barrier. Now they were to carry on to the base of the Beardmore Glacier, something for which they were not provisioned. Supplies were redistributed and Meares's team continued.

At the bottom of the Beardmore, Scott decided to kill the last of the horses and store their meat in a depot. Wary of Shackleton's experiences, he had no intention of having the ponies and their precious cargo fall down a crevasse, threatening the whole expedition. At the base of the glacier, the dogs were also sent back—it would be man-hauling from now on.

Film shot earlier by Ponting indicates how hard this was: men are shown roped to the sledges, connected to a denim harness that spreads the load across the shoulders and stomach. Hauling their loads across the snow, they repeatedly stumble, weighed down with the effort. Cherry summed up the experience: 'Polar exploration is at once the cleanest and most isolated way of having a bad time which has been devised.'

As the expedition pushed on, small teams of men peeled away. Two groups were sent back along the barrier; another at the top of the Beardmore Glacier. One and a half degrees of latitude short of the pole, Scott suddenly announced he would go on with a team of five men—not four—for the final assault. Bowers was to join him from the other sledging team and second-in-command Evans was to be sent back with naval personnel Tom Crean and William Lashly. The three men were bitterly disappointed—Evans was furious, convinced Scott had never intended to take him and had appropriated Bowers to make his sledge-pulling easier—but their return to base proved more than eventful. On the barrier Evans fell down, ill with scurvy. Dumping geological samples to shed weight, Crean and Lashly dragged him on their sledge. Finding they could pull no further, Crean walked, weak from exhaustion, the remaining fifty-six kilometres to Ross Island and returned with help, saving Evans's life.

———•———

The pole party's scientific work continued unabated. The surrounding mountains were mapped and geological formations recorded—all precisely fixed by theodolites and compasses. Weather observations were a major focus, and meticulously taken each day. For the sledging teams, however, there would be none of the automatic measurements enjoyed by Simpson back at base. Instead, as *Hints to Travellers* suggests: 'On the march, or whenever good shade cannot be had, it will be found a good plan to attach a string to the top of a pocket thermometer, and whirl the instrument round at arm's length for about half a minute.' Breakfast, lunch and dinner a sling thermometer was religiously brought out, swung vigorously round the body and the temperature noted.

Changes in altitude and atmospheric pressure were monitored by barometer readings. As the men slowly approached the Antarctic Plateau temperatures dropped, routinely hitting -30°C and lower. The tents tested on Cape Crozier proved invaluable.

Fatigue, though, brought about mistakes. As the men approached the pole the two chronometers were found to be off by twenty-six minutes. The difference in time was not merely inconvenient: a precise time-keeping device meant the men could accurately place themselves on the ground. The watches were kept individually in small leather pockets attached to the inner vest and close to the body, shielding the mechanism from extreme conditions to maintain a regular beat. This was critical to fixing the time when the sun hit the highest point in the sky each day, and from this the men's location.

The basic premise is that the sun moves overhead at an average speed of 15° of longitude per hour. By measuring the time when the sun is at its highest point in the sky it is possible to calculate an observer's location relative to the agreed meridian in Greenwich, London. If the time of local noon happened one hour after midday at Greenwich, the longitude would be 15°W. But an error of just a few minutes can lead to a serious miscalculation—so Scott's men brought two chronometers, to cross-check. They were meant to be wound up twice a day, before and after a march.

With the watches now disagreeing, there was a question over location and with it the prospect of the British reaching the pole by the most direct route. Scott was furious, convinced Bowers had not taken care of his device. Bowers recorded in his diary that he 'got an unusual burst of wrath in consequence, in fact my name is mud just at present. It is rather sad to get into the dirt tub with one's leader at this juncture.'

And yet Scott pushed on with increasing confidence. By 6 January the British sledging team was beyond Shackleton's

furthest south. Hopes were high—they were on the verge of
reaching new territory. But, ten days later, a heart-breaking
discovery: Bowers spotted a black flag on an upright sledge in
the snow. It could mean only one thing.

On 17 January a dispirited Robert Scott and four companions staggered towards their long-sought goal and discovered
a solitary small tent flying the Norwegian flag. After seventy-
eight days of dragging equipment and food over fourteen
hundred kilometres, they had managed to reach the last great
unclaimed geographical record—but had arrived second.

Amundsen's team had trumped Scott and his men by the
slenderest of margins. Wilson wrote in his diary: 'all agreed that
he [Amundsen] can claim prior right to the Pole itself. He has
beaten us in so far as he made a race of it. We have done what
we came for all the same and as our programme was made out.'

Captive South Georgian king penguins strapped in corsets by the
German polar expedition of 1882–1883. From Karl von den Steinen,
in *Die Internationale Polarforschung 1882–83: Die Deutschen
Expeditionen und Ihre Ergebnisse* (1891).

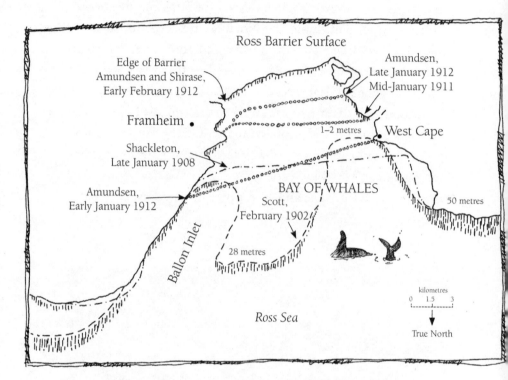

The changing face of the Bay of Whales (1902–1912).
Map inspired by a lantern slide used in Edgeworth David's 1914
Royal Geographical Society lecture 'Antarctica and some of its problems' (LS/333).

CHAPTER 4

OF REINDEER, PONIES AND AUTOMOBILES

Roald Amundsen and the Norwegian Bid
for the South Pole, 1910–1912

Nobody except a demented scientist would want to melt ice on the tops of
mountains, and even if he did, who cared what the temperature was?

WILLIAM ERNEST BOWMAN (1911–1985)

In the lead-up to 1912 Roald Amundsen was already something of a household name. Born in 1872, the Norwegian was obsessed with polar travel from an early age. Reading stories of the doomed Franklin expedition, and later inspired by Fridtjof Nansen's crossing of Greenland in 1888, he was keen to emulate his heroes. But Amundsen, born into a family of shipowners, was devoted to his mother, who from all accounts had a strong personality and was intent on her fourth son becoming a doctor. Amundsen's heart wasn't in it, but he dutifully enrolled at university as a medical student. Barely attending lectures, he received terrible grades and it looked likely he would be asked to leave, when his mother unexpectedly died. At twenty-one Amundsen was suddenly able to escape his obligations, and he promptly went off to sea.

The Norwegian soon had the opportunity to develop as a polar explorer, becoming first mate on the *Belgica* expedition of

1897 to 1899. Under de Gerlache, Amundsen gained valuable leadership skills during the long Antarctic winter dark. It was a turning point. Amundsen's efforts were subsequently highly praised and his standing soared, allowing him to attempt what his hero Franklin had failed to achieve: to find the Northwest Passage.

Busily raising money from numerous sources, Amundsen was aware that a new route was not in itself enough to open the wallets of the wealthy. He needed scientific credibility and support to give the trip cachet. Just as Shackleton had realised that scientific results would help justify his travels, Amundsen worked hard to get recognition from learned societies. No one had reached the North Magnetic Pole since Ross, seven decades before. Had it remained in the same location or moved, as many supposed? Here was a hook to justify the jaunt. Funding continued to prove difficult to source, but there was enough interest for Amundsen to muster a team and start gathering supplies for a two-year trip.

Careers and lives had been lost in the quest for the Northwest Passage. It was a formidable task for any explorer. Most had tried using large ice-breakers to punch a path through the sea ice. Amundsen had neither the resources nor the enthusiasm for such an approach, and instead settled on a different strategy.

Outside the impressive Fram Museum in Oslo, in a dry dock, sits a low, narrow wooden trawler. The *Gjøa* is one of the world's great exploration vessels—but it is largely ignored by visitors today, who walk by to the viewpoint of the local fjord. Amundsen, however, saw this doughty ship offered an alternative method to those tried before. It was capable of taking seven men and enough supplies to survive at least one winter in the ice. More importantly, the *Gjøa* could hug the coast and work through the shallows: crucial for finding a way through the sea ice.

He consulted widely with scientific groups and individuals: Nansen wrote an exhaustive book of instructions on what measurements to make at sea and why, which Amundsen diligently studied; for guidance on magnetism and navigational equipment Amundsen travelled to Hamburg and spent time with the great German scientist Georg von Neumayer. Amundsen was not above asking fellow adventurers for advice, either, writing to Frederick George Jackson about the Burberry waterproof linen he had used in the Arctic.

Funding remained tight. So much so that, his boat stocked with supplies and scientific equipment, Amundsen left Europe in 1903 with creditors chasing him to the quayside. No one was to hear from him for three years.

Setting off towards Baffin Bay, the ship made the long journey past the myriad islands that straddle the Canadian Arctic. Taking advantage of the shallows, the *Gjøa* pushed on until it could go no further, then spent the winter months locked in sea ice. The time was not wasted: on 26 April 1904 Amundsen became the first to reach the position of Ross's North Magnetic Pole, and found it had indeed moved. The scientific community would later scramble to understand these new findings—but for now they remained unknown. Cut off from the rest of the world, Amundsen would not finish the journey that so many others had failed to complete until 1906.

When news broke of his success in negotiating the Northwest Passage, Amundsen stepped onto the international stage. At only thirty-four he had ploughed the first new route into the Pacific since Magellan and Drake worked their way around the opposite end of the Americas. Yet the trip had not been as lucrative as he hoped. An American military officer had intercepted Amundsen's telegram to Nansen reporting his success. The American had enthusiastically let the rest of the world know before the exclusive could be delivered to newspapers willing to pay for it; and, once the cat was out of the bag, editors were not interested in paying for old news. Amundsen had also hoped to claim the British government prize of £20,000 offered in 1745 to discover a sea route for the Northwest Passage. Nansen made enquires but found it had been awarded to those searching for Franklin. Amundsen felt cheated but learned a valuable lesson: secrecy was the key to future success.

The Royal Geographic Society remained enthusiastic about Amundsen's success. Its secretary, Scott Keltie, wrote to Amundsen and suggested that if 'things are properly managed you ought to make a considerable sum' from articles, lectures and a book on his journey. Keltie proposed bringing the *Gjøa* up the River Thames to London—which, after Amundsen 'practically circumnavigating America...would produce a very great effect upon the British public'. The Norwegian was impatient to get back and rejected the advice, travelling straight to Europe and leaving the *Gjøa* to make its way home under another captain.

On his return Amundsen began planning his next sojourn into polar waters, a scientific exploration of the Arctic. He was to follow in Nansen's footsteps and finish what the great man had started: to drift across the Arctic in the *Fram* and claim the North Geographic Pole. Complementing the ship's crew, an expedition team of nine men was brought together. Included was Hjalmar Johansen, who had made the attempt on the North Pole with Nansen. On getting home, Johansen had struggled as a captain in the army and as a family man, regularly finding solace in alcohol. On 24 November 1908 he applied to join Amundsen on his venture. Nansen strongly supported his application and the deal was done, though Johansen was not Amundsen's first choice.

Two months later Amundsen made a pilgrimage to the RGS and received its blessing for the trip. When challenged, he agreed the sole objective of reaching furthest north had in the past led to an unnecessary waste of money and life. Publicly, the main object of the expedition would be a scientific study of the polar ocean.

And yet it was implicitly understood that capturing a pole was popular and financially lucrative. Amundsen was not a scientist, though he understood the value of science in making expeditions happen. The RGS secretary was very supportive. On 28 July 1909 Keltie wrote to Leon Amundsen—Roald's brother, who was managing the expedition—and encouraged him to negotiate with the British papers. The *Daily Mail* and *The Times*, in particular, would be 'disposed to give a very handsome price should your brother actually get to the Pole'.

But the events of September 1909 changed all this. With the news that Cook and Peary were claiming the same goal, Amundsen was in a conundrum. He had secured money for an attempt on the north, but the pole had apparently been taken and his backers were getting antsy. On 9 October Keltie commented that it would be hard to get 'any very big price' after the 'Peary–Cook business'. In spite of this, Amundsen wrote to his friend Cook in early September, congratulating him on his success but informing him he was not able to join the American's European tour of triumph. He needed time to think.

After Peary's announcement on 7 September, Amundsen assiduously avoided sending the new claimant a letter of compliment. 'Peary's behaviour fills me with the deepest anger and I want to proclaim publicly that Dr Cook is the most reliable Arctic traveller I know and it is simply unreasonable to doubt him and believe Peary,' he recorded. Amundsen caught the next train to Copenhagen, to see Cook. With one claim he might have been able to justify a trip north, at least on scientific grounds; but with two, Amundsen needed advice. And who better to offer it than his old confidant?

Precisely when Roald Amundsen changed his mind about heading north is unclear. Years later Cook wrote in his controversial memoirs that he had suggested Amundsen go for the South Geographic Pole when the two met in Copenhagen. Amundsen was more circumspect, but there is no doubt something happened in Denmark to change the Norwegian's mind. There was a flurry of letters to expedition members after Amundsen met Cook, informing them that the expedition would not depart until July the following year. No specific reason was given.

One geographic record remained to be claimed: the South Geographic Pole. Amundsen had to keep quiet. He was all too aware of what had happened in London to Arctowski, after the Belgian's rumoured 1907 plans for an assault on the Antarctic. As far as anyone outside Amundsen's immediate circle was concerned, the Norwegian explorer was intending to take the *Fram* south around Tierra del Fuego, then north up the American west coast, to enter the Arctic through the Bering Strait. The route would avoid Nansen's troubled path and allow a better starting point for the *Fram*, from the Siberian coast, for the approach on the pole.

Amundsen's preparations might have seemed odd to the more careful observer. For a start, the explorer had 120 Greenland dogs, and he insisted on these being sent to Norway rather than picking them up en route, in Alaska; the dogs would have to suffer the tropical heat twice. Then there was the wooden hut he was taking. If Amundsen was intending to spend the time on the *Fram*, designed to keep a large team in relative comfort, he did not need a base on the ice. If he needed to ski—as Nansen had done—he would not require a hut. It was all a bit strange, and some of his team questioned what was going on. They were fobbed off with excuses.

Outside Norway the scientific equipment Amundsen was ordering gave a hint of the change in plan. In early 1910 he wrote to Shackleton's British Antarctic Expedition headquarters and asked for supplier details of their hypsometers. Up to this point the correspondence had mainly been about fabrics; this enquiry was entirely different. Hypsometers are an elegantly simple device for measuring height above sea level. Traditionally, bouts of rheumatism had been used as an indirect measure; hypsometers are altogether more scientific. These contraptions are made up of a small metal column tightly fitted over a metal bowl filled with snow, which is melted and then boiled by a small spirit burner. A thermometer set within the device gives the temperature of the boiling water. Because atmospheric pressure changes with height, the boiling temperature of water also changes, making it possible to calculate altitude. The higher you are, the lower the atmospheric pressure and the lower the boiling water temperature. For every gain in altitude of twenty-five metres, the boiling temperature drops 0.1°C. It is not altogether reliable, and *Hints to Travellers* suggests that to minimise errors 'at least four or five readings should be taken, at half-minute intervals.'

Hypsometers were the principal way of measuring altitude on expeditions in mountainous areas, alongside increasingly accurate barometers. There was no need to determine altitude on the Arctic sea ice, and Shackleton may have known, or at least suspected, something was afoot. But no one said anything publicly. It was a sensitive time: Britain had supported Norway's separation from Sweden, in 1905. Nansen, instrumental in the dissolution, had been dispatched to Britain as Norway's first independent ambassador, serving between 1906 and 1908. Amundsen's incursion in Antarctica could easily be regarded as an insult to a country that had encouraged the young nation's self-determination.

When Scott's decision to head south was announced, on 13 September 1909—just after Peary's reported return from the Arctic—Amundsen was suddenly aware there was competition for the south. Nonetheless, the Norwegian felt his plan was justified: no one had the right to claim anything until they got there. Anyway, he had overwintered in the Antarctic region before Scott had even been made leader of the *Discovery* expedition.

Amundsen now had to tread a fine line. 'At all costs we had to be first at the finish. Everything had to be concentrated on that,' he later wrote. The Norwegian was keen to differentiate his work from the scientific efforts of Scott; it had to be a different sort of expedition. 'On this little détour, science would have to look after itself'—but 'we could not reach the Pole by the route I had determined to take without enriching in a considerable degree several branches of science.'

There was more science to the Norwegian effort than was generally supposed. But some of the planned research would never come to pass, thwarted at the last moment. Probably the most significant casualty was the magnetic work. On 5 August 1909 a young American, Dr Harry Edmonds, wrote to Amundsen agreeing to the Norwegian's invitation to join the *Fram* on its quest for the North Geographic Pole, for what was described as the 'most important part of the scientific work of the trip'. The son of a judge in San Francisco, and claiming 'inherited powers of endurance in pioneer work', Edmonds had an unusual but useful skill set. He was a trained medical doctor, had been on an Arctic expedition and had also run a magnetic observatory. Amundsen was delighted, and confirmed the American's position as lead magnetic observer and expedition doctor. Edmonds and his equipment would be picked up in San Francisco by the *Fram* on the way north.

Later that year Amundsen contacted one of the world's leading centres for magnetic research: the Department of Research in Terrestrial Magnetism at the Carnegie Institute of

Washington. Because of Edmonds's experience in magnetics, the institute agreed to employ him for six months to design and construct the equipment needed on the *Fram*. Equipment lists were drawn up; magnetometers and dip circles were identified. Then the Norwegian wrote to Edmonds, confirming a delay in the expedition, though not giving the real reason. Edmonds felt his time at the institute had been 'without any value whatever to the expedition'. By July 1910 he was ready to go.

Despite Amundsen's insistence, Edmonds was not keen to join him in Christiania by the Norwegian's deadline of 1 August. He could not understand the need for it. Colleagues had told him any measurements travelling around the Horn would be worthless; the *Fram* would have to be swung to take measurements at sea and these would be of little value, given that measurements had already been made on land by people at the institute. The plan, as Edmonds understood it, had been to take observations once the *Fram* was frozen in. Edmonds claimed he was 'absolutely in the dark...about the trip'. He sat tight, and refused to travel until the *Fram* reached San Francisco.

Amundsen was furious, claiming he would 'now have to start without medical service on board which is very annoying'. The Carnegie Institute could—or would—not intercede, and Edmonds was unmoved. Amundsen had run foul of his own secrecy.

———•———

For the trip north there were plans to use polar bears for dragging sledges; now even the ever-ambitious Amundsen could not justify attempting to take them south. The Norwegian was also developing man-bearing kites. The idea rapidly lost its appeal when, in the summer of 1909, the expedition's second-in-command, Captain Ole Engelstad, died when he was struck by lightning. Yet Amundsen was ahead of the game: today kite skiing is hugely popular; in 2008 the Norwegian Ronny Finsås set the record for kiting from the South Geographic Pole to the coast, in just five days.

As some of Amundsen's plans—though not his final destination—leaked out, the media asked other explorers their opinions. Borchgrevink was one of the more vocal. He had advised Scott to use reindeer in the south, and criticised Amundsen for not taking them north.

Amundsen convinced Nansen to let him borrow the polar vessel *Fram*, though he knew his mentor also wished to make an attempt on the South Geographic Pole; when Amundsen decided to switch to the south, he did not tell Nansen. And when Scott twice called on Amundsen to discuss scientific collaboration during the different polar bids, the Norwegian hid. The subsequent arrival of British scientific equipment was deeply embarrassing, but Amundsen was committed to heading south and kept quiet. Amazingly, when the expedition departed few of the crew knew the true destination, most still believing they were heading north via the Bering Strait.

The *Fram* left Norway on 9 August 1910 but only once the ship reached the Atlantic Portuguese island of Madeira, some four weeks later, did Amundsen tell his nineteen-strong expedition of the new objective. Though given the option of returning home, all agreed to proceed. Leon Amundsen had gone with the *Fram* to Madeira and, once all had been settled, returned to Europe clutching a packet of letters and telegrams with the explosive news.

One was a three-page typed apology from Roald to Nansen, explaining his motives and need for secrecy, fearing the titan of Norwegian exploration would attempt to dissuade him; in it Amundsen did not reveal where he would set up a base but said that he would try to meet Scott in Antarctica, and tell him of his plans. The telegram to Scott announcing the Norwegian's plans was sent on 3 October 1910, and reached the British leader in Melbourne. The secret was out, leading *The Times* to comment that Amundsen had not 'played the game'.

The Norwegian expedition members were aware of how much was at stake. The explorer and scientist Bjørn Helland-Hansen wrote to Leon Amundsen, 'Now we must just hope that all goes well with the dogs and the disembarkation then everything will be fine, in spite of reindeer, ponies and automobiles.' The race for the South Geographic Pole was on.

———•———

In mid-January 1911 the Norwegians were pleasantly surprised to find the pack ice in the Ross Sea was not as bad as expected. The sun's warmth had already much weakened it. Travelling nearly a month later than Scott had given Amundsen a tremendous edge: it took five days, as opposed to three weeks, to cover almost the same stretch of ocean. Knowing the British were working in the McMurdo region, Amundsen sailed for Shackleton's Bay of Whales.

The team got to work fast. They erected the hut that had caused consternation in Norway and christened it Framheim. Meanwhile, the sledges and dogs were immediately put through their paces in preparation for the journey further south. Within two weeks the new home was built, the provisions were safely on the ice and the *Fram* was sent north to explore the depths of the southern Atlantic Ocean.

In an age where we can effortlessly—albeit virtually—explore a vast amount of the world's surface from the comfort of a warm home, it is easy to forget that the Norwegians were off the map. When Amundsen was heading to Antarctica, there was still debate over whether it was a continent or a string of islands covered in ice. Unlike Scott, Amundsen could not follow an established route—he had to blaze a new path through an unknown landscape.

The immediate challenge was the Great Ice Barrier. In Scott's 1903 attempt to reach the geographic pole with Shackleton and Wilson, the British team had reported reaching 83°S and finding the barrier kept going. In the process, Scott and his men had discovered the mountain chain that formed the backbone of Victoria Land continued to the south, and apparently bordered the barrier, holding back a vast high-altitude plateau. Scott believed that most of the barrier was floating, but how much further it extended beyond Shackleton's later route was unknown. Closer to the pole, Scott wrote in 1905, it was 'extremely improbable that the full height of the ice-cap of Victoria Land could be seen anywhere from the sea or from the barrier surface. It is certain that the ice-cap is of very great extent...[and] that it maintains a great and approximately uniform level over the whole continent.' Shackleton's findings seemed to bear this out.

But from Amundsen's perspective no one had any idea where the barrier ended and the plateau began. The Norwegian had no desire to be accused of using the 'British route'—which meant starting further east, heading into uncharted territory. And yet there were significant benefits. It also took best advantage of the relative proximity of the Bay of Whales to the geographic pole: Framheim was 1° of latitude closer than Scott's base, equivalent to more than one hundred kilometres that would not have to be covered by sledges, skis or dogs. Early on, Amundsen suspected the barrier was an enormous glacier, and that 'after a steady climb, we will reach the pole at around 7000 ft, perhaps a bit higher', offering the prospect of an easier route. If the mountains did continue south, as Shackleton had suggested, it meant less time spent on the high-altitude plateau. And with more of Antarctica to explore, the Norwegians would be able to proclaim genuine discoveries to learned societies on their return.

There was, however, one big risk: the Bay of Whales. Shackleton had visited the same spot just a few years earlier, and felt it distinctly unsafe—a view also held by Victor Campbell, when he had visited in the *Terra Nova*. In his book *The South Pole* Amundsen later downplayed any concerns and suggested the Bay of Whales had changed little in shape since Ross had visited in the 1840s.

The Norwegian leader popularised the idea that this part of the barrier sat on land. But some expedition members felt movement—something that signalled there was sea below and the location unsafe. If this was true, Framheim risked being cast adrift into the Ross Sea. Amundsen noted their observations but maintained publicly that if Shackleton had based his operations there he would have probably made it to the pole.

We now know the ice around the Bay of Whales is floating and fundamentally unstable. Shackleton was correct: the configuration of the Bay of Whales changes continuously, sometimes drastically. The bay is formed downstream of a prominent ice-covered feature known as Roosevelt Island. A survey in the 1930s found Roosevelt Island lies at the meeting point of two separate ice systems, which flow north nearly half a kilometre a year. The result downstream is a jumble of ice that frequently collapses into the sea. At times the bay almost completely disappears, rendering it unsafe to use, even as a temporary harbour.

━━◆━━

Amundsen set about monitoring the weather from his new home at Framheim, and a routine for observations was soon established. The Norwegian had brought the latest instruments to make automatic measurements—although these were not as sophisticated as Simpson's contraptions. For atmospheric pressure, the barometers were housed indoors behind the open kitchen door, to shelter them from the heat of the stove and prevent jarring. In the living room was a barograph, a device with a stack of small bellows that were highly sensitive to the pressure of air overhead. These would inflate or deflate over time, recording the changing conditions on a slowly rotating barrel of graph paper.

Outside, Amundsen placed a weather station in what he thought was a 'lucky position'. Fourteen metres from the hut, it was far enough away to be unaffected by any heat leaking from Framheim. Henrik Lindstrom, the cook, built a Stevenson screen to house the instruments outside. Made from an old wooden *Fram* model, the screen had four louvred sides, which allowed the air to circulate while keeping the devices out of direct sunlight. Into this were placed two thermometers; a hydrometer, for measuring moisture in the air; and a thermograph, an instrument similar in principle to the barograph but which was comprised of a bimetallic strip of brass and steel that flexed with changes in temperature. Thermographs regularly choked with snow during blizzards. Set apart was a weathervane and an anemometer to measure the wind.

In case the thermometer broke, Amundsen had a regular competition for guessing the temperature. Each team member was required to estimate the temperature every day and the figures were diligently entered into the expedition book; the closest one at the end of each month won its predictor a few cigars. It provided a brief distraction during the long winter wait. Over the winter, when the night sky was clear enough, Amundsen was still able to make geographic discoveries from his base, remarking: 'the dark, heavy water-sky was visible in a marked degree, leaving no doubt that a large extent of the Ross Sea was open the whole year round.'

Before the assault on the south could be made, supplies had to be laid on the barrier for the following summer. In the final sun of early 1911 depots were placed at every degree of latitude across the barrier to 82°S. Totalling more than a tonne and a half, this was enough food for eight men. An organisational genius, Amundsen prepared for the worst. Aware that the paraffin used as fuel for the Nansen cookers could 'creep' out of stoppered containers at low temperatures, he made sure the caps were soldered secure to prevent leakage. It was remarkably effective: while tracing the Norwegian Antarctic route in 2011, the British Army officer Henry Worsley found a can of Amundsen's paraffin, still full.

In anticipation of poor conditions, the depots had a system of black flags to help orient the travelling team. Ten bamboo poles with flags were planted up to nine hundred metres on either side of each depot; each was numbered, giving the direction to the supplies. It was a superb piece of planning that minimised the chance of getting lost.

By March the Norwegian leader found he had not done all of his homework, discovering that the temperature sometimes hit -40°C. 'We were astonished to find this low temperature while summer ought still to have lasted,' Amundsen wrote, 'especially when I remembered the moderate temperatures Shackleton had observed on his southern sledging journey.'

During the British *Discovery* expedition, Scott had undertaken a similar program of weather observations, led by the hapless Royds. On returning to Europe, Scott had invited the Austrian meteorologist Julius von Hann to take a look at the data. Hann realised that in Antarctica, unlike anywhere else on the planet, once the sun dipped below horizon temperatures plummeted and stayed low until the sun rose back above the skyline. Temperatures almost flatline the whole winter; March temperatures are as cold as July. This is in marked contrast to the Arctic, where the coldest temperatures are restricted to the few months around the shortest day of the year.

In 1909 Hann described the Antarctic winter as *kernlos*, coreless. Simpson's observed temperature inversion and the lack of any surrounding land meant Antarctica received no benefit from warming at lower latitudes and went straight from summer to winter, where it remained cold; there was little spring or autumn to speak of. It was a classic example of how northern concepts had no real meaning in the south. But now Amundsen made a finding of his own. He realised he was working in a much colder location than Ross Island: he had inadvertently discovered another pole, this one marking the location of the most frigid conditions in the south. Due to the limited observations made before 1911, Amundsen had come across the latest contender for the Pole of Cold—in the eastern part of the Great Ice Barrier, right where he had chosen to reside for winter.

None the wiser, the English-speaking press talked admiringly of the Norwegian team using the winter moonlight to reach their ultimate destination. Amundsen sensibly stayed in Framheim.

———————◆———————

The Norwegian expedition knew that their presence in Antarctica might cause consternation among the British based in McMurdo Sound. The stakes were high, with paranoia to match. One of the *Fram* sailors wrote, 'Well, if they are planning something bad (we were constantly asking ourselves in what light the Englishmen would view our competition) the dogs will manage to make them turn back...I had better be armed for all eventualities.'

But when the British expedition ship *Terra Nova* came across the Norwegians in the Bay of Whales, it was all peace and calm. They had tea and coffee, and gave each other guided tours of the two vessels. This offered Amundsen the opportunity to allay one of his fears about the British effort. Although 1911 was early for long-distance wireless telegraphy, Amundsen knew Scott was interested in the technology. In the race for the geographic pole the spoils would go to the person who reported success to the world at large, even if he came in second. The Norwegian could breathe a sigh of relief: there was no wireless on the *Terra Nova*.

Amundsen was, though, also aware of the motor sledges' potential for accelerating the British push to the pole. He asked Campbell about them and the reply did nothing to calm his fears: one of them was already on 'terra firma'. Campbell was referring to the sledge lost on the seabed, but he was not going to give the Norwegian the satisfaction of knowing it. Amundsen and his men reportedly fell silent. The British departed, leaving a parting gift: bad head colds for the Norwegian expedition.

Back in London, Leon Amundsen was desperately trying to secure a deal with a British newspaper for exclusive rights to the scoop from his brother's journey. During these negotiations he met many of the protagonists of 1912. Captain John King Davis, who would be second-in-command of the Australasian Antarctic Expedition led by Mawson, declared his hope that Amundsen would beat Scott. The new president of the RGS, Leonard Darwin—son of Charles—happily exclaimed, 'let the best man win.' But there was little love lost with Markham, Leon describing the older man as a 'jabbering idiot'. Shackleton worked hard on the Norwegians' behalf, too, negotiating with different newspapers in London. Leon finally managed to secure an exclusive deal with the now-defunct British *Daily Chronicle* for £2000, which Shackleton felt was good, 'as Polar news is somewhat at a discount'.

In April 1911 the journal of the RGS reported that the

Fram had reached Buenos Aires after leaving Amundsen at King Edward VII Land, and was expected to return south in early October to collect him. The same issue announced that Congress had passed a bill to retire Commander Peary with the rank and pay of a rear admiral in gratitude for his services to America. It was a timely reminder that in exploration terms the north was settled; the south was all that mattered now.

———————— • ————————

By the end of August, Amundsen was champing at the bit to start for the pole. The thought of the British explorers gave him no peace. One of the Norwegian team wrote while at Framheim, 'if we were not first at the Pole, we might just as well stay home.' By early September 1911 they recorded a third day of relatively mild temperatures, hovering around a fine -32°C. Though the sun was not permanently over the horizon, Amundsen could wait no more. Leaving Lindstrom to make weather observations while they were away, the other eight Norwegians headed south.

For transportation Amundsen followed the advice of his mentor, Nansen. The great Norwegian innovator had set out the principles for sledging in polar regions, and Amundsen embraced them wholeheartedly. The wooden sledges were European ash and made up of two wide flat runners bent at both ends, like skis. These were connected by a series of uprights and crossbars to form a frame, topped off with lengthwise slats that were capable of bearing half a tonne. The sledges were lashed with strips of leather—known as greenhide—that allowed the body to flex and follow the contours of the frequently uneven surfaces: a design feature that made it hard to beat on the Antarctic ice. Distances were measured by a sledgeometer, a wheel attached to the back of each sledge specially calibrated for distance. Spurning many of the British choices, the Norwegians decided to use skis and dogs to transport them and their supplies; the men wore fur to keep warm. It was a powerful combination for covering ground quickly.

The warming at Framheim was a false dawn. Temperatures quickly plummeted, reaching -56°C just a few days later. Man and dog alike suffered from the extreme cold and, to top it all, the alcohol froze. By 14 September it was too much. Two of the men were suffering frostbite, and were at risk of losing their heels from the extreme cold. Amundsen decided to return to base. The supplies were quickly stashed and the men fled back to Framheim. Two days later the second-in-command, Kristian Prestrud, was in a terrible state and could ski no longer. Johansen waited two hours and let him ride with his dog team. The Arctic veteran had managed to secure a tent from one of the others but with no stove or food, save for a few dry biscuits, the two men had to push on as best they could.

They reached Framheim at half-past midnight, six and a half hours after the rest of the team. Lindstrom made them coffee but no one else stirred from their sleep, though Prestrud could easily have died on the journey. Amundsen later downplayed the affair, questioning where the two men had been: 'Heaven knows what they had been doing on the way!' The most charitable view is that Amundsen had thought everyone could look after themselves—not a great philosophy for a leader—and had returned to Framheim without looking back.

In his diary Johansen describes it as a 'sad aftermath'. Asked at breakfast why he and Prestrud had been so late, Johansen 'expressed amongst other things my opinion about this strange way of travel and that I had never done anything like this before'. Told patronisingly 'that I would learn as long as I lived and that I would learn more later', Johansen felt 'the arguments were harsh.'

Amundsen claimed in his diary that 'unflattering statements regarding my position as leader for our actions here' had been made. 'During the morning the Chief [Amundsen] walked around and became angry about these statements,' Johansen recorded. It was then that Amundsen showed a single-mindedness that saved his leadership and, arguably, the expedition—but at a cost. Amundsen talked each man round, including Prestrud. Johansen was isolated. 'Naturally after what has taken place, he is completely barred from the 3rd Fram voyage,' Amundsen wrote in his diary. He decided to split the team—he could not risk mutiny during the second attempt on the pole.

With the British gone, Amundsen could use the spare men to achieve another first for the expedition: to explore King Edward VII Land. Prestrud would lead a three-man expedition and Johansen would participate as 'a private person'. Johansen later lamented, 'I have been found incompetent for participation in the expedition to the South Pole and so I have been excluded.'

Amundsen's lapse of judgement in the recent attempt on the pole had unintended practical benefits. The depots laid at the end of the previous summer with the dumped supplies from the aborted effort meant there was a far larger amount of food cached than had been planned, and it was now available for those who would make the next assault on the South Geographic Pole. With only five men now making the journey, the team was well stocked for food.

———•———

On 19 October, Amundsen and his men left with fifty-two dogs pulling four sledges and enough supplies for sixty days. The conditions were now far warmer than September; typical daily minimum temperatures were reaching a relatively balmy -18° to -12°C—ideal for sledges. Because their runners were made using a metal alloy—confusingly called 'German silver', despite it containing no silver—the sledges did not stick to the surface ice. Metal running over ice at these temperatures generates sufficient friction to melt the surface crystals and form a thin film of liquid water, which serves as a lubricant. Too cold and the system falters, as the Cape Crozier effort had found.

Cherry-Garrard, on Scott's team, concluded years later that the most favourable surface for pulling sledges was at -9°C, and they would continue to work reasonably well down to -40°. Colder than this and the water molecules can still form on the surface of the snow crystals, but there are fewer of them and sledging becomes less efficient. Colder still and it is almost impossible. Amundsen was a master in this regard. The Norwegians averaged thirty-seven kilometres a day across the barrier using dogs. They would often cover this impressive distance in just five hours or so, giving the men plenty of time to pitch the tent and rest for the remaining part of the day before the next effort. Boredom was a common complaint.

Amundsen took no longitude sights during the journey, depending instead on a single longitude fix at Framheim and then sticking with latitude observations alone, noting the distances covered each day, courtesy of the sledgeometers. In the early twentieth century there were two schools of thought on how best to navigate off the map in Antarctica. Some, like Scott, felt precise measurements of both latitude and longitude were important if you were to claim a geographical first. But at high latitudes the meridians converge—so much so that a degree of longitude changes drastically across the globe; at the equator it is 111 kilometres, while at 86°S the difference shrinks to just six kilometres and at the pole, of course, it is nothing at all.

In a specially convened session of the RGS in 1910 the British geographer and surveyor Arthur Hinks had argued that it was not always necessary to pay much mind to longitude in southern-polar exploration. Unlike in the Arctic, where moving

sea ice can wreak havoc with bearings, in the south latitude
could suffice: all you had to do was to measure the distance
covered each day and keep to a bearing. The simplicity of this
approach had impressed Amundsen.

Whichever way you decided to reach the pole, you needed
a precious book called the *Nautical Almanac*. Amundsen had
written to the British Admiralty to find out when it would
be available, and was reassured to learn in July 1910 that the
'almanac for years 1910–1913 inclusive will be ready and be on
sale'—and then promptly forgot to take the 1912 issue to Antarctica. Still produced today by the UK Hydrographic Office, this
formidable tome is full to the brim with columns of figures
describing the angles of the sun and other stars, planets and
phases of the moon, for different times of the day, at different
latitudes. For Amundsen and his rivals in the south the almanac
was a must: because of the round-the-clock summer light, the
sun's reported movements were the only way to know precisely
where you were.

As we saw with Scott and the mistimed chronometers, the
most practical way to use the sun was to observe the time it
reached the highest point in the sky, known as local noon, to fix
your location on the ground. And for measuring local noon, the
simplest method was the sextant: it required little training, only
patience and a steady hand. The sextant was traditionally used
on ships, but because of the difficulty of getting a clear line of
sight on the skyline—for example, in mist or fog—it was often
necessary to use an artificial horizon to get an accurate fix. In
Antarctica the conditions are exacerbated by the lack of contrast
between the snowy surface and the sky.

In 1912 artificial horizons were a small box filled with
mercury; in these more enlightened days you have to use
water—no use in freezing conditions—or motor oil as a substitute. A clear line of sight of the sun is taken; then the sextant's

index arm is used to measure the sun's angle in the sky, by looking at its reflection in the artificial horizon. To measure as precisely as possible, and to avoid being blinded, a combination of filters removes the worst of the glare and maintains a sharp image. Following this procedure every few minutes allows you to track the rise and fall of the sun across the sky.

Accurate chronometers were essential. Set to Greenwich Mean Time—commonly known today as Universal Mean Time—these watches played an important role in the calculation. The figures in the *Nautical Almanac*, in tandem with the user's notes on the angle and time of the sun at its highest point, allowed the latitude to be fixed to an accuracy of just a few minutes. It was remarkably effective, and far easier than the British-preferred method of setting up a heavy tripod and making the same measurements with a theodolite. But both approaches depended on the sun being visible.

When cloud obscured the sun, preventing sextant readings, compass readings could play an important role. They presented numerous problems at high latitudes but offered benefits to the explorer who knew what he was doing. Thanks to the efforts of David, Mawson and Mackay on Shackleton's *Nimrod* expedition, the position of the South Magnetic Pole was already reasonably well established. By taking the difference in the compass reading from true south, Amundsen could make the compass a valuable tool for following a particular direction during a day's march. Perversely, it meant heading north when going polewards.

———◆———

As the team relentlessly forged their way across the ice a massive mountain range slowly came into view. It was the same one that in 1909 Shackleton had spotted extending from Victoria Land, but Amundsen and his team had come across it considerably further southeast. The barrier was not going to rise steadily to the pole, as the Norwegian had originally hoped. Driving onwards they found a glacier that appeared to pour off the plateau, through the mountains—which Amundsen named the Queen Maud Range, in honour of his monarch. He named the ice stream after one of the expedition's major patrons, Axel Heiberg, a Norwegian industrialist, and took his sledges and dogs up it.

As they went they made continual weather observations and mapped the land: peaks, glaciers and ice tongues were discovered and recorded. Amundsen also sketched the skyline. These unpublished pencil drawings of the mountain route are housed in the National Library Archive in Oslo, and are evidence of a man acutely aware that he was exploring new terrain, searching for recognisable features that would bring him and his team safely home.

At 85°S the men still had forty-two dogs and had decided to take all of them up to the plateau. Near the top they killed twenty-four, nicknaming the spot Butcher's Shop, and fed the surviving dogs the meat, storing the leftovers. Scott's troublesome ponies had needed their own feedstock; these dogs could feed on one another.

The Norwegians pushed on, but in the rush the expedition crampons were accidentally left at the site of the slaughter. The omission was not spotted until the team faced crossing an area of heavily crevassed ice that became known as the Devil's Ballroom. Amundsen weighed up whether to go back to retrieve them. It was tempting to return: the crampons would make travelling easier. But the estimated time lost was a price Amundsen was not prepared to pay. They struggled on over the ice as best they could, dogs and men regularly falling into crevasses. Lives were nearly lost in the desperate bid to reach the pole. The travelling eventually became easier, though the temperature was now routinely -20°C.

Now the hypsometer—about which Amundsen had contacted Shackleton's office—came into its own. The Norwegian leader needed to know when he had reached the plateau itself. This piece of kit was invaluable: so important, in fact, that Amundsen took four thermometers in case of breakages. On 6 December, at 88°S, the team took the boiling-point temperature and found they were around 3300 metres above sea level: 'Are we now on the final high plateau?' Amundsen wrote in his diary. 'I think so.' They were no longer climbing the Axel Heiberg Glacier and were through the fractured ice—they had reached the Antarctic Plateau.

———•—•———

In polar environments the body quickly becomes dehydrated. Amundsen's men were now frequently complaining of feeling parched during their travels, as well as suffering from headaches and breathlessness brought on by altitude sickness. For the men on the plateau, the effects were exacerbated by the thinner air at that elevation, increasing metabolic and respiration rates. The dry air and increased body temperature in Antarctica means your body sweats more profusely when doing any arduous work; even driving a sledge can become thirsty work. During breaks you have to drink considerable amounts of liquid. And yet eating snow can be fatal: it is not possible to digest enough to meet the body's daily water needs without dangerously lowering its core temperature. Fortunately, the Norwegians had enough fuel to melt snow and drink their fill.

But they were suffering. Three of the men, including Amundsen, had frostbitten faces, with 'sores, inflammation and scabs all down the left side', while the dogs were becoming increasingly threatening. Amundsen considered them 'dangerous enemies when one leaves the sledges...although strangely enough they haven't tried anything'.

On 7 December they were getting close and the sun's angle in the sky was becoming ever more critical to their enterprise. It was five days since their last sighting: 'It took time for "Her Ladyship" to show herself,' Amundsen wrote in his diary. 'But finally she came, not in all her glory, but modestly and sedate... We took a bearing, we made no mistake, and the result was exactly 88°16'; a wonderful triumph, after a march of 1½° in thick fog and snow drift.' They were close to their goal.

The team passed Shackleton's record furthest south on 8 December. Emboldened, and aided by good weather, the Norwegians reached the pole area just six days later and made camp. It was mid-December, close to the summer solstice. The sun's position in the sky was still increasing slightly, though not obviously to the naked eye. Keen to avoid controversy, Amundsen surveyed the area until he was satisfied they could prove their success. The team was split in two, Amundsen making observations with his sextant over twenty-four hours while another group drove 18.5 kilometres out from where the observations were being made, effectively boxing the pole in. They wanted to avoid the debacle of Cook and Peary in the north, and ensure everyone could testify to the readings made.

Their final latitude was recorded as 89°59'S. Those present countersigned the entry for the day, testifying to the measurements and agreeing they had claimed the South Geographic Pole. Contrary to the Norwegian explorer's diary entry, the men reached the pole on 14 December 1911. Just as Phileas Fogg gained a day during his journey around the world, so Amundsen had crossed the dateline sailing to Antarctica and thus was a day off in his log.

'It is quite interesting to see the sun wander round the sky at the same height day and night,' Amundsen wrote in his diary on reaching the pole. 'I think we are the first to see this strange sight.' Regardless of what he had publicly stated, Amundsen does not seem to have believed that Cook, let alone Peary, had made it to the North Geographic Pole.

The Norwegians erected a tent, which they called Polheim, to mark their visit, and left in it some spare gear and, in anticipation of the imminent British arrival, a short letter to King Haakon. Amundsen requested Scott deliver the latter, in case anything should happen to the Norwegian party on the return journey. The letter, with the dark expedition logo of the *Fram* in the top left-hand corner, is preserved today in the National Library Archive in Oslo.

—————•·•—————

With their task achieved, Amundsen and his men enjoyed a smoke, then raced back to the *Fram*. The Norwegians did not wish to meet Scott, and feared the British were hot on their heels. Everything now depended on getting the news home first. Yet they continued to make weather observations on the journey north and also collected rock samples as gifts for their colleagues at Framheim.

Although Johansen and Prestrud had been sent away, ill feeling still bubbled to the surface during the mission. Amundsen felt the pressure of his task—and it did not help that he was suffering from haemorrhoids, a common problem for polar explorers, who lived off constipating high-protein diets. Amundsen's short temper and unwillingness to be contradicted were a constant source of irritation for the rest of the team. On the ascent of the Axel Heiberg Glacier the skier Olav Bjaaland had questioned Amundsen's instructions; the leader then ordered his subordinate to return to Framheim. Bjaaland was no navigator, so one of the other men, Sverre Hassel, was instructed to escort him back once they had reached the plateau. Only by pleading on his knees was Bjaaland allowed to stay on.

Hassel wrote in his diary that he and Bjaaland were also rebuked for having snored in the tent: 'That's O.K. by me but things can be said in several ways. Mr. A. always chooses the nastiest and most haughty one.' Sometime later he mused, 'One might think the man has a screw loose. He has many times in the last few days actually initiated quarrels, an extraordinary stand to take for a Governor and leader for whom peace and good camaraderie should be the main target.' Even Helmer Hanssen, who had managed to avoid falling out with Amundsen for most of the expedition, argued with him just a week short of Framheim, when he suggested one of the dogs stank and the Norwegian leader insisted she did not. The two men did not speak for days.

The successful team reached Framheim on 26 January 1912, having taken ninety-nine days to cover the three thousand kilometres. The original schedule proved remarkably accurate, down to the supplies, number of dogs and time needed for the journey—in fact, the team made it back eight days sooner than expected. Because of the extra supplies in depots, most of the men had actually increased their weight during their return trip. It was an incredible achievement, and the dogs—in spite of their sometimes threatening demeanour—had shown their worth beyond doubt.

With the Norwegian flag flying over the barrier to signify Amundsen's return, the *Fram* returned to the Bay of Whales. No time was wasted. By 30 January the remaining dogs were on board and Framheim left behind. It was time for Amundsen to tell the world of his success.

On 6 March 1912 the *Fram* quietly dropped anchor in Hobart, southern Tasmania. Word quickly leaked out that Amundsen— at first thought a tramp in one of the local hotels—had made it back to civilisation, but it was unclear whether he had been successful in his quest. Desperate journalists swamped the Norwegian leader, to no avail. He had an exclusive deal with the *Daily Chronicle* and he had learned his lesson from the Northwest Passage. Amundsen sent telegrams in code to the king, his brother Leon and the *Daily Chronicle*. To Nansen, he sent the message, 'Thanks for everything. Mission accomplished. All well.' Then he tried to hide.

With little to go on, the other newspapers gossiped away, speculating that Scott may have beaten Amundsen. Out of the loop, the *Manchester Guardian* declared in frustration, 'In Christiania they know that a telegram has been received saying Amundsen has reached the Pole; in Wellington, New Zealand, they know that Amundsen has telegraphed the news that the man who has reached the Pole is Scott.' Norwegian papers, meanwhile, emphasised their man's experience and his 'sterling personal qualities': 'These are a guarantee that he will have made exact and complete meteorological, magnetic and geographical observations, which together with Scott's observations, will give important scientific results.'

On 7 March 1912 the *Daily Chronicle* proclaimed the news of Roald Amundsen's success. Letters and telegrams of congratulations poured in from around the world. Some in the British press expressed outrage; most were more restrained. Outside Europe, interest was equally intense, with the *New York Times* managing to obtain word of Amundsen's triumph and reporting it on the same day as the public announcement in Britain.

Intrepid explorer though he was, Amundsen was not a natural storyteller, and the trip was accounted in a clinical fashion. Moments of danger were brushed over, told without the

excitement the public had come to expect from Nansen, Shackleton and Scott. Amundsen made a virtue of being prepared:
'I may say that this is the greatest factor—the way in which
the expedition is equipped—the way in which every difficulty
is foreseen, and precautions taken for meeting or avoiding it.
Victory awaits him who has everything in order—luck, people
call it. Defeat is certain for him who has neglected to take the
necessary precautions in time; this is called bad luck.'

True—but Amundsen seemed to have little sense of the
story people wanted to hear. And though the Norwegian team
was remarkably well prepared and had planned for almost every
eventuality, success was not a foregone conclusion. Spectacular
arguments had broken out among the men, threatening their
main objective, while crevasses were an ever-present threat,
even if Amundsen played down the risks. Little of the expedition's tension and danger came across in the reports.

The photographer Anders Beer Wilse, who had taught the
expedition members to expose and develop film, found that
Amundsen had largely ignored these efforts, preferring instead
to use his Kodak and declare, 'If I take six pictures with various
aperture and shutter speed, one of them will probably turn out
right.' Today the old cameras appear a wonderful mix of buttons,
bellows and strange attachments, but they are unforgiving. I
tried using a similar camera in Antarctica and, despite the enormous amount of help I received before heading south, I ended
up adopting the Amundsen method, taking a range of shots and
hoping the odd image would work. Most didn't. Glass plates
added another level of complexity, and the extra weight, along
with the need to change the plates in a suffocating sleeping bag,
did not endear them to many explorers.

Wilse believed that Amundsen's poor images cost him
several thousand kroner in lost revenue. The press had to rely
on photos taken by others—in particular Bjaaland, who took

the most famous photo of them all at the South Pole. In it four men stand in a white void, Amundsen on the far left, facing the Norwegian flag flying over the dark tent, Polheim. Most versions of this image are copies of copies. Some are fuzzy, and the fuzziest of all shows a relatively slimline Amundsen and the flag rippling. For his lectures Amundsen understandably seems to have preferred these, the most retouched and flattering copies of the image. To the new nation of Norway, the shot was more than evidence of a world first: it was a public statement that Norway had arrived on the global scene.

The glass plate that gave birth to this famous photograph was developed in Hobart; unfortunately, it seems to have long since disappeared. In 2009 a copy of the closest thing to the original was discovered in the National Library of Australia, in Canberra. A large dog-eared dark-brown album labelled *Tasmanian Views* contains an eclectic collection of photos developed by a professional Hobart photographer, J. W. Beattie, and his assistant, Edward Searle, who Amundsen records having visited. Inside is a strikingly detailed copy of the glass-plate photo taken at Polheim. Amundsen is shown, full-bellied, as one of four bareheaded, sunburnt men saluting the Norwegian flag; the limp pennant suggests the wind was considerably weaker than depicted in the better-known, reproduced versions; even the horizon is discernible.

After his first lectures in Australia, Amundsen did not attract positive comments. When the American promoter Lee Keedick heard rumours that Amundsen had 'made a poor figure on the rostrum', he wrote to Leon and recommended the polar explorer find an English teacher. He warned against including too many scientific elements in public lectures, and suggested Amundsen concentrate more on the humorous aspects: 'Shackleton did this with the most satisfactory results.'

In response Amundsen worked hard on his presentation

style and language skills, peppering his talks with photo slides and film footage from the expedition. By Sydney, things were markedly better. Edgeworth David hosted, speaking highly of Amundsen's achievement and defending his decision to head south. During the Norwegian's numerous talks there was frequent applause, particularly when Amundsen announced that 'he was quite certain that Captain Scott had been to the South Pole, and was now safe and sound in his winter quarters'. It was invaluable practise before Europe.

———•———

Working ferociously on his return to the northern hemisphere the same year, Amundsen wrote *The South Pole* and delivered it to his Norwegian publishers. Within two days of the announcement of Amundsen's success, William Heinemann, founder of the esteemed Heinemann Press, had tried to secure a deal for the English translation of this much-anticipated title—previous polar exploration books had sold well, and Amundsen's account was expected to prove highly profitable. Heinemann asked Nansen to act as an intermediary. But by 18 March he had revoked his offer. The publisher was shocked by a second interview in the *Daily Chronicle*, writing to Nansen: 'I must say I am so disappointed with the want of imagination he displays and the blindness he seems to have for a pictorial attraction in even so thrilling a thing as his achievement that I have decided not in any circumstances to compete for his book...I cannot help feeling that however great Amundsen's feat is, he is not likely to write a good book; and even if he were, it has been so seriously hurt by the wretched cable interview that it is pretty certain to be a disappointment.'

Fortunately for Amundsen, others were willing to take the risk. In Amundsen's English version the weather observations made at Framheim were included for the first time and the units converted from metric to imperial measurements, so they could be understood by the English-speaking scientific community. And when Amundsen returned to Norway he submitted his latitude observations to an astronomer, to be independently checked. The calculations proved correct: Amundsen had made it to the pole, and the report was included as an appendix.

Sales of *The South Pole* were disappointing and reviews were mixed. In the appendices was also a report of the oceanographic cruise made by the *Fram*. During July and August 1911 the vessel had sailed thousands of kilometres, from Buenos Aires to Africa and back again, taking temperatures and salinity measurements as it went. 'Valuable as they are,' wrote one reviewer, 'we feel it somewhat disappointing that a ship like the *Fram* did not do this work in higher southern latitudes in the South Atlantic where the work is even more required, and where the ordinarily constructed ship could not work with the same safety and success as the *Fram*.' The RGS review was positive but expressed amazement that Amundsen had not taken any medical support—it was 'extremely fortunate that the necessity for surgical assistance did not arise'. Dr Harry Edmonds, the American doctor who had missed the journey, appears to have kept quiet.

Other comments were more comical. The *Observer* remarked: 'One is struck by the wealth of infernal nomenclature in Captain Amundsen's narrative. He arrived, he tells us, at "The Devil's Glacier"; and a particularly difficult corner he named "The Devil's Dancing Room." But perhaps, in the Antarctic Circle, the most illicit suggestion of warmth is welcome.'

Amundsen had included a map of his route, drawn up shortly after the polar party had returned to the ship. Commenting on the mountains ascended by the Norwegians, a reviewer remarked, 'Amundsen made the most important discovery that the main line of peaks from there is continued not towards Graham Land [the Antarctic Peninsula], but towards Coats Land [the eastern edge of the Weddell Sea], in the range named after Queen Maud, while in about 86°S., 160°W., another range strikes away to the north-east: this bears no name on Amundsen's map, but in the text it is called Carmen Land.' Amundsen was nervous about whether Carmen Land was real and preferred to describe it as having the 'Appearance of Land'. The reviewer was not sympathetic. 'Such caution is admirable, but it will likely enough result in some explorer in the future taking unto himself the credit for the discovery of this land.'

But Amundsen was right to be careful. Tricks of light are common in the south, giving the appearance of land. The best known are mirages, where light is refracted through the atmosphere, causing a range of unusual effects. Most of us are familiar with movies showing thirsty, desperate explorers seeing images of oases in the desert, the result of a rapid drop in air temperature above the surface. When the opposite happens, with the air cooling towards the surface, objects on the horizon can appear to float above the ground.

Antarctica has an impressive record of claims for new coastlines and mountain ranges caused by this effect, exaggerated by the exceptionally clear skies and low levels of dust in the air. Images can be thrown up above the horizon, frighteningly clear and seemingly closer than where the object is located. Importantly, in exploration stakes, it is not considered a true observation unless you have a direct line of sight; it is not enough to claim a new discovery from a mirage, as some have been shown to appear as far away as 450 kilometres from their true locations, causing much subsequent confusion. So, when Amundsen and his team thought they had seen a mountainous region they called Carmen Land about one hundred kilometres away, they rightly voiced their doubts. And whether this land was real or not would have major implications for our understanding of the make-up of Antarctica.

———•———

Amundsen was the hero of the day, and many wanted to bask in his reflected glory. One of the first was his former Antarctic colleague Frederick Cook, who was visiting Europe in the summer of 1912 in a final attempt to convince the public that he had been the first to reach the North Pole. He asked Amundsen if they might meet and be photographed together, billed as the discoverers of both poles. Amundsen dared not risk it: Cook was falling from grace, and it would not do to be seen publicly with him during his long and bitter argument with Peary; it risked detracting from Amundsen's achievement and drawing comparisons to the Norwegian's decision to compete with Scott. Cook was on his own, and shortly afterwards went into hiding.

What had happened to Scott at the time of Amundsen's return remained unclear. Some newspapers questioned whether both teams had reached the pole and not seen each other. Others wondered when news would be received from Scott. Privately, many connected to the expedition expressed their frustration. Sir Clements Markham's journals were typical of the feeling in Britain. On 12 March 1912 he wrote, 'News that Amundsen had got to Hobart, asserting that he had been to the south pole. We shall hear the truth when the "Terra Nova" arrives.' Markham referred to Amundsen scornfully as a 'gad fly' and his actions as a 'dirty trick', and resolutely refused to acknowledge what the Norwegian had done beyond stealing Scott's thunder.

Other colleagues were more supportive. Scott Keltie of the RGS expressed his relief that the pole had been claimed. Nansen concurred: 'it is a blessing that both Poles have at last been conquered. Now has the time come for solid scientific work in the Polar regions, and there is indeed much to be done both in the one way and the other.' There was some concern over the manner in which it had been conducted, but Nansen was magnanimous. 'I gave up my South Polar expedition (planned exactly as Amundsen's expedition has been now carried out) in order to let Amundsen have the "Fram" for his North Polar expedition,' Nansen later wrote to Keltie. 'This fact may also have made it a little difficult for him to speak to me about it before he left, as I had told him that I considered his North Polar expedition more important than any attainment of the South Pole, and that I therefore gave up the "Fram" to him.'

Nansen would not let Amundsen forget that he was still committed to reaching the North Pole, and insisted his protégé make an attempt. Most financial backers had invested in a Norwegian expedition for a scientific study of the Arctic, after all, and not its southern equivalent. On their return journey Amundsen approached the *Fram* crew to see if they wished to join him for an assault on the original objective. Most were desperate to get home and not enthusiastic. The explorer had to use all his powers of persuasion to talk each individual round— save Bjaaland, who was not having any of it.

Meanwhile, the relationship with Johansen was now irreparable. Amundsen described him in correspondence as a 'rascal' and, on reaching Hobart, Nansen's old friend had left the *Fram* and made his own way home. At the time of public celebrations of the Norwegian success, Johansen went to Solli Park in Oslo and shot himself—a tragic end to the life of one of the great polar explorers.

For all the criticism, awards too were heaped on Amundsen, and invitations were soon forthcoming from Britain. The RGS was particularly keen to host the Norwegian at the end of the year. But, by July, some of the negative comments in the British press were starting to irritate Amundsen and, after an ambiguous report by Lord Curzon, now president of the RGS, the Norwegian wrote a stinging letter, forcing Keltie to protest that there was no bad feeling. Keltie assured Amundsen he would be met in London 'with the most friendly and sympathetic reception', adding, 'Personally I have great pleasure in congratulating you on what you have done. It was a very brilliant feat.'

Reassured, Amundsen went ahead with the visit. In anticipation of his RGS talk he wrote a report on his findings that would be published in the society's journal, variations of which were reproduced around the world. There were concerns over Amundsen's writing and doubts raised about some of his unit conversions. The manuscript was in a 'somewhat colloquial style', prompting Keltie to suggest Amundsen 'omit all mention of what he calls the "butchery" of the dogs'; and, later, observe: 'I suppose he has a right to name part of the Plateau after King Haakon although it is really a part of King Edward Plateau.'

The RGS lecture was not the great success it might have been. In wrapping up the event, after hearing Amundsen's praise for his canine transport, Lord Curzon, the former viceroy of India, allegedly concluded his speech with, 'Therefore, I take the liberty to propose three cheers for the dogs'—while at the same time gesturing to Amundsen to keep calm. Whether the story is real or apocryphal is unclear. At the time, most of the comments concerned the quality of Curzon's delivery, with one journalist complaining that the lord 'mumbled' and 'did not utter a single sentence I could quote in my reports', his report concluding: 'It might have done in India; it actually does in the House of Lords, but it won't do before great meetings of the R.G.S.'

It is difficult to tell whether Curzon's comment about the dogs was a pointed joke or misunderstood, but Amundsen took it as a public insult. In his 1928 memoirs he wrote, 'I feel justified in saying that by and large the British are a race of very bad losers.' Certainly Amundsen was sensitive about the lecture, even going to the length of taping over one half of the Polheim slide, hiding the four Norwegians facing the flag. It was probably a relief for all concerned when the night was over.

———•———

Beyond disgruntled rivals, and uneven book and lecture reviews, there was widespread recognition that Amundsen's was one of the great achievements in world exploration. He had done more than just claim a pole. Through meticulous planning and innovative ways of exploring the south he had revealed profound insights into Antarctica.

William Speirs Bruce, in thanking Amundsen for his RGS lecture, singled out 'the valuable scientific work Captain Amundsen has done in the South Polar regions...Most important is it that he has found the mountain range that Shackleton discovered extending to the south-east as far as 80°S., and also that from a point in 86°S. he has found a range stretching to the north-east.'

Carmen Land was fast becoming a major outcome of the expedition. It was more than just a curiosity, for it appeared to resolve an important problem. Bruce explained: 'there are two theories of the Antarctic continent which have been advocated in recent years. The one is that there is one land-mass, and the other that there are two land-masses divided by a barrier running from the Ross sea to the Weddell sea...now Amundsen has thoroughly cleared up the matter, for he found the great mountain range bounding the inland Plateau to the north continuing north-east to Edward Land, thus shutting the Ross Barrier into a bight. That is a scientific result of the greatest possible importance.'

Bruce seemed more convinced than Amundsen, but the question remained: was Carmen Land real?

CHAPTER 5

THE DASH PATROL

Nobu Shirase and the Japanese South
Polar Expedition, 1910–1912

---

*Each sacrifice on the altar of science has driven man onwards
in the wake of his philosophy, until science has conquered the
pioneer work of the last terra incognita on the Globe.*

CARSTEN BORCHGREVINK (1864–1934)

Cook's and Peary's 1909 claims in the Arctic did more than
cause the Norwegians to switch their sights south. They also
inspired another team—one largely forgotten today—to set out
for Antarctica. But, unlike the Norwegian effort, this expedition
came from a nation that had almost no tradition of exploration. The planned Japanese attempt on the North Pole, led by
Nobu Shirase, was quickly derailed by the announcements of
the two American explorers on their return to civilisation. And
with Shackleton just falling short of the southern counterpart,
Shirase turned his attention to Antarctica, deciding to seek
scientific discovery and adventure there. The result was one of
the most extraordinary of all Antarctic ventures.

Shirase prepared for his expedition with a determination
and zeal that impressed the harshest of critics. Unlike the other
teams of 1912, the Japanese had almost no contact with other
explorers, gleaning what little they could about Antarctica from

books and news reports. Reports of their impending effort went largely unnoticed outside Japan—so much so that the rest of the world was blithely ignorant of their plans until the Japanese suddenly turned up in New Zealand late in 1910. Perhaps most amazingly of all, save for Shirase, the team had no polar experience. The team assembled comprised sailors, enthusiasts, military men and one scientist: all said to have vowed to reach the South Pole or die.

Born in the small town of Konoura, northwest Japan, in 1861, Nobu Shirase was the eldest son of a Buddhist priest. Konoura is now part of the city of Nikaho, and the birthplace of the technology giant TDK, but at the turn of the twentieth century it was a backwater in Japanese affairs, best known for a thousand-year-old temple and a popular annual fish festival celebrating the local cod. And yet, even here, tales of early European explorers, particularly Franklin and his search for the Northwest Passage, reached the young Shirase's ears, inspiring a lifelong passion that would lead to his own expedition.

Like Amundsen, however, Shirase was destined to first follow a different career path, leaving school in 1879 and training to become a Buddhist priest. He soon decided that it did not fit with his plans to be an explorer. Leaving the temple, Shirase signed up to become an officer in the army, and the honour of becoming a priest fell to the family's second son. Shirase's military experiences, while horrific, led directly to his later Antarctic journey.

Shirase's proposal to reach the South Geographic Pole came during a momentous period in his nation's history—a tumultuous time, politically and intellectually. Four decades earlier the Meiji Restoration of 1868 had overthrown the Tokugawa government, ending centuries of self-imposed Japanese isolation. For more than two centuries under the Tokugawa leadership, the Sakoku Edict had made it illegal to go overseas and return to Japan.

To the Tokugawa shoguns the outside world offered only uncertainty, which would lead to internal instability, benefitting overseas powers. With the advent of the Meiji Restoration, Japan decided the best way to deal with the rest of the world was instead to open itself up. Although some saw the new era as threatening—understandable, after such a long period of isolation—others considered it an unparalleled opportunity. Western science was of particular interest: Japanese intellectuals argued that the nation should take science more seriously if the country was to talk to the rest of the world as an equal. Dedicated research institutions were established and progress was swift. The country had its first Nobel Prize nomination by 1910—the same year that Nobu Shirase proposed his expedition.

Shirase was determined that his exploration of the south would help show that Japan was a world power: it could compete for the last unexplored continent. Success in Antarctica would announce that Japan had rejoined the global community.

———•———

Shirase came to Antarctica by a circuitous route. In 1875 Japan had acquired the Chishima Islands from Russia in return for recognising their neighbour's rights elsewhere. Now known as the Kuril Islands, this archipelago stretches from the northern coast of Japan's second-largest island, Hokkaido, all the way up to southern Kamchatka, in far-east Russia. Four years after joining the military, Shirase found himself in the Chishima Islands on his first polar expedition, led by one Naritada Gunji. Between 1883 and 1885 the party would explore the new territory and establish an all-Japanese colony. Poor planning, though, led to the deaths of ten of its members during the first winter, and the following summer Gunji left to fight in the First Sino-Japanese

War, leaving Shirase to spend the second winter with five new expedition members.

Things did not improve. Of the six men, three died from scurvy and the survivors pulled out the following August. Shirase was incensed at Gunji's disorganisation; they had achieved little, at the cost of many lives. He wrote a stinging attack, publicly accusing the former expedition commander of poor leadership. Yet Shirase stayed in the army, and became a veteran of the Russo-Japanese War of 1904–1905. He was one of the few Japanese figures who could claim significant polar experience, invaluable for his planned Antarctic expedition.

Shirase petitioned the government in early 1910 to support his proposed South Pole venture. 'I believe it is the proper course of action to boldly accept this challenge [of polar exploration],' he wrote. 'The powers of the world ridicule the Empire of Japan, saying we Japanese are barbarians who are strong and brave in warfare, but timid and cowardly when it comes to the realm of science. For the sake of bushido [loosely translated, honour] we must correct this regrettable situation.'

It was time to use science to show how progressive Japan was. 'For this reason, from July or August of this year, I humbly propose to...set out to explore the Antarctic accompanied by scientists of various specializations. In addition to scientific contributions, within three years I vow to raise our Japanese Imperial flag at the South Pole and to solve this most formidable challenge of the world'—and to 'expand the nation's territories and become a rich and powerful nation'.

It was a bold vision—or foolhardy, depending on your point of view. Certainly the Japanese government was not particularly impressed. Shirase later wrote that the response was: 'First, we don't have the money and second exploration isn't exactly in our line.' Eventually Shirase argued round the doubters, and was offered a healthy ¥15,000 and a vessel from the naval fleet. First

impressions die hard, however, and the support did not mate-
rialise: the navy was unhappy with the idea of giving one of its
ships to an army man and the government's promised money
never came through.

'I might as well argue with dumb Buddhist idols as with
Government officials,' Shirase later commented. He turned
to others to help finance the trip. In a canny move, he went to
Count Shigenobu Okuma, one of the young samurai who had
started the Meiji Restoration, later becoming finance minister
and then prime minister. By this time well into his seventies, this
national treasure was excited by Shirase's plan. Ignoring government ridicule and hoping to overcome widespread uncertainty,
Shirase made a public call for funding. Speaking to a large and
enthusiastic crowd in Tokyo in July 1910, Okuma announced
the formation of the Antarctic Expedition Supporters' Association, with himself as president.

With Okuma's backing, public funding started to flow in.
The government, though, seemed to take delight in trying to
thwart the nascent Antarctic effort with what Shirase described
as its 'frequent officious meddling'. And yet Shirase showed
aptitude for fundraising, cutting deals here, seeking sponsorship there. He negotiated with the popular magazine *Expedition
World* to advertise his polar activities, in return for the rights to
publish the expedition's first reports.

Unlike his European counterparts, Shirase found it hard to
obtain the sort of support from the learned societies that may
have helped leverage further funds. Whereas the other expeditions of 1912 received the stamp of approval from their national
geographical fraternities, Shirase failed to get the backing of
the Tokyo Geographical Society. Given the parlous state of
the expedition's funding, so dependent on public subscription,
Shirase's scientific program had to be scaled back. Reaching the
South Geographic Pole was the priority.

Not only this, but without official backing few professional scientists would risk their careers—or lives—on the proposed trip. Of the hundreds of applicants, only two of the men accepted could be said to have any sort of scientific background, and one of those had cold feet and fled the day before departure, leaving Terutaro Takeda, a teacher with a background in Earth sciences. Nevertheless, the expedition team obtained a serious amount of scientific gear, much of it for measuring the weather while travelling south and on the ice.

Things were not helped when the British expedition members Cecil Meares and Wilfrid Bruce visited Japan in August 1910, en route for New Zealand, with Scott's ponies and dogs. The Japanese press interviewed the men, and Bruce was reported as saying that without scientific experts any expedition south would have no value, and that the Japanese effort was a 'mistake'. Whereas the local scientific community had been lukewarm, it now became hostile. Indeed, while the journal of the Tokyo Geographical Society would report details on the numerous planned international polar trips, both north and south, it did not mention a word of the home-grown effort.

There was some support from military quarters. An army general, Tsuchiya Mitsuhara, was disgusted with the scientific community and argued that, like his soldiers, scientists should 'be prepared to die for the cause of their work' instead of favouring a 'comfortable livelihood'. Similarly, in the House of Representatives Kokubo Kishiichi gave the profession a public dressing-down, saying: 'in truth, no men are more feeble-minded than scientists.' But, Kishiichi said, Shirase's Antarctic expedition had no need for them anyhow. Ultimately 'anyone can record meteorological conditions…and bring back fossilized things or indigenous wildlife specimens.'

If Shirase was going to counter his critics and avoid cancelling his Antarctic effort like the Americans and the Scottish, he had to leave with his team by the end of 1910—even if they were not fully prepared. In September, Shirase found a ship that would fit the bill. It was a wooden three-masted vessel, the *Daini Hoko-maru*, weighing just 204 tonnes. This was small compared to the others used in Antarctic waters: Amundsen's *Fram* weighed in at four hundred tonnes, while Scott's *Terra Nova* was seven hundred. Designed for fishing the northern waters of the expanding Japanese empire, the *Daini Hoko-maru* was only a year old and large enough for the planned twenty-seven men, supplies and equipment. There was only one problem: the vessel's captain was Gunji, Shirase's former leader in the north.

Time had not healed all wounds and Gunji was not delighted at the prospect of helping his former subordinate. Count Okuma stepped in, buying the *Daini Hoko-maru* for ¥25,000 and registering it in his own name. They renamed the ship the *Kainan-maru*, meaning Southern Pioneer, overhauled and refitted it with an eighteen-horsepower auxiliary steam engine, and buttressed it with iron plating.

The British enthusiasm for horses in Antarctica had not escaped the notice of Shirase and his team. The plan was to follow Shackleton's approach, and use ten Manchurian ponies to reach the South Geographic Pole. After all, Shackleton had nearly reached his goal; it was widely believed that if the horse Socks had not fallen down a crevasse on the Beardmore Glacier with most of the supplies, the team would have made it. But the *Kainan-maru* was too small for horses, and the team decided to switch to dogs. It turned out to be an inspired move, even if there had been little choice.

Preparations started straight away, testing the dogs' capacity to drag sledges along dirt tracks. Shirase was convinced, and the official report of the expedition commented, 'A dog can pull one and a half times as much as a man can on just one man's ration of food, whereas horses are comparatively useless.'

The day of departure had been set for 28 November, the same date Magellan had left Europe on his famous expedition around the world. The crew would re-provision in New Zealand and go from there to Antarctica. This was far too late to credibly reach the Antarctic and establish a winter base that summer, but the public did not know any better and remained upbeat about the enterprise.

The expedition members swore on a scroll 'on which the vow of our intent was sealed with our own blood' at the official farewell ceremony, in front of 'the milling throngs of tens of thousands of well-wishers'. But the *Kainan-maru* was not ready to sail, and few people turned up the following day, causing Shirase to remark it was the 'most dismal sort of send-off ever accorded to any polar explorer'.

There was much to be nervous about—not least that the expedition was ¥10,000 in debt. 'Skimming south like an arrow', though, the *Kainan-maru* headed for New Zealand, aiming to cross the equator by the end of December. Not everyone was convinced they would make it to Antarctica.

───•◆•───

While the Japanese had been frantically preparing for the journey south, the rest of the world was oblivious. After crossing the Pacific, Shirase's team had their first major challenge: facing the international press. Nothing could have prepared the Japanese for the incredulity they faced in Wellington on their arrival, on 7 February 1911. To New Zealanders and to the wider western world, the Japanese plan did not make any sense. There were several expeditions making an attempt on Antarctica; they had all left civilisation by December to give themselves time to work their way through the sea ice, establish a base on the icy continent and lay depots south for the following summer's work.

Scott had come through the New Zealand port of Lyttleton the previous November, while Amundsen had headed into Antarctic waters in January. Yet here were the Japanese turning up in New Zealand in February, with all their dogs dead from the Pacific crossing—most likely from parasitic worms. Perhaps most suspicious of all, they did not seem overly concerned that time was pressing.

With hardly any of the crew speaking English, confusion was rife. Rumours spread that the Japanese were spies; they were publicly mocked. Shirase later wrote, 'The New Zealand press viewed our attempt with ridicule. The *New Zealand Times* was particularly poignant in its comments upon us. It remarked that we were a crew of gorillas sailing about in a miserable whaler, and that the polar regions were no place for such beasts of the forest as we. This zoological classification of us was perhaps to be taken figuratively, but many islanders interpreted it literally.'

Unpleasant as much of the commentary was, there is no doubt that the expedition was at this point a comedy of errors. The Japanese were not aware of what faced them in Antarctica. And from the locals' point of view, their presence did not add up; given Japan's recent military engagement with Russia, the press saw a risk of Asian political interests expanding south.

The men spent much time on shore, looking for books and newspaper reports that might help them with their efforts on the ice. Some of the local press were won over. After the Japanese had restocked supplies and pushed on southwards, New Zealand had 'the honour of offering the last Godspeed to the plucky little band of explorers from the Far East', in the more gracious words of the *Lyttleton Times*.

Being 'helplessly late in the season', the *Kainan-maru* struggled to make headway, carrying on as best it could. On

17 February the Japanese had their first experience of a penguin, which swam towards the ship. The unlucky creature was captured in a bag and assessed: 'It walked upright, looking for all the world like a gentleman in an overcoat. We immediately instructed the ship's carpenter to make a cage for it and we gave it something to eat. As it showed no interest in the food offered we crumbled up some bread to make pellets which we forced into its beak.'

Eleven days later they saw their first ice floe and berg, which 'resembled a gigantic bullock with its head submerged and only its back and hindquarters showing above the surface of the water.' By the morning of 6 March the mountains of the Admiralty Range in Victoria Land 'towered into the sky like the pointed cones of inverted *suribachi* mortars'. The men were so excited that 'they were girding their loins for a landing before we had even thought of dropping anchor.' Alas, icebergs passed by—'with their flat tops they looked like the batteries out in Shinagawa Bay'—and on 9 March the sea started to freeze. 'At first the ice took the form of small lotus leaves, which as we watched gradually spread out over the sea so as to cover the whole surface.' To make matters worse, the compass needle started to swing wildly. They were beginning to experience the effects of proximity to the South Magnetic Pole.

By now winter was fast on its way. 'The ice started to form as particles...and these would at first be about one *shaku* [thirty centimetres] in diameter and one *sun* [three centimetres] thick. They then gradually turned into disks of ice with an area approximately two *ken* square *shaku* [four metres] which drifted on the surface of the sea,' the official account of the expedition later stated. 'As far ahead as the eye could see the surface of the water was completely packed with these disks, and it was now quite probable that they would bring the ship to a halt.' Recognising the risk of becoming trapped, the Japanese tried to find an alternative route. 'The sea was silver white as far as the eye could see, waveless and flat as the surface of a frozen lake.' By 12 March the sea ice had thickened to two *shaku* (sixty centimetres) and the vessel could go no further. 'The crunch and crack every time we smashed through a floe were not at all pleasant.'

The crew attempted to turn the *Kainan-maru* around quickly, desperate to avoid the fate of de Gerlache, who had been beset by the Antarctic winter. Shirase realised they were in no position for such a stay, and headed for Australia. This was easier said than done, and the pack ice caused considerable damage to the hull as the vessel was swung north. The *Kainan-maru* had reached 74°16'S, a respectable latitude for the time of year.

———·•·———

After a rough passage the Japanese limped dejectedly into Sydney on 1 May 1911. The Australian scientist Edgeworth David interceded on their behalf, and the authorities were supportive, giving a berth and exemption from harbour dues.

Newspaper coverage, however, remained tainted by scorn and suspicion. Britain's *Observer* commented dryly that the Japanese had fallen nearly 15° short of Shackleton's efforts: 'The whole incident illustrates the inadvisability, not to say danger, of attempting great undertakings with inadequate means. In the opinion of most observers, the Japanese Government would have been well advised had they interdicted the departure of the expedition until at least they were satisfied that, although there might be failure, there would be no fiasco.' A minor American paper, the *Tacoma Times*, led with the impressive headline 'Swore by Buddha they'd find South Pole but Jap expedition was miserable failure' and wrote of mutiny, with Captain Nomura allegedly taking over from Nobu Shirase and a Japanese government embargo supposedly slapped on the crew once the expedition reached Sydney.

While waiting for the next Antarctic season and for their ship to be refurbished, the expedition members were granted permission to settle in Parsley Bay. The site today is surrounded by dense bush rolling down to the water's edge, with a stunning view of Sydney Harbour. In 1911 the area was largely clear of bush, with more of an English-lawn effect. The Japanese set up their camp among the few remaining tall eucalypts. The main hut and tents, all originally intended for the ice, were used for storage and bathing.

With few funds, the men 'lived almost a beggar's life'. Shirase later wrote: 'There were some who criticised our endeavours, some who mocked us, and some who were even downright abusive.' The shortage of money concerned Shirase, who was not sure the expedition would be able to muster a second attempt the following year. In May, Nomura was sent back to Japan with a report on what had been achieved and the team's future plans: a renewed attempt on the pole, to be reached in February 1913. The expedition's supporters maintained that to give up now would mean Japan 'will be ashamed'—a desperate bid to secure extra funds.

The Australian military became twitchy over the presence of a foreign expedition so close to the fort at South Head. Extra pickets were mounted and all leave was cancelled. The newspapers were keen to know whether an official complaint had been lodged at the Japanese consulate. The *Clarence and Richmond Examiner* published a short piece entitled 'Japanese Espionage', indignantly reporting that a Japanese representative had declared rumours of spying to be 'too ridiculous to entertain seriously'.

Calmer heads prevailed. On 15 May, under the title 'The Mysterious Japs', Sydney's *Sun* wrote that 'Shirase and his merry men' could not be spies: 'No nation—and certainly not a shrewd and intelligent nation like the Japanese' would attempt such surveillance. Describing the Japanese as scientists, Edgeworth David argued in a *Daily Telegraph* interview that 'to raise an outcry against them on the purely imaginary grounds that they are spies is worse than inhospitable—it is sheer nervous stupidity.'

The intervention did the trick, and the hysteria subsided. Now the Japanese camp was swamped with visitors and supporters, many keen to have their photos taken with the team and even getting Shirase to pose with their children. He enigmatically observed that the Japanese were the 'enviable recipients of bouquets from many admiring maidens of the island'.

At home, news of the Japanese return to Australia spurred the organising committee to raise more funds. The risk of disgrace in having to abandon the expedition in Sydney was too much to bear. Count Okuma again spearheaded the effort, and expedition supporters lectured across the nation. In a July interview with the *Japan Times*, Okuma lambasted the government for its broken promises and its reticence to support the team in the field:

> There are men on board the ship who have sufficient knowledge of astronomy and navigation. What more is necessary?… only strong physique, unflagging determination, and the money to back them up are what are wanted, and not learned men. This being the case, we appeal to the generosity of our countrymen…Only the small sum of 70000 yen is needed. We are not Europeans: we need a fifth less provisions and clothes than they do. We have wonderful stomachs whose chemistry can produce much energy from a little amount of food. And our constitution can stand almost any kind of

hardship. When we are thus fitted for the task better than any people, why should we abandon the hope of reaching the Pole and let foreigners get the glory? Some may ask 'What's the use of finding the Pole'? Did the Americans get any benefit from the North Pole? If they succeed in the attempt this time, they will bring back a chart of the seas around the Pole which task has not been done by anybody. When well explored the Antarctic seas will offer us a rich field of fishery. When things are becoming harder for us in the northern seas, a new field of freedom will be welcomed. As to the distance there is but a difference of two thousand miles. Is 70000 yen too big a price to pay for the seas of inexhaustible wealth?

The hyperbole seemed to work. In October, Nomura returned to Sydney with the news that they had at least enough money to continue, bringing with him fresh provisions and other supplies. Shortly after, some of the crew were sent home sick, dogs were delivered and two new expedition members joined the team: Masakichi Ikeda, who bolstered the scientific side of the expedition with his degree in agricultural science, and Taizumi Yasunao, a cameraman from the Japanese film company M. Pathe (not to be confused with the international Pathé Film Company). Shirase could prepare for his second attempt south.

The expedition's original aim was to dash to the South Geographic Pole, but Scott and Amundsen were now firmly ensconced in Antarctica and had a significant start. Shackleton was sceptical of the Japanese bid for the pole and, by 1912, so was Shirase. The expedition duly changed its focus, and science became the primary reason for the trip.

Meeting Edgeworth David was fortuitous for the Japanese. Not only did he alleviate fears in Sydney about their expedition; he also spent considerable time bringing them up to speed on Antarctica, particularly on how best to approach to the continent, the ocean depths, the currents, and its known geography and geology. Shirase and his men finally had access to one of the few experienced Antarctic scientists.

With news that at least some of the funding was secured for a second attempt, Count Okuma telegrammed Shirase in Sydney: 'Go forth. Set sail anew. Though you perish in the attempt, do not return until you have achieved your aims.' The official account of the expedition later stated, 'How did the twenty-seven gallant men of the expedition feel when they received the Count's instructions? There is no need to ask!' Indeed.

On 10 November 1911 the Royal Society of New South Wales gave a farewell dinner in Sydney for the Australasian expedition to Antarctica, led by Douglas Mawson. Attending were representatives of the Japanese expedition, for which a toast was proposed by the University of Sydney's registrar. Japan's Vice-Consul Miho responded that 'they had all one common object in their search after scientific truth—the advancement of humanity.'

By the time Shirase and his men left Australia they were considerably better placed to make a scientific contribution to the exploration of Antarctica. In a letter later published in Sydney's *Daily Telegraph*, Shirase and several key team members wrote to Scott, informing the British leader of the Japanese expedition's intentions. They also wrote to Edgeworth David, thanking him for his endeavours:

Dear Sir,

As you are aware, we are leaving Sydney to-morrow on our journey to Antarctica; but we cannot go without expressing our heartfelt thanks to you for your many kindnesses and courtesies to us during our enforced stay in this port.

When we first arrived at Sydney we were in a state of considerable disappointment, in consequence of the partial and temporary failure of our endeavour. To add to this we found ourselves, and in some quarters, subjected to a degree of suspicion as to our bona-fides, which was as unexpected as it was unworthy.

At this juncture you, dear sir, came forward, and after satisfying yourself by independent enquiry and investigation of the true nature of our enterprise—which no one in the world at the present day is better able to do—you were good enough to set the seal of your magnificent reputation upon our bona-fides, and to treat us as brothers in the realm of science.

That we did not accept all of your kind offers to bring us into public notice was not from any lack of appreciation of the honour you desired to do us. But we felt there was a danger that your generosity and magnanimity might unwillingly place us in a position to which we could only regard ourselves as entitled when our efforts should have been crowned with success.

Whatever may be the fate of our enterprise, we shall never forget you.

We are, Dear Sir, Yours most sincerely
Signed
Nobu Shirase Commander
Nackichi Nomura Captain of the 'Kainan-Maru'
Terutaro Takeda Scientist
Masakichi Ikeda Scientist
Seizo Miisho Physician

On 19 November, their last day in Sydney, Shirase's men bestowed a tremendous honour upon Edgeworth David. For the only known time, a samurai sword was willingly given to a non-national. Its blade measuring only a few millimetres in thickness, the weapon had been forged by the master swordsmith Mutsu no Kami Kaneyasu in what is now Osaka, sometime between 1644 and 1648. It is now held in the Sydney Museum, and is a beautiful thing to behold.

The sword had been presented to Shirase by his sponsor in 1910 as he embarked for Antarctica, with a dedication: 'In admiration of the expedition's courage.' It had seen innumerable battles—but after his first experience in the South Ocean, and the media frenzy in New Zealand and Australia, Shirase felt a huge debt to David. The Australian professor was touched.

The gift-giving over, the *Kainan-maru* departed Sydney Harbour for its second attempt to reach Antarctica. This time the Japanese were better prepared—they had provisions for twenty-seven men and thirty sledge dogs—and heading south at a far more sensible time of year.

Hopes were high among the members of the Japanese team. Although they were a year too late to make a bid for the South Geographic Pole, they could still carry out valuable scientific work. And at least this time they were arriving at the start of the season. Instead of the Southern Ocean threatening to trap the *Kainan-maru*, as it had at the end of the previous summer, 'the floes that now assailed us were all half melted and extremely varied in shape,' according to the expedition report. Working through the pack ice, however, was still fraught with danger: 'The noise the ice floes made as they banged into the ship would be followed by an interminable grating as they scraped their way along the hull followed by yet another bang. Lying in one's bunk listening to these noises was like being shut in a barrel while somebody on the outside attacked it with a stick. With every bang the ship shuddered and seemed to jump astern, and rolled in a most unsettling way.'

Working through the pack, they frequently met enormous icebergs: 'With a ferocious tiger at the front door and a vicious wolf at the back, one peril was followed by another in quick succession.' The pressure was sometimes too much for those on board. Most arguments would blow over, but others were terminal. Shirase fell out badly with Keiichi Tada, the secretary to the expedition, who had argued with the captain and many of the ship's officers during both voyages. Shirase finally had enough: he relieved the secretary of his duties and took him off the expedition roster.

In just a few days they were through the sea ice and into the open water of the Ross Sea. The *Kainan-maru* made good progress and, by 3 January, the Admiralty Mountains of South Victoria Land were sighted. Antarctica was in reach. What would the Japanese do now? They did not have sufficient supplies to reach the South Geographic Pole, but they could explore as far and as widely as possible. In addition to measuring the weather and ocean conditions, Shirase decided to focus part of his expedition's efforts on King Edward VII Land. Scott was known to be working in Victoria Land and some research had already been undertaken there by earlier expeditions. Unaware of the Norwegian disagreements during the aborted attempt on the South Geographic Pole, Shirase felt King Edward VII Land would offer the best return.

Here was a part of Antarctica that Scott and Shackleton had only seen from afar. Neither had managed to land a ship there, and it was uncertain how the region related to the rest of the continent. One possibility was the popular theory that the Great Ice Barrier might be one end of a vast ice-filled strait, stretching across to the Weddell Sea, splitting Antarctica in two. If Shirase could explore this area, and define its boundaries and geology, the Japanese would provide important insights. Quite possibly David had encouraged the Japanese to consider this option, given their limited resources and time. The ship set sail east for King Edward VII Land.

The official expedition report does not quite have the

eloquence of Shackleton's or Scott's writings, but the descriptions are often effective as well as lyrical: as they approached the coastline on 10 January, for instance, the Japanese had seen a glowing 'dim white of light, reflected from the ice' and then, shortly afterwards, a cry went up of 'Barrier ahoy' and they saw it like the 'sinuous length of the Great Wall of China, stretching in an unbroken line from the virgin snows of morning to the moon-white light of evening before our very eyes'.

But the conditions suddenly changed. Temperatures dropped—so much so that the ink on the nibs of their pens froze. The *Kainan-maru* was attacked by a school of twenty killer whales, perhaps believing it to be prey. The two Ainu dog drivers declared the whales messengers of the gods, and were soon lost in fervent prayers during the attack. Thankfully it ended quickly, with the whales withdrawing.

The official expedition narrative indicates a predilection for fighting with the local wildlife. Whether the Japanese had read *Hints for Travellers* is unknown, but they seem to have taken to heart its list of equipment for collecting biological samples. Almost all interactions with the fauna involved a gun or a stick, and were undertaken with almost militaristic zeal.

In the sea, on the ice and in the air, nothing was safe. Albatrosses were regularly caught; one was 'killed by having its head pushed into a barrel of water, sentenced to death by drowning'. They shot at seals on nearby floes, and the expedition report recounts the story of a young crew member diving half-naked into the sea to fight a wounded seal in the freezing water. The man was rewarded for his efforts with a tin of fruit.

It was the penguins, though, that captured the expedition's imagination. Shirase and his men saw many Adelie penguins and decided to take some home for scientific research. The process of capturing these unfortunate creatures was recounted as a tongue-in-cheek military engagement. Going 'penguin hunting', four of the men disembarked from the *Kainan-maru* and, 'armed with just one gun between them, they set off gallantly, rowing towards the crystal island' where the birds stood. The men disappeared behind a mound on the surface of the floe, 'a battle plan cleverly devised to prevent the enemy from detecting their approach'.

After capturing a couple of the birds, they found two remaining penguins were not so easy to grasp and a couple of men were required for the task. The expedition report remarked, 'This made it an excellent match...It was a fight well worth watching, with both men and birds falling over and scrambling to their feet again and again. Though it is hard to give a proper account of this action, the best word is probably comical and we in the audience all fell about the deck laughing.' They later captured another four penguins, described as 'a formidable enemy', and built an enclosure for these 'important guests' outside the research cabin.

On 15 January, after the expedition found a cove in the barrier at 78°17'S and 161°50'W that they called Kainan Bay, four men were sent ashore to explore. The area was far too heavily crevassed to become their base. Deciding to move on, they sailed westward until a ship unexpectedly hove into sight some forty kilometres ahead. A cry of 'pirates' went up. Chaos ensued as the crew tried to get a clear view of the vessel. Shirase prepared his men for action, but they soon made out the Norwegian flag and realised it was the *Fram*, waiting patiently in the Bay of Whales for Amundsen's return later that month.

The *Kainan-maru* sailed past and anchored just a couple of kilometres from the Norwegian ship. It was an ideal location: the bay was close to the barrier edge, and brimming with penguins and seals, which would provide a welcome extra supply of food to supplement their provisions. No one was more surprised than the Norwegians that two expeditions should meet like this at the bottom of the world—they had last heard the Japanese were in Sydney. Amundsen's team could understand little of Shirase's plans, and only managed to solicit enthusiastic statements such as 'nice day' and 'plenty ice' from his men.

———•———

Unlike the Norwegians, the Japanese had no intention of staying over the winter. They were at the Bay of Whales to get as much work done as possible in two weeks and return home. On the ice the crew went 'hunting penguins, seals and suchlike to dissipate the weariness of the long journey, like little birds let out of their cage'. The Norwegians were horrified.

Stores were unloaded, and equipment moved off the sea ice and onto the barrier. Cutting a route up through the ice, Shirase took six men with him to establish a base camp. Capturing moments like this, the official expedition report has a fine sense of the poetic, describing the snow and ice layers that made up the barrier as being like 'Mother Nature herself had painted this mural, this infinite masterpiece, which had been conjured into existence by heavenly beings with celestial pigments of unearthly hues'.

After a few days the Main Landing Party had broken a route up on to the barrier and transported the supplies there. The official report later called this 'indescribably difficult and fraught with danger…without doubt the worst of all the trials and tribulations we had experienced since we left our mother's womb'. The *Kainan-maru* left the seven-man party with an agreement to return in a couple of weeks, during which time the vessel would explore the coastal side of King Edward VII Land and attempt a landing.

Heading south on 20 January, Shirase led four men on sledges pulled by dogs for a dash into the interior. Never realistically intending to reach the South Geographic Pole, Shirase instead aimed for the Dash Patrol to explore as far south as possible, in an area to which no one had been. So, rather than head directly south as Amundsen had, the group went south-east. The two other men remained to continue making weather observations at the base camp.

The Japanese were entirely dependent on the dogs and sledges. They had no knowledge of skis and were amazed when they later saw Amundsen's team using 'special Norwegian snow shoes made from long, narrow boards of wood'. Instead, wearing felt-lined boots, the five men forged on through strong winds, snowstorms and temperatures as low as -25°C, covering the ground as best they could. And yet, despite their inexperience and the frequent need to halt—staying in dog-fur-lined sleeping bags inside their tents—the Japanese made good time. As they went they made observations of the weather and ice.

Condensation in the Japanese snow goggles was a common complaint. Even today this is an occupational hazard in Antarctica: perspiration regularly leads to glasses fogging up and dimming. There is nothing for it but to take them off and wipe them with a cloth. The relief at being able to see clearly makes it tempting to leave the glasses off, even knowing the risk of snow blindness. For those teams on the ice for weeks on end, even the most disciplined eventually succumbed. Snow blindness was a common and painful experience for all of the expeditions of 1912.

By 28 January the Dash Patrol had reached as far as it could safely manage. Shirase was nervous about missing the *Kainan-maru* and getting trapped in Antarctica for the winter. The Japanese had covered 237 kilometres after travelling for just eight days—remarkable, compared to the distances achieved by earlier expeditions. Scott's attempt on the South Geographic Pole, during the *Discovery* expedition, covered four hundred kilometres but in fifty-eight days. The Japanese put much of their success down to the dogs.

Reaching 80°5'S and 156°37'W, they buried a cache: a copper casket containing a list of those who had supported the expedition. A bamboo pole with the Japanese flag was planted in the ice and, after three *banzai*—an exclamation meaning 'ten thousand years of life', and used as a salute to the emperor—Shirase claimed the area for Japan and declared it Yamato Yukihara, or the Japan Snow Plain. After taking a few photographs, the men quickly packed up their gear and headed north, back to the Bay of Whales and, they hoped, the waiting *Kainan-maru*.

———•———

After dropping off the Main Landing Party the *Kainan-maru* left the Bay of Whales on 19 January and headed towards King Edward VII Land, sailing as far east as 155°W—a record unsurpassed until 1934. The Japanese later considered this part of the expedition to be 'far more fortunate and successful'. They became the first people to land on the coast of King Edward VII Land, finding a bay further east than either Scott or Shackleton had reached—which in turn allowed them to be the first to explore the interior from the seaward side.

Scaling the ice barrier, two members of the expedition managed to reach the Alexandra Mountains, first described by Scott. Looking beyond they saw a new mountain range branching off south-southeast. It was not necessarily Carmen Land, but it was yet more proof that King Edward VII Land formed the eastern limit of the Great Ice Barrier. They left a memorial post with a list of those on this part of the expedition, announcing their visit, and the *Kainan-maru* headed back west to the Bay of Whales.

In a bid to help finance the expedition Shirase had sold film rights to M. Pathe, which sent a junior technician from its Tokyo office for the second voyage. Cameraman Taizumi Yasunao was only twenty-three when he joined the expedition in Sydney, and was not keen on the trip to Antarctica. But he was at least partly placated by a twentyfold increase in his monthly salary and ¥5000 in life insurance.

Taizumi may not have had quite the same eye as some of the better-known Antarctic photographers of the time, but he managed to capture the essence of the expedition. Unfortunately, a large amount of the footage was lost on the return journey due to poor conditions; but there was enough to make a unique film of almost an hour's length that was a huge success when shown back in Japan. The silent black-and-white flickering images are an eerie but enchanting record of this unusual expedition and its work in Antarctica.

In the M. Pathe film is one of the funniest—and also more alarming—pieces of Antarctic footage, an 'experiment' that went largely unreported at the time. The film was not distributed overseas, and before the recent publication of the complete English translation of the report on Shirase's expedition, most of the Japanese team's activity was related to outsiders through a brief summary translated by an enthusiastic Norwegian whaler, Ivar Hamre, which was published in 1933. In this article Hamre reports that, after the *Kainan-maru* reached King Edward VII Land, the expedition members encountered 'a flock of Emperor Penguins showing no signs of fear. One of the men presumed to "shake hands" with one of these beings so human in their behaviour. But his patting seems to have been taken up in a way quite their own, for the result was a round of beak-strokes from one individual to another until it came back to the starting-point and the circuit was closed.'

The new translation is quite different. After finding more than half a dozen emperor penguins, 'One of the expedition members punched a penguin to see what would happen. The

stupid creature did not seem to grasp the fact that it was one
of the men who had punched it, and assuming that it had been
pecked by the penguin standing next to it, it pecked its neighbour back with its long thin beak. That penguin in turn pecked
the next penguin, and so on until finally all six penguins had
been pecked.' Later attempts to do the same thing were recorded
in Taizumi's film, with Japanese team members herding groups
of penguins, and apparently punching and kicking them as they
try to get away. No doubt, when shown to the public, it must
have caused much amusement.

After considerable interaction with the local wildlife the
Kainan-maru hugged the coast and made one last, major
discovery: the team reached the very edge of King Edward
VII Land and the start of the Great Ice Barrier. Now, finally,
the eastern limit of the barrier was firmly fixed. Ross had first
found this impressive feature of Antarctica in 1841 and defined
the westernmost edge at McMurdo Sound; Shirase's expedition located the last piece of the puzzle at what they called
Okuma Bay. For a small ship it was an impressive achievement:
the Japanese succeeded where Ross, Scott and Shackleton
had failed.

In Okuma Bay the men observed an unusual phenomenon.
On 29 January they saw large bergs with rocks embedded in
them. As early as 1839, before Charles Darwin became a household name, the great scientist had observed that few if any
icebergs in the northern hemisphere had been found to contain
rocks, and yet this appeared quite common in the Southern
Ocean. In another of his prescient contributions, Darwin
described some of the early sealing expeditions and suggested,
'Transportation of fragments of rock by ice throws light on the
problem of erratic boulders which has so long perplexed geologists. If one iceberg in a thousand or ten thousand transports its
fragment, the bottom of the Antarctic Sea and the shores of its

islands must already be scattered with masses of foreign rock, the counterpart of erratic boulders of the northern hemisphere.' The rocks on the seabed signified past convoys of bergs had been released into the Southern Ocean from an undiscovered land in the south.

By collecting a sample the Japanese hoped to improve their understanding of the geology of King Edward VII Land. Much as Shackleton had collected geological samples on the Beardmore Glacier, this was a chance to collect material from the largely inaccessible coast. A small boat was sent out; frighteningly, after the crew had collected mud and gravel samples from the floating ice, one of the nearby bergs rose dramatically out of the ocean, having calved off the shelf floor, accompanied by the sound of thunder. Ice and water were thrown violently into the air—miraculously, the men survived.

There were other ways to collect scientific samples that were considerably safer, at least for the expedition members. Today we are not supposed to approach any animal so that it alters its behaviour, but in 1912 all the Antarctic expeditions captured seals and penguins for food and scientific samples. During much of the Japanese explorers' time in the Antarctic, penguins were caught. One of the 'important guests' captured earlier was strangled for food and the contents of its stomach analysed. Three stones were found, each around six millimetres in diameter. Finding the rest of the stomach was made up of small fish and realising they could not feed their new guests, the men killed the other birds using chloroform; but, as the official report remarked later in rather macabre fashion, 'it still took a long time for them all to die.'

Penguins have long been known to have stones in their stomachs. Even today, though, the reasons for this are uncertain. Ideas range from helping with ballast while diving, to digesting stones to help break down food in the gizzard, to accidentally mistaking rock fragments as fish. Regardless, many of the stones collected seem to come from the seabed, providing a handy way of gaining insight into the local geology below the ice and waves.

Reaching the Bay of Whales on 1 February the Japanese were shocked to see that the bay had changed completely. In two weeks most of the sea ice that had covered the area on their arrival had broken up and drifted out of the bay, to be replaced by drifting floes and ice lumps of different sizes. With the conditions too poor to get Shirase and his men off the ice, the *Kainan-maru* stayed offshore overnight. Unlike Amundsen, the Japanese feared the stability of the barrier around the bay.

Shirase and his six men were hurriedly loaded on board over the next two days, when conditions temporarily improved. Once again the weather deteriorated and the ship was forced to leave in haste on 4 February. Twenty dogs were left behind, marooned on an uninhabited ice shelf, chasing the departing vessel with howls of anguish. The loss was felt deeply: Shirase remembered them in his morning and evening prayers to his final days. With heavy hearts the Japanese turned north and headed home, via New Zealand.

———————

Shirase and his men returned heroes: 'we left the country out of favour of the people and were welcomed back into public favour and recognition.' Despite there being no national tradition of exploration or whaling in the Antarctic region, the team had come home safely after making a sizeable contribution to the scientific understanding of Antarctica. Shirase was immediately invited to regale the imperial family with stories from the expedition. The achievement was widely celebrated and a parade in Tokyo was dedicated to the returning explorers. Telegrams were received from afar, including one from Edgeworth David, written as soon as he heard of their safe return to Wellington, congratulating Shirase on his scientific success in the south.

Shortly after, the M. Pathe film of the expedition was shown around Japan and China, raising the profile of the expedition still further. It also raised a phenomenal amount of money, esti-mated to have been in the order of ¥100,000, but this all went to M. Pathe; Shirase had sold the rights for a fraction of this amount. And yet, even with all the publicity, not everyone was convinced of the leader's claims about his exploits. No doubt to Shirase's chagrin, his home town was highly sceptical, and it was only when the film was shown that the locals believed him.

A Record of Antarctica, the official expedition report, hints at a Japanese territorial claim while inviting the reader to 'the wonderful realm of Antarctica, where the wild ice of moun-tains towers high into the sky and the rising sun now shines in splendour by both day and night, and shall never set'. But the expedition's story and almost all of its discoveries were, natu-rally, reported in Japanese. Few overseas were aware of their findings, beyond a small number of individuals who had contact with Shirase's team—most prominently, David—or who read the occasional brief report in western newspapers and journals. The film of Shirase's expedition was not distributed globally. Books were the primary means of telling the world about the Japanese exploits, and they were in a language not many outside Shirase's homeland understood.

Consequently, an expedition that had left for Antarctica amid much controversy returned to applause and, almost as quickly, to anonymity. The bulk of the scientific results were published as a series of appendices at the back of the official account of the expedition, and remained largely untapped. Although an English translation of these reports was released as a series of discrete papers in the Japanese journal *Antarctic Research* during the late

1950s, the papers were only picked up by the small research community that is Antarctic science. The rest of the world carried on much as if the Japanese expedition had never happened.

The language barrier is typified by the expedition's original public claim to succeed or perish in the attempt on the pole. In Japanese the word *Nankyoku*, the objective of the expedition, means both Antarctica as a whole and the South Pole. To those in the English-speaking world who took notice, the effort appeared a failure: the team did not reach the pole. But in Japan the expedition was billed a success and public statements stressed the great significance of the discoveries.

The team's findings made a particular contribution to understanding King Edward VII Land, and how it and the barrier related to Antarctica as a whole. The Norwegians had collected samples from King Edward VII Land, and reported, 'They consist of granitic rocks and crystalline schists, and are identical with those brought by the southern party from Mount Betty beside Axel Heiberg Glacier in 85°S. Moreover, they agree so closely with the rocks of South Victoria Land that we can now say that an identity of structure has been established all round the Ross Barrier. Edward Land undoubtedly seems to belong to the Plateau formation of Victoria Land, and the presumption grows in strength that the Ross Sea is a rift valley.'

The Norwegians were only partially correct. The samples the Japanese collected around Antarctica, including those found within the penguin stomachs, were not entirely the same as those taken in Victoria Land. The volcanic rocks supported the evidence of rifting in the Earth's crust, but pointed to an early formation of King Edward VII Land, separate to the eastern Antarctic. The failure of the Japanese to find the most recent rock types of Victoria Land only reinforced this conclusion. Hints of a geological connection to New Zealand suggested a much more complex history than first thought.

Fortunately, because of his friendship with Edgeworth David, Shirase had been happy to send examples of his geological samples to the Australian. The results of David's analysis were incorporated into a later report on the geological work of Shackleton's *Nimrod* expedition, guaranteeing at least some of the Japanese science was known to a wider readership.

There were other equally important findings. Alongside the weather and ocean observations, the Japanese were able to show just how quickly the ice scape could change. After the Norwegians had departed in the *Fram*, the Japanese were in the area long enough to report that the Bay of Whales was considerably larger than had been supposed. By the time Shirase left, the bay had opened up fifty kilometres into the interior.

The expedition also provided observations on the make-up and movement of the Great Ice Barrier. During the Dash Patrol, halfway to their furthest point south, Shirase crossed what we now know to be Roosevelt Island, in the eastern part of the barrier. At the time, this prominent feature in the landscape was not known to be an island. Conditions were poor and the gradient uncertain, but the 300-metre-high 'small hill' was south of a towering 'ice cliff' that 'looked as if it had been thrown up by some cataclysmic event, such as a volcanic eruption'.

The Norwegians had also been intrigued by the area. They felt this same snow-covered rise to the south of the Bay of Whales must be land, and the hummocks in the immediate area were disturbances caused by the flow of ice around it. It was a fundamental observation. Today, this 'small hill' is the origin of some of the largest tabular bergs released into the Southern Ocean.

Scott's suspicions about the region had been right: the eastern Ross Sea was an important part of the Antarctic story.

Not six weeks after the Tokyo parade for Shirase's men, Emperor Meiji died and the nation went into mourning. The emperor who had heralded a new start for Japan had passed away—and so, it seemed, had the nation's interest in Antarctica. This could not have come at a worse time for Shirase. There had been talk of continuing the research in the Southern Ocean for a further two years, but the funding simply was not there: the extra year south had added a lot to an already huge bill. Though Shirase had returned home a hero he was also met with bad news. Fundraising had continued after the expedition sailed, but there remained a major shortfall: ¥53,000.

There was not enough money to pay the salaries owed, and rumours circulated that the Supporters' Association had spent far too much on entertainment. True or not, it still meant Shirase was left to meet the commitment. Unlike Shackleton's case, the government did not step in, and with no imperial champion Shirase was left largely on his own, financially crippled. The *Kainan-maru* was sold to its previous owner, Gunji, for ¥20,000 and returned to fishing. The remaining money had to be raised through a string of different ventures.

Shirase spent the next five years touring Japan, giving lectures. He sold his house in Tokyo, too—but it was not enough. During the years 1921 to 1924 Shirase returned to the Kuril Islands to put his knowledge of foxes to good use. By managing a fur farm he was able to earn some of the money owed. He returned to mainland Japan and grew his own vegetables to live off. Yet Shirase's interest in Antarctica did not wane. In 1927 he finally met Amundsen, when the Norwegian visited the imperial family in Tokyo to show them the details of a planned flight over the North Geographic Pole.

In an attempt to gain wider recognition of the Japanese effort, Masakichi Ikeda appears to have assumed the role of the official expedition scientist. He sent a map to the Royal Geographic

Society in London, incorporating the Japanese Antarctic findings with those of Amundsen. In it, Ikeda names two prominent
mountains in King Edward VII Land as Mount Nobu and Mount
Okuma, while the inlet at the eastern extremity of the Great Ice
Barrier was declared to be Murakami Inlet, after one of the major
expedition supporters—though it eventually became Okuma Bay.

The map was duly noted, filed away in the archives, and
forgotten. Indeed, the society and its most senior people seem
to have ignored the expedition after this. The secretary of the
RGS, Scott Keltie, wrote to Lord Curzon in September 1912
and remarked, unimpressed, 'A member of the Japan Antarctic
Expedition has sent to the President a note of some of their
discoveries, which do not amount to very much. I suppose I
had better acknowledge it?' Sir Clements Markham's history
of polar exploration, *Lands of Silence*, makes no mention of the
Japanese effort and no reports on their findings were made in
the society's journal for years.

—————•————

It would be another two decades before Japan's effort in the
south was properly acknowledged. In 1929 the pioneering
American air explorer Richard Byrd flew along the edge of the
Ross Sea and named many of the features he saw on the way.
Bays identified and reported by the Japanese were renamed,
and when alerted to this they protested loudly. It was not really
Byrd's fault, as no English translation of the expedition report
was available at the time, and he dutifully published an article in
the American Geographical Society's *Geographical Review* that
gave the names Kainan Bay and Okuma Bay to two of the most
prominent spots.

It was probably as a result of this renewed attention that, in
the same year, the Norwegian Ivar Hamre published his short

summary of the expedition. The Japanese were finally finding their way onto the map, long after the other 1912 expeditions had received credit for their work. Shirase petitioned his government to accept as a gift the region of the Ross Sea where the Japanese flag had been raised, allowing it to make a territorial claim. The offer was turned down. Shirase saw tremendous opportunities to exploit the south, later writing: 'Study the treasures under the Antarctica and make use of them even after my death.'

By the early 1930s Japan's presence in the Southern Ocean was increasing: whaling vessels frequently headed south, prompting interest in the region at home, while the Japanese Polar Research Institute was established in 1933 and Shirase appointed honorary president. But the government still would not settle Shirase's final debts and these were only fully repaid in 1935, not long before he died. In 1981 a statue of Shirase flanked by penguins was placed in the grounds of the temple close to where he was born, and in 1990 a dedicated museum was opened in Nikaho. Today the circular building and its staff provide a unique insight into the Japanese expedition. Each year, on 28 January, there is a festival dedicated to Shirase called the Walk in the Snow: a tribute to a man who briefly inspired a nation and never gave up his belief in the importance of Antarctic exploration.

The official narrative of the expedition summed up the Japanese effort: 'Leaders in unity unify their followers.' This was not strictly true, as there had been some notable disputes on board—but these were nothing compared to the German Antarctic Expedition of 1911 to 1912, led by the hapless Wilhelm Filchner. Although not hamstrung by debt, as the Japanese had been, the German expedition south saw attempted murder, mayhem and a hefty dose of madness. And yet it was one of the most important expeditions of them all.

Modern weather station in the Heritage Range of the Ellsworth Mountains, 2011.
Photo taken by Chris Turney with an Eastman Kodak No. 2
Folding Autographic Brownie (model 1924–1926).

CHAPTER 6

LOCKED IN

Wilhelm Filchner and the Second German
Antarctic Expedition, 1911–1912

Facts send theories to the four winds.

Sir Clements Markham (1830–1916)

On the morning of 16 July 1910 change was in the air. The fine
summer weather southern England had enjoyed during the first
half of the month was on the wane. London awoke to a fresh
northerly breeze and reports of an impending storm. But the
poor conditions did little to dampen the enthusiasm of a small,
select crowd at Waterloo station, gathered to officially send off
Robert Scott and the British Antarctic Expedition. Flowers and
gifts were presented; there were huddled exchanges.

Shortly before the train was due to set off for Southampton
and a waiting ship, the British leader and his wife boarded, with
Ernest Shackleton crying out, 'Three cheers for Captain Scott!'

Scott looked back and, with a wave of his bowler hat,
shouted: 'See you at the Pole.'

But the call was not directed at Shackleton. It was to a
smartly presented army officer planning to lead a German expedition south at the same time, Wilhelm Filchner.

Born in the Bavarian town of Bayreuth in 1877, Filchner seemed destined for a career in the arts. As a young man he had displayed an uncanny talent for painting copies of master-pieces. But the call to adventure proved too strong. By fifteen he had turned his back on canvas and oils, and joined the Prussian Military Academy.

Filchner first came to public prominence at twenty-three after an infamous lone journey on horseback through the Pamir Mountains of central Asia. Sponsored by the army, his sojourn led to accusations of spying and a ban from travelling in Russia, making his book *Ein Ritt über den Pamir* a national bestseller— and his name as a daring German explorer.

Buoyed by success, Filchner went on to develop an impres-sive scientific background, studying among other things geophysics and the latest surveying techniques. His newfound skills were soon put to good use when he was given the leader-ship of a national mapping expedition of the Earth's magnetic field in Tibet. Commendations and honours swiftly followed the successful expedition, and Filchner's reputation for success-fully blending science and adventure was assured.

Shackleton's efforts in Antarctica greatly appealed to the young German. Although the British team had blazed trails around McMurdo Sound, the other side of the Antarctic remained largely unknown. The sealer James Weddell had seen birds during his furthest-south voyage, in 1823, but could only speculate he was close to land. In 1902 the Scottish scientist and explorer William Speirs Bruce had fallen well short of Weddell's mark, due to particularly thick sea ice, but had discovered Coats Land in the eastern Weddell Sea. Filchner's plan was in the Shackleton mould: to push through the Weddell Sea ice and cross the interior of the unexplored continent, all the way to the Ross Sea.

Although the limits of Antarctica were still hazy at best, this had not stopped scientists around the world continuing to theorise. Some, like Nansen, considered Antarctica to be a number of ice-covered islands. Others, among them Shackleton, thought Antarctica was a single landmass.

A third view was championed by Friedrich Albert Penck, a colossus in German science who held the prestigious Chair of Geography at Berlin University. To Penck, there was no doubt a continent lay in the south; but it was divided in two by a frozen strait, of which the Weddell and Ross seas formed the extreme ends. Antarctica was made up of two large landmasses, east and west.

Penck's idea depended on what the known Antarctic mountain chains did in the interior. Before 1912 it was fairly clear that what we now know as the Antarctic Peninsula was a geological continuation of the South American Andes. The question was whether the Antarctic Andes joined up with those in Victoria Land, or went elsewhere—and if they did not connect, might Bruce's Coats Land be joined in some way? Penck made an enticing case for two continental-sized landmasses.

Filchner was intrigued and resolved to test the idea, travelling via the South Geographic Pole. Unlike the Norwegians and Japanese, however, Filchner was determined to gain as much knowledge as possible on the journey to Antarctica. Major questions remained about the surrounding regions. How did the various oceans in the south link up—if at all—and what effect did this have on the world's climate? Scientific observations would start from day one of the voyage. Filchner approached the Berlin Geographical Society in 1909, and received a positive response. Penck was so enthusiastic that he took Filchner's plan to the public in March 1910.

———•———

Filchner was not the first to lead a German expedition south. One of his renowned predecessors was Eric von Drygalski, who travelled a decade earlier. A contemporary of Scott's *Discovery* expedition, von Drygalski's *Gauss* party nobly agreed to forgo McMurdo Sound and investigate an unknown part of the East Antarctic coastline, near where the American Charles Wilkes had claimed to have been sixty years before. Aiming to be the first to the South Magnetic Pole, the Germans never made it. Reaching the edge of the Antarctic in January 1902, the *Gauss* became locked in sea ice.

The Germans were prepared for winter. Drawing on the local wildlife—especially penguins, as both food and fuel—they set about making as much of the situation as possible. All manner of scientific observations of the elements were made, carefully arranged in advance to be directly comparable to Scott's. Alongside these efforts a hot-air balloon was sent aloft and, reaching a height of nearly five hundred metres, von Drygalski saw what appeared to be ice-free land to the south. Sledging there, the Germans discovered an extinct volcano and ramparts of rubble that spoke of an ice sheet considerably larger than today's.

Though the summer sun returned, the ice remained stubbornly opposed to releasing the *Gauss*, and no amount of dynamite would free the vessel. Only when ashes from the ship's boilers were put on the ice did the surface warm and weaken. Although the Germans had been frustrated in their efforts to reach a high latitude, they could at least show that in the south Indian Ocean there did indeed exist land—to which they attached the moniker Kaiser Wilhelm II Land. They returned home to international acclaim.

Filchner sought to repeat the success of von Drygalski with an equally well-organised and well-equipped expedition. Ambitiously, he wanted the Germans to work in an entirely different part of the Antarctic, addressing a great scientific question while also claiming the South Geographic Pole for his nation.

A common theme of Antarctic expeditions is a shortage of funds, and Filchner's was no exception. The original proposal for two ships came in at a cost of two million mark. With limited funds from the outset, the expedition was looking decidedly rocky. Where others gave up on their Antarctic ambitions, though, Filchner would prove to be considerably more imaginative in raising money.

In early 1910 the expedition organisers hosted a formal dinner for the Kaiser, with the aim of gaining royal approval. To one outside observer, the German monarch was not impressed. 'So, you want to go to the South Pole?' he reportedly said. 'Wait, if you please, till Zeppelin gets that far with his airship. He'll do in a couple of days what takes you three years. You will not make this expedition—understood?'

Filchner is said to have replied, 'Majesty, I have resolved already to lead the expedition'—and the Kaiser turned his back and left the hall. Afterwards Filchner was diplomatic about the exchange, remarking that the Kaiser listened 'benevolently' to his plans before turning him down.

The day after his tête-à-tête with the Kaiser, Filchner travelled to Munich for an audience with Prince Regent Luitpold of Bavaria. At the time Luitpold was effectively ruler of Bavaria, in place of his nephews Ludwig II and Otto, who were considered too mentally incapacitated to fulfil their formal roles. Luitpold presided over a cultural renaissance in central Europe, with Munich the capital. He was considerably more excited by the prospect of a German Antarctic expedition and agreed to assume the role of 'honorary patron'.

The expedition's plans were scaled back to one ship, costing 1.1 million mark. A national committee was set up and fundraising efforts were re-energised. One of the most successful was a public lottery. By the following year Filchner had his money: the Germans had the best funded expedition of 1912.

Keen to maximise scientific effort and avoid duplication on the ground, the German leader worked hard to develop research links and reassure other national groups heading south. Leaders of these efforts responded in kind, freely giving advice on planning and equipment—even those who were in direct competition for the South Geographic Pole. Shackleton was particularly keen to be involved and visited Germany, giving public lectures and advising on the ice-strengthening of the expedition vessel, the *Deutschland*. Less usefully, Shackleton also passed on Jackson's obsession with horses; Filchner was so enthused that he immediately went out and bought a number from northeast China to complement his Greenland dogs.

The media were aware of the rights Scott and Bruce might claim for their attempts on the South Geographic Pole. By focusing on the other side of the Antarctic, Filchner hoped to avoid any misunderstanding with the British explorers, much as von Drygalski had done. He need not have worried. Filchner travelled to meet the two leaders in the spring of 1910 and found both remarkably relaxed about this new European expedition.

In Edinburgh, Filchner agreed to work west of Coats Land and leave the region east to Bruce's proposed Scottish expedition. The Scot's plans were similar to Filchner's and included an extensive oceanographic survey of the Weddell Sea, from where he intended to cross to the Ross Sea. Bruce, though, believed Penck to be wrong and argued that the mountain range of Victoria Land continued across to the Antarctic Andes. While waiting on funding that never came, Bruce generously gave the German leader ideas for research and equipment to use while at sea.

The meeting in London was arguably even more successful. Scott was keen to share ideas, equipment—including the latest plans for motorised sledges—and even men with the German expedition. Scott was later quoted as saying, 'Lieutenant Filchner and I have agreed, as far as possible, to work our scientific programme in unison.' As a final goodwill gesture, Scott invited Filchner to the official British Antarctic Expedition farewell at Waterloo station on 16 July.

Returning to Germany with an expedition that was now gathering serious momentum, Filchner set about gaining polar experience. He wanted to test his men and equipment—including the ponies—on icy mountain passes, and soon headed off to the Arctic archipelago of Svalbard. Filchner found the shipping space he had bought for transporting his ponies north was too small and the animals had to be sold en route, forcing him to fall back on the first part of his motto, 'Optimist in execution, pessimist in preparation.'

Once there, he found the conditions were considerably worse than anticipated, and the men had to hunker down for longer than planned, cut off from the rest of the world—leading to news reports they had perished. And yet there were positives: the men survived and the equipment seemed up to the task.

When news of the German expedition south was announced, there was a flood of applications. Filchner could pick from an impressive list of scientists: there was a German astronomer, Erich Przybyllok; an Austrian biologist, Felix König; and the rising star of German oceanography, Wilhelm Brennecke. Other applicants were less welcome; some were arguably outrageous. One of the most bizarre was a former Tibetan expedition 'colleague', Albert Tafel, who had first approached Penck about joining the expedition. Tafel seems to have been Filchner's nemesis.

There had been problems almost from the start of their travels in Tibet. Tafel, from all accounts an angry man, seemed keen to fight the locals whenever a problem flared, and Filchner reportedly spent a considerable time talking him down, so that the two men could pass along peacefully. On their return to Germany, the junior man had accused the expedition leader of cowardice and public flatulence, and openly questioned the authenticity of his maps. Now here he was asking to join the Antarctic expedition and threatening to undermine it from afar if refused. Filchner was not having any of it. Tafel's application was rejected.

Shortly after, rumours started circulating about the expedition and its leader, many harking back to Filchner's trips in Asia. Threats and counter-threats followed, many involving the ship's captain for the German expedition, Richard Vahsel. On paper Vahsel seemed a good appointment. He had been second officer on the *Gauss*, giving him invaluable Antarctic experience, which few other German naval captains possessed. On learning of the appointment, however, the *Gauss*'s former captain, Commodore Ruser, wrote to warn Filchner: Vahsel was trouble.

The expedition committee insisted on Vahsel and, further confusing matters, made the *Deutschland* fly under the Imperial Navy flag. The captain was in charge of the vessel and the lives on board while at sea: Filchner had suddenly lost absolute leadership of the expedition. With his appointment confirmed, Vahsel soon started throwing his weight about, threatening to put Filchner 'in irons' during the voyage if he felt it necessary. The early promise of success in the south was fast disappearing.

Deciding to ignore his problems, Filchner instead concentrated on what he could control: the expedition's plans in Antarctica. He reasoned that it would be easiest to answer the question of a two-part Antarctica by travelling over the Great Ice Barrier, and could not understand why the British or Norwegians were not tackling the issue. When he heard the Japanese were also in the Ross Sea, Filchner felt the last thing needed was another expedition operating there. Instead he bravely decided to try somewhere different: the Weddell Sea.

The *Deutschland* would go via Buenos Aires and use South Georgia, in the South Atlantic, as a springboard for the Weddell Sea in December 1911. Following the coastline of Coats Land south, Filchner hoped to establish a base as far south as possible, making scientific measurements through the winter. With the onset of summer, four men would then push on to the South Geographic Pole, sledging with dogs, the much-vaunted Manchurian horses and motorised sledges—though the last ended up being dropped.

Meanwhile, having delivered the men in Antarctica, the *Deutschland* would return north, making oceanographic measurements as it went, supported by the latest wireless tele-graphy, which would allow contact with the outside world. If the worst came to the worst, the ship was stocked with enough supplies to survive a winter trapped in the ice. Not much was being left to chance.

Filchner's thinking on the Weddell Sea was remarkably clear. He had heard reports that conditions in the region were favour-able. Large numbers of icebergs had been seen in the north, calved from the Antarctic the previous summer. After consulting Shackleton and others, Filchner decided the stock of ice in the Weddell Sea would not have had time to rebuild and the way should remain relatively clear. If ever there was a time to beat Weddell's record in the south and make landfall, this was it.

Seeing off the *Deutschland* from Bremerhaven in May 1911, Filchner was left to finish the expedition paperwork and set out later in a fast boat to Buenos Aires. It was a disastrous mistake. Although the *Deutschland* collected a wealth of oceanographic data as it travelled south, Vahsel argued with the scientific director for almost the entire journey. Things were so bad that Filchner received a telegram while travelling to Argentina: the expedition captain was resigning his post. Filchner must have been mightily relieved, given Vahsel's disturbing behaviour.

Filchner met a promising naval officer called Albert Kling aboard his passage ship and, not one to miss an opportunity, offered him Vahsel's post. But by the time Filchner reached Buenos Aires, in September, Vahsel had changed his mind and the scientific director had walked instead. Frustrated, Filchner was forced to accept the situation; but Kling stayed, keen to continue with the expedition, albeit not in charge of the vessel.

Reaching Buenos Aires the *Deutschland* met the *Fram*, recently returned from Antarctica having dropped Amundsen and his team off at the Bay of Whales. The Norwegians were about to start a survey across the Atlantic, to Africa and back. The teams apparently got on well, and the *Fram* saw the Germans off with three cheers. If Amundsen and Scott failed to reach the Pole, Filchner was ready to make his bid; in the meantime, the scientific work would continue. Filchner had prepared meticulously—but it remained to be seen whether things would go to plan.

German interest in the Antarctic had blossomed in 1882, during one of the first global scientific endeavours: the International Polar Year. Affectionately shortened to IPY, this global effort was designed to focus research on the polar regions during a single year and share the resulting data. Its revolutionary idea was the pursuit of scientific knowledge through international co-operation and not geographic conquest, which had been the norm up to that point. Unlike the Magnetic Crusade, which focused on magnetic observations around the world, the IPY was limited mainly to high latitudes and looked at the gamut of scientific interests. Two expeditions went south, one of which was a German team that based itself in South Georgia and undertook the infamous corseting of penguins, tethering them for research.

These early efforts also looked at the make-up of the oceans. But the teams involved were hampered by instrument failure, as the equipment was rarely up to scratch. First attempts involved dropping thermometers over the side, unprotected, to obtain maximum and minimum temperatures. Unfortunately, the changing salt levels and higher pressures experienced in deep water skewed the results. At two thousand metres below, for instance, the pressure is two hundred times greater than that at the surface, distorting any measurement made by an unprotected instrument. Different designs were tested, with varying degrees of success, culminating in an effort led by the great Nansen, who with his team designed a deep-ocean thermometer that could withstand the tremendous pressures and preserve the measurements accurately.

By the time of the *Deutschland* expedition it was understood that ocean properties were not the same the world over. The *HMS Challenger* expedition of the 1870s had gleaned that south of 65° the surface water was cold and remarkably low in salt; deeper down below, the opposite was true. In the tropics, however, the same cold, fresher water was just below the surface. By measuring the temperature and saltiness it was possible to map these water masses relatively easily.

In the seas surrounding Antarctica, de Gerlache's *Belgica* party had fleshed out more detail using modern, deep-sea reversing thermometers and showed the cold surface water extended all the way south and sat over a warmer layer below, which was in turn underlain by yet more cold water towards the bottom. It suggested the oceans were made up of different masses of water that originated in different parts of the world and were modified as they moved around the planet. But how this happened was still a mystery.

On the way to Buenos Aires, along with recording the ocean-water temperature and how much salt it contained, the *Deutschland* team was interested in other characteristics, especially how biologically active the ocean was. Even before the ship had reached South America, the tropical cold-ocean mass that the *Challenger* had suggested originated from Antarctica had been shown to have unusually high amounts of nitrate. Nitrate is a crucial nutrient, sustaining small, single-celled organisms known as phytoplankton. In the past we called these plants, but things get hazy when you are dealing with single cells; today the problem is bypassed by describing them as protists. These particular protists photosynthesise carbon dioxide dissolved in ocean water and are the food of choice for krill, a small shrimp-like crustacean found in Antarctic waters. In the summertime melting ice and constant daylight fuel massive plankton blooms, which support huge krill populations—and with them most of the Southern Ocean food chain. The *Deutschland* measurements implied the Antarctic waters were some of the most productive in the world. And yet, somehow, the nutrient levels of the Southern Ocean were being replenished.

———•———

Leaving Buenos Aires the *Deutschland* pushed on through some of the planet's most feared seas, towards the 170-kilometre-long island of South Georgia, which lies in a vast belt of waves and wind that encircles the mid-latitudes of the southern hemisphere. The region has acquired all sorts of dramatic names—the 'screaming sixties', the 'furious fifties', the 'roaring forties'—because of the temperature difference of several degrees over a relatively narrow band of latitude. Combined with the spin of the Earth and the vast expanse of ocean, this means the wind almost always blows from the west, and with prodigious force.

South Georgia sits in a perfect position to be hit sideways by this continuous blast. Because the island is immediately downwind of a relatively small gap between South America and Antarctica known as the Drake Passage, the circulating ocean waters can combine with the wind to create extraordinarily rough seas. It is also something of a gateway to Antarctica. On 20 January 1775, as part of his second expedition, Captain Cook fought through these same South Atlantic waters in *HMS Resolution* to explore the southwest coast of South Georgia, hoping it would continue south and prove to be part of the hitherto undiscovered *Terra Australis Incognita*. The *Resolution* rounded a headland at the southern end and Cook, to his dismay, saw land heading northeast. South Georgia was an island and not the tip of a great continent: it was another false dawn. The British captain would have to continue polewards.

Cape Disappointment was preserved forever on the world's maps, a testament to Cook's frustration. He later wrote of South Georgia that it was 'doomed by Nature to perpetual frigidness… whose horrible and savage aspect I have not words to describe'. But, after his remarks on the rich abundance of its wildlife, especially the seal colonies, South Georgia became a significant location in the Southern Ocean.

Reaching South Georgia today is fraught with difficulty. There is no airfield, and visiting cruise ships, while frequent in the summer months, are not a cheap way to travel. For scientists, the principal way of reaching the island is by a Fishery

Protection Vessel operated by the South Georgian government. Known as the *Pharos*, this distinctive red ship ploughs the waves between the Falkland Islands, South Georgia and beyond. Day in, day out, it searches for poachers of the famed delicacy the Chilean toothfish. To survive, like many other Antarctic fish, the toothfish have glycoproteins in their body fluid that effectively act as an anti-freeze, allowing them to rove in waters as cold as -2°C. Adaptations like this allow the Southern Ocean to support vast—but rapidly depleting—fishing populations.

You are guaranteed a rocky journey on the *Pharos*; save for the almost constant company of albatrosses, there is nothing to see beyond the succession of rolling waves and the inside of a toilet bowl. Travelling there is one of the closest experiences you can get to the expeditions of 1912, even though it is only four days' journey each way. In 1912 the men had weeks of this, and in far more vulnerable vessels. But reaching South Georgia is worth it. It is like travelling to the fabled land of Prester John, the mythical kingdom in the Southern Ocean, a place rather like the Scottish Highlands but with glaciers. If you are fortunate enough to arrive with a break in the clouds, you are greeted with a vista of mountains and ice, shrieking flocks of sea birds, pods of dolphins and, in among the floating mats of seaweed, harems of seals.

Wildlife is so abundant here because South Georgia sits just south of a prominent boundary between very different masses of ocean water known as the Antarctic Convergence, or the Polar Front. Critically, there are two different forms of ocean circulation in Antarctic waters. The best known is the drift in the surface waters from the west, driven by the pervasive westerly winds; but there is another, deeper type that travels south–north, suggestions of which were first made by the men of the *Challenger* and *Belgica*.

To understand the latter we have to look south, at what is taking place around Antarctica when sea ice is formed out of the freezing surface waters. Because the newly formed ice contains little salt, the water left behind becomes heavier, sinking to the sea floor and flowing north, taking with it dissolved gases and the decaying remains of ocean-dwelling plants and animals. The sea ice left behind is blown north and, as it melts, forms a cold, fresh ocean mass. By the time this Antarctic Surface Water reaches South Georgia it meets a considerably warmer body of water heading in the opposite direction and is forced to sink before it can carry on to the tropics. More importantly for South Georgia, a warmer ocean mass is drawn south to replace the surface and deep cold waters heading north, bringing the nutrients to the surface that are essential in supporting the island's remarkable wildlife.

Today South Georgia is teeming with fur and elephant seals—most lying among the shoreline tussock, including surrounding the research station at King Edward Point, next to the old whaling station of Grytviken. After Cook's reports reached home sealers poured in to the subantarctic, lured by the rich pickings. Fur-seal skin was particularly prized for hats, while elephant seals were hunted for their blubber. The damage was colossal: populations plummeted and in turn new hunting grounds were pursued. In 1821 the Russian explorer Fabian Gottlieb von Bellingshausen was staggered to find eighteen American and British sealing ships lying at anchor at Deception Island, a small piece of rock off the Antarctic Andes that had only been discovered the previous year.

Fur seals were some of the worst hit by over-hunting: in 1825 James Weddell calculated that around 1.2 million fur seals had been killed on South Georgia alone. He realised the devastating impact of indiscriminate killing and proposed that, by not killing the females until the young were capable of taking to the Antarctic waters, the southern sealing grounds could provide a sustainable yield of one hundred thousand furs per year. It was a radical thought about sustainability, way ahead of its time, and it was largely ignored. When Wilhelm Filchner reached South Georgia, decades later, fur seals numbered in the low hundreds, while elephant seals survived only as isolated communities scattered across the island. Today, South Georgia's seal population has largely recovered, with the number of 'furries' estimated at three million—probably their highest level.

By the late nineteenth century the most lucrative financial endeavour in the Southern Ocean was whaling. In 1851 Herman Melville's fictional Captain Ishmael opined, 'For many years past, the whale-ship has been the pioneer in ferreting out the remotest and least known parts of the earth. She has explored seas and archipelagoes which had no chart, where no Cook or Vancouver had ever sailed.' Where governments had been largely uninterested in exploring polar regions, whalers had carried on regardless. The increasingly industrialised world had become hungry for whale oil and the North Atlantic could not keep up with demand; supplies were dwindling fast, and South Georgia soon became a whaling centre.

These days the whaling station of Grytviken lies empty, save for a museum catering for tourists. But a century ago it was a hive of industrial activity. Between late 1904—when a Norwegian, Carl Anton Larsen, established a whaling factory—and 1914, almost thirty thousand whales were caught there. Dead whales were moored in the bay, waiting to be processed; when finished with, the abandoned carcasses would drift towards the shore. Even today, if you disturb the surface shoreline the smell of rotting meat and oil is overwhelming.

It was against this backdrop that the Germans arrived in October 1911. Larsen's stunning financial success meant the island now supported twelve hundred people. The Germans found Grytviken was a Scandinavian preserve, with only a small British contingent, but they were warmly welcomed.

Although disgusted at the level of waste, Filchner got along famously with Larsen and the Norwegian lent him a ship to ferry his men around.

Over the next two months the Germans frenetically studied the island. They returned to the former International Polar Year station and took magnetic measurements to see how the Earth's field had changed over the intervening thirty years; they took meteorological measurements for comparison with those they planned to gather in Antarctica; and, in their little spare time, they visited the outer islands of the Scotia Arc, the island system around the Scotia Sea that includes South Georgia.

When not making measurements, Filchner was busy readying equipment and organising supplies for their time south. The preparation was marred by the disappearance of one of the crew while fishing in the bay off Grytviken. The man fell overboard—some said accidentally, but others suspected suicide. And the ship's doctor, Ludwig Kohl, was diagnosed with appendicitis and could not continue to Antarctica, staying behind to be nursed by Larsen's daughter, whom he later married.

Despite this, the *Deutschland* left on time, departing South Georgia in December 1911. But, with conditions changing fast, Shackleton worried that the Germans now ran the risk of getting caught in the sea ice.

———•◦•———

Heading south into the Weddell Sea the *Deutschland* made good time and in just a week sighted pack ice. But Filchner's hope that the way might be clear was soon dashed: the Weddell Sea was crowded with bergs. Slowly, the Germans pushed on, and their efforts were rewarded. By 28 January the amount of ice suddenly lessened, allowing the *Deutschland* to make considerably faster progress. By 29 January they had reached further south than the pioneering British sealer Weddell, ninety years before.

There came hints they were near land. Sounding measurements continued to show great depths below the ship but the dead weight now routinely came back to the surface with blue clay attached, showing the seabed was covered in fine sediments laid on the ocean floor by vast ancient glaciers—something not possible far from shore. Shortly after, the water rapidly became shallower and, by the following afternoon, a gently rising icecap more than two hundred metres high and crowned by a pinnacle of rock loomed on the horizon. It was the first hard evidence of land in the far south Weddell Sea. The German team named the new coastline Prinzregent Luitpold Land, in honour of the expedition's sponsor.

After catching several penguins that made the mistake of approaching the *Deutschland*, the Germans were able to follow a similar approach to the Japanese and analyse the birds' stomachs, finding only basalt stones, implying the recently discovered mainland was all the same rock type. Hoping to find a more suitable landing place, the German expedition pushed on south from Luitpold Land, but reached just a little north of 78°S before they met an eight- to fifteen-metre-high ice cliff surrounding a small bay. The situation here was different: at a depth of more than 1150 metres, the seabed was considerably futher down. The party had discovered a hitherto-unknown ice shelf, a cousin to the Great Ice Barrier in the Ross Sea.

Keen to get as far south as possible, the expedition tried heading west—but there was no way through. To the Germans' dismay, the ice shelf directed them towards the northwest and conditions looked decidedly more threatening, risking the safety of the *Deutschland*. They could go no further; the ice shelf was a true barrier to the south. Reluctantly, Filchner realised they had to return east, from where they had come. The Germans had found the southernmost extent of the Weddell Sea and, in spite of their monarch's lack of support, named it the Kaiser Wilhelm Ice Barrier.

Returning southeast on 2 February, the *Deutschland* edged into the recently discovered bay at the junction between Luitpold Land and the new ice barrier. Behind, the ice sheet continued to the south, the surface broken by impressive nunataks that continued off over the horizon. Filchner baptised their new anchorage Vahsel Bay.

Just as the expedition appeared to be on the verge of success, personality clashes threatened its survival. Fights broke out on board and Filchner started recording in his diary that some of the expedition members were plotting against him. Part of the problem was the frustration the men felt in seeing the land and not being able to reach it. Behind the pack ice of the Weddell Sea is one of the world's most inaccessible coastlines, and landing to explore the interior proved far more difficult than the Germans had anticipated.

Filchner's book on the expedition only hints vaguely at problems on board. *To the Sixth Continent* is a remarkably dry account that gives almost no insight into what happened behind the scenes. Filchner was a Prussian officer, and had no desire to air his dirty laundry in public. It was only towards the end of his life that he published his *Exposé*, with signed affidavits testifying to his account. Since then his diary has become available to scholars and, read together, the two accounts give a totally different insight into the expedition.

It was clear early on that Filchner and his captain were different in character and that, thanks to the expedition committee, the line of command had become confused. Filchner drank little and considered tobacco a vice, while Vahsel liked alcohol—a lot—and had a host of health problems: colds, rheumatism, exhaustion, heart concerns and, if those weren't enough, syphilis, which no doubt made all his other complaints considerably worse in the frigid conditions. Filchner had hoped the individual cabins on board the *Deutschland* might help, so that 'the personal tensions inevitable on polar voyages should rarely reach a dangerous level.' It was not to be. The ship's officers and crew split down lines of allegiance to the two men.

With its unenviable atmosphere of tension and suspicion, the team was in danger of falling apart. Summer was nearing its end and the expedition was falling drastically behind schedule. Yet more problems surfaced. The captain now insisted the main aim of the journey was to beat Weddell's southernmost record of 1823, and this had been achieved. Given all the preparations for sledging and scientific observation on shore, Vahsel's new stance bewildered Filchner. Landing was anathema to Vahsel. Perhaps, because of his experience in the sea ice on the *Gauss*, he feared being caught a second time. Filchner pleaded with the captain to land, so they could set up a base from which scientific exploration might start.

Finally, in February, Vahsel yielded—but the chosen site was controversial. The captain had suggested they place their base on an iceberg attached to the shelf, where it would be within easy reach of the ship and connected to the inland ice. Filchner was not so sure: it seemed too close to the sea edge and at risk of falling into the ocean. Vahsel maintained it would be okay; but with Filchner desiring a second opinion, the captain reluctantly agreed to consult the Norwegian ice pilot Paul Björvik, one of the few seamen on board who had any experience of ice. Vahsel went away and returned shortly after, confirming he had Björvik's word that this was the best spot. Filchner consented. The next phase of the expedition could start.

With the site chosen, supplies were hurriedly unloaded in preparation for the winter. Seeing Björvik, Filchner remarked on its fine location. 'Very bad,' Björvik replied. 'I have always had the opinion that you should build no station on a floating iceberg but only on the inland ice, and if possible a couple of kilometres inland.' When the bosun also voiced displeasure and accused Filchner of making decisions without listening to experienced men, the German leader realised Vahsel had never asked Björvik his opinion.

Filchner was furious. He challenged Vahsel, who retorted angrily that the crewman had lied. Filchner wrote wearily in his diary on the 13 February, 'I don't trust the captain any more.' It was too late to do anything. The expedition was committed to the decision and the location would have to do.

In four days the hut frame was raised and the roof completed. For a brief moment, concerns over the wisdom of the site were forgotten. Cigars were lit, beers cracked and chocolates eaten in celebration. By 17 February the expedition hut was completed: animals, provisions, coal and scientific equipment had been unloaded for a winter of work and the following year's attempt on the South Geographic Pole.

The celebrations did not last long. Within twenty-four hours there was an explosive boom and the expedition was in crisis. Filchner would later write ruefully, 'In the Antarctic ice one should never celebrate too loudly if, for once, everything is going well for the moment; generally things soon turn out differently.' It could not have been much worse: a sudden spring tide had exposed a weakness in the shelf and a large part had broken off, taking the new base with it.

The berg cast adrift was a staggering size, close in area to Singapore and containing the equivalent of some fifty billion cubic metres of water. It must have been an awe-inspiring sight for the men on the *Deutschland*. Filchner had been incredibly unlucky: even today a berg of this size is a rare sight in the south.

The *Deutschland* fired up its engines and set off in hot pursuit, chasing the berg that was floating away with the expedition's raison d'être. The Germans worked tirelessly towards a single aim: to salvage as much of the equipment and animals as possible, and ferry them back on to the *Deutschland* using the ship's lifeboats. Incredibly, most of these were saved.

With admirable optimism, they immediately started another base on the ice, intending to move a tonne of supplies on shore, led by the loyal Kling. Vahsel's delays and intransigence over landing, though, prevented this modest plan being completed; on 4 March the captain declared they must return to South Georgia if the ship was to escape being frozen in. The *Deutschland* would have to return next year for a second attempt. Filchner somehow kept calm in front of the men as the vessel turned north.

Because of all the delays, the German expedition had left it too late. By 15 March 1912 the *Deutschland* was trapped in the sea ice. Picks and dynamites were tried, to no avail. It was hopeless. The ship's engines were turned off and the vessel quickly lost warmth.

This was the worst outcome of all. No Antarctic base was set up for the winter and now everyone was trapped on the *Deutschland*. Yet their predicament seemed to galvanise the men. They quickly set up a research station on the sea ice and made measurements as originally intended. They drilled holes to observe and record the growth of ice and the ocean temperature; to collect samples of water and plankton; and to measure the speed, direction and depth of the water below their feet. On the surface they established a weather station, from which kites and balloons with self-recording thermometers attached were sent up every few days. And by early April a magnetic observatory was established, completing the scientific set-up. The activities kept everyone busy and, for a while, their minds off the situation.

But science could not heal the party's bitter divisions. Some confrontations were relatively harmless: at one point, 'König used a wet sponge this morning to wake Przybyllok who then angrily beat König's door in with climbing boots. He acted afterward as if nothing had happened.' Some tried to play music to entertain, but it was not a huge success. Filchner wrote later that 'in this remote wilderness one's musical ear becomes more strict rather than uncritical. Unfortunately we did not have a single musician on board and hence accordion concerts turned into dreadful ear-torturing trials.' The men withdrew to spend a greater part of each evening in their cabins.

Other problems were considerably more serious. Criticisms were met with threats of duelling. In Filchner's book on the expedition there is barely any mention of alcohol. He claims he gave control of the expedition's stocks to the navigation officer, a teetotaller, while individuals kept 'modest private stocks of alcohol in their cabins'. 'I can heartily recommend fruit juices, mineral water, soda drinks etc and do not consider light wines for special occasions harmful.' If only this were the case. Filchner regularly remarked in his diary upon the damage alcohol did to the expedition's collegiality. It was a way of escape, and some of the characteristics it unmasked in the men were not to Filchner's liking. Vahsel apparently indulged in an 'abundant consumption of whiskey' and would insult Filchner in front of the other officers. He wrote of the captain, 'He is a sly fox.'

Some of the allegations are extraordinary. 'This drunkenness is a cancer,' Filchner declared, writing after one of the captain's soirées. 'The captain is always in the thick of it.'

One evening Filchner was woken at ten o'clock by the expedition doctor, Wilhelm von Goeldel, shouting. 'He fought with the carpenter and the boatsman,' Filchner wrote. 'Goeldel was totally drunk, threatening with a pistol. Przybyllok was also drunk. I brought them both to bed with the help of König. I myself got to sleep at around 2 am.'

By April, Filchner and Vahsel were no longer speaking. 'The captain opposes me wherever he can,' Filchner declared. Von Goeldel and the ship's first officer, Wilhelm Lorenzen, were now also openly hostile to the German leader. After the expedition Przybyllok commented, 'The expedition doctor...had twice threatened members of the expedition that he would shoot them down with his revolver. And one had to sit daily at table with such gentlemen!' The others on board were 'a bunch of pigs' and their behaviour towards Filchner was 'shameful'. Meanwhile, Brennecke had instigated a Great Ship's Council, supposedly as a means of representing the crew's views to Filchner. It soon became an opportunity to bypass the command and openly judge the leadership.

One of the most important issues the council investigated was an incident involving König, who claimed he had been shot at on the ice. The Austrian had brought news of the shooting to Filchner and showed him the bullet he had retrieved. Word got out and König was asked to explain himself to the Great Ship's Council. Filchner was worried. Von Goeldel was 'behaving like a madman' and had declared he would place König in 'a strait jacket at the first opportunity'. At the council König was interrupted with frequent jeers and declarations of 'Fool!', 'Crazy Man' and 'Strait Jacket'. It was touch-and-go. Filchner only managed to keep the mob at bay by declaring the shot had been accidental. In the end, von Goeldel did not follow through with his threat and the matter was dropped. Who had shot at König remained a mystery, though Filchner had his suspicions.

———•———

By June the bad feeling was too much for Filchner and he desperately needed to get off the ship for a while. He might not have made landfall on the Antarctic coastline, but he could at least make another contribution. Filchner decided to test one of the more controversial claims made about the Southern Ocean. In 1831 the eccentric American sealer Benjamin Morrell had returned from a purported journey south and subsequently published a popular account of his travels, *A Narrative of Four Voyages*. The book is highly entertaining, full of flamboyant claims and outlandish descriptions of the lands and people Morrell allegedly visited. In it he describes taking his schooner, the *Wasp*, south into the western Weddell Sea, where he found a 480-kilometre coastline he dubbed New South Greenland— though some later called it Morrell Land.

Pushing on south, Morrell subsequently claimed that, because of a shortage of cooking fuel at 70°, he was 'compelled to abandon, for the present, the glorious attempt to make a bold advance directly to the South Pole. The way was open before me, clear and unobstructed; the temperature of the air and water mild, the weather pleasant and the wind fair. Under such tempting auspices, it was with painful reluctance that I relinquished the idea...The vassals of some petty despot may one day place this precious jewel of discovery in the diadem of their royal master. Would to heaven it might be set among the stars of our national banner!' Morrell's pleas in America fell on deaf ears.

Despite concerns about its colourful discoverer, the existence of Morrell Land excited debate for decades. At a meeting of the RGS in 1870 a paper on Morrell's claims incited fervent discussion. Francis Galton, editor of the bible of exploration, *Hints to Travellers*, was suspicious. Morrell, he said, had claimed to have made an excursion into the interior of Africa at about 23°S, describing it as 'consisting of rich valleys, with large herds of cattle roaming over them, whereas it was a barren desert'. Charles Enderby, the former owner of a sealing company that had funded the discovery of one of the few known parts of the Antarctic coastline at the time, thought Morrell 'appeared to be a kind of Baron Munchausen'.

The most stinging comment, however, came from a Captain Davis: 'No doubt the work was a very remarkable one, and also very amusing…southward of that parallel [50°] it was evident that Morrell was out of his latitude…had Mr. Morrell restrained his tongue and pen, a great part of his narrative might have been believed…He visited Auckland Islands, having made the voyage from Kerguelen Land in twenty-two days, or at the rate of about 180 miles a day [in icy seas]…Mr. Morrell then wound up with what may be considered a "clincher", by characterising the island as "a delightful retreat for a few amiable families". Of the same spot, Sir James Ross said, "Well adapted for a penal settlement."'

By mid-June the *Deutschland*'s northwesterly drift had brought her sixty-five kilometres east of Morrell's alleged sighting. Filchner grabbed the opportunity. Here was a chance to achieve something and dodge any future shots from his trigger-happy colleagues. Filchner left the ship on 23 June and, with two companions he could trust—König and Kling—made off with enough provisions for three weeks of unsupported sledging. With just two to three hours of daylight a day, the three men slowly worked their way over the sea ice and around open patches of water, much of the time by moonlight, with temperatures regularly approaching -35°C. Kling later wrote, 'We proceeded at a rapid pace through the ghostly shadows thrown by piled-up floes and snow hillocks. We glided along noiselessly, as if we were heading for Valhalla. Everything around us was as silent as the grave; only the monotonous crunching of the sledges and König's shouts to his dogs broke the demonic silence.'

Acutely aware of what had happened to Nansen after he left the *Fram* in the Arctic, Filchner took frequent sightings of their latitude and longitude. The three men pushed on and, dragging their sledge of supplies and equipment, managed to get fifty kilometres from the ship. There was no sight of land. Finding a break in the ice, they dropped a lead weight and reached a depth of sixteen hundred metres before the line snapped. There was no hint of a shallow seabed: there was no coastline anywhere in the immediate vicinity. During their trip the three men saw 'phenomena on the western horizon which looked like ice-covered land; later it turned out that we had been deceived by mirages'. Filchner was convinced that, if Morrell had made it this far south, he had most probably seen a mirage. The American sealer had been wrong, or had made the whole thing up.

Filchner and his two accomplices headed back to the ship. Correcting for the drift of the sea ice, they successfully intercepted the *Deutschland*. The small team had covered 160 kilometres in three weeks. For a while, Filchner's success seemed to surprise those on board: this was not the action of a coward, as Vahsel was now portraying Filchner to the crew. It was not long, however, before the situation on the ship changed irrevocably.

On 8 August 1912 Vahsel died. Filchner is circumspect about the cause in *To the Sixth Continent*, and suggests it may have been a heart attack. But on board it was common knowledge that the captain suffered from syphilis and, privately, Filchner considered this the most likely culprit. Vahsel was given a sailor's burial on the Antarctic Circle. The question now was who to put in charge of the *Deutschland*. There was little choice, and Filchner feared for his life. With the level of suspicion on board, he could hardly set about putting his preferred man, Kling, in the post. In the end Filchner chose Lorenzen, a man he disliked almost as much as Vahsel. But when Lorenzen had signed his name in the log book with the title Captain, Filchner made a point of striking out the title, leading the sailor to faint—or pretend to—in shock. Przybyllok described him as acting 'like a young girl who wants a new outfit'.

If Filchner had hoped things would improve with Vahsel's death he was to be bitterly disappointed; if anything, morale worsened. Filchner and Lorenzen argued constantly. By mid-September the *Deutschland* had edged far to the north, and Filchner was desperate to start the ship's engines and get going; Lorenzen would not hear of it. Filchner wrote in frustration, 'Lorenzen is not able to lead a ship, every time he is challenged by decisions, he wants to faint (by purpose!). Shit gang here on board.'

Dr von Goeldel became ever more frustrated with König, who was struggling psychologically. The doctor was even suspected of trying to poison the Austrian biologist. Meanwhile, Filchner was suffering from constipation and haemorrhoids, a situation well known to von Goeldel. Because of the continued poor relationship between the two men, the expedition leader asked Kling to get his medication for him—but the doctor would not acquiesce. 'Kling was supposed to get laxatives from von Goeldel,' Filchner wrote. 'Von Goeldel made him swallow the double ration (although he didn't need it!).'

Their relationship did not improve. By 17 October, Filchner was writing in his diary, 'At night I slept on the bench in my room so that von Goeldel can't shoot me through the walls. I locked the door and have a gun and cartridges next to me...I will sleep always on the floor, gun loaded.'

Finally, on 26 November at 63°S, the *Deutschland* broke free of the ice and headed straight for South Georgia, leaving behind its prison of eight awful months. The ship had covered a staggering 10° of latitude, drifting north in a clockwise direction around the Weddell Sea.

On 19 December the inhabitants of Grytviken greeted the
return of the *Deutschland*. But the relative calm of the whaling
station was soon shattered by shouts of alarm and the sound of
scuffles on board. The chief of police went on the *Deutschland*
and asked Filchner whether he needed help to restore order.
Fearing how this would be interpreted at home, the German
leader declined. Lorenzen screamed that he wanted Filchner off
the vessel: 'I am the commander. He has no more say on board
this ship.' Many of the crew were utterly demoralised. Hearing
an untrue rumour that they would not be paid, they fell in
behind Lorenzen and announced, 'We don't want anything
more to do with Dr. Filchner.'

The Norwegian whaler Larsen attempted reconciliation, but
failed. The bad feeling ran too deep. The mutineers were taken
off the *Deutschland* in South Georgia and sent home via Buenos
Aires, completing their journey on a passenger steamer. It was an
ignominious end to what had promised to be a fine enterprise.

———————•———————

Ever ambitious, Filchner soon reported to the American
Geographical Society that he was keen to give the south another
go. 'About May the *Deutschland* will reach Buenos Aires and then
go into dry dock in order to carry out a trip to the Sandwich
Islands southeast of South Georgia, during the current year.
At the end of the year the second trip to the newly discovered
land can be made again and the explorations in the Antarctic
continue according to the original program.'

It was not to be. Those sent back to Germany early had
returned with tales of poor leadership and low morale. The
fallout reached Filchner's superiors, and he was ordered to
return home and answer charges. His plans for further work in
Antarctica were quietly shelved. The Siberian dogs and horses

were left behind in South Georgia and died from lack of food, victims of a thwarted expedition.

In Germany the recriminations came swiftly. Accusations raged in the press and a Court of Honour was established. All accusations were heard. Although the court was not legally binding, the disputes it addressed were intended to be settled privately, instead of in the media. The verdict was not what Filchner's opponents wanted: he was not castigated for his leadership, and several of the scientists continued to back him.

Filchner wrote, 'The verdict of the Court of Honour included, among other things, the clause that the scientists who were aboard *Deutschland* had refused to publish their expedition results in co-operation with me. This representation did not correspond to reality, since the expedition astronomer Prof. Dr Przybyllok had not been in agreement with this protest; for his part he rejected the unfair demand that he should publish his results along with the other scientists.'

The protagonists appear to have ignored the court's verdict and continued to make public accusations. Filchner later remarked, 'When, after this failure, my enemies circulated the story, that I had achieved nothing scientifically on the polar voyage, this rhetoric did not especially disturb me, since it was familiar to me.'

Not everyone was convinced by the denouncements. The Kaiser invited the German expedition leader to his castle at Doon and gave him his backing. Penck wrote a public essay on the expedition in early 1914, defending Filchner and the mission's success. To him, it was clear where the blame lay: Vahsel and the naval leadership imposed on Filchner.

Still rumours abounded, with von Goeldel claiming that Filchner was not 'a man of honour'. In the traditional Teutonic way, he was challenged to a duel and the comment was swiftly withdrawn.

After her return to Europe the *Deutschland* was sold to
Austria, so that a restored König could lead another trip south
and finish the job. Filchner was invited to take part, but felt
'for the time being I had had enough of "Antarctic Doings".
Moreover, many experiences had convinced me that truly great
successes in the polar ice are granted only to members of those
nations where polar research has tradition, namely the Scandi-
navians, the Russians, the British and the Canadians. I [have]
decided to return to my original field of work: Central and East
Asia.' First, Filchner got on with writing up the scientific output
of the Antarctic expedition as best he could.

Filchner's efforts in the south became synonymous with failure
in Germany, but were followed with interest overseas. Early
in the expedition many commentators pondered what had
happened to the *Deutschland*, with one writing, 'A guess may be
hazarded. Lieutenant Filchner is probably wintering somewhere
under the lee of Coats Land. For aught we know to the contrary,
there may be another range of mountains there pointing towards
the South Pole; at any rate, it seems probable that Filchner will
have better weather than…Scott, and that this may aid him in
breaking a new trail to the South Pole.'

On the Germans' return, the international enthusiasm was
undiminished. Learned societies and individuals were effu-
sive about the expedition's achievements. The Germans had
heroically fought their way to the southernmost end of a vast
Atlantic-facing ocean. And after traversing the extent of the
Weddell Sea, Filchner had reached a previously undiscovered
shore that set a northern limit to the continent.

The discoveries seemed to show there was no strait
beyond the Weddell Sea. Instead, the ocean was backed by an

enormous ice shelf that soon lost the regal name bequeathed to it and became known as the Filchner Ice Shelf. On the other side of Antarctica the Japanese and Norwegians appeared to have sighted peaks to the east of the Great Ice Barrier. There was little if any room for a connection between the Ross and Weddell seas. It looked like Penck was wrong.

Sir Clements Markham was particularly positive about Filchner's efforts. Although Markham did not recognise the scientific outcomes, the German's bravery appealed: 'There was no impenetrable pack for him. He put the ship's stem straight at it, somewhere near Weddell's furthest, and forced her through. After battling with the pack over 120 miles the ship came out into open water and land was sighted in 76°35' extending to 79°. There was an ice barrier to the westward.'

The Scottish were equally enthusiastic. On the scientific front Robert Mossman, who had been part of Bruce's team, remarked, 'The German Antarctic expedition under Dr. Filchner is the most recent, and in some respects, the most interesting, of expeditions in the Weddell Sea area...It was Dr. Filchner's intention to winter on this land and make sledge expeditions in a westerly direction with the view of testing whether Penck's theory of the division of the Antarctic continent...was correct.' And, 'Apart from the discovery of new land, the drift of the ship demonstrated the general circulation of the air and ocean currents of the Weddell Sea area.'

The balloon releases showed the same sort of temperature inversion the British were finding in the Ross Sea, suggesting this was a common feature of the Antarctic, while the route taken by the *Deutschland* gave a remarkably clear indication that the Weddell Sea flowed in a clockwise gyre. The Germans thought that this was driven by a low-pressure system which sat over the region, driving the air currents and ice in a clockwise direction, parallel to the coastline. 'The ice fields follow these air currents, although they are sometimes pushed slightly out of the general direction,' Filchner later wrote. 'They respond quickly, however, to temporary changes in the wind direction, so that the direction of the drift always corresponds to the direction of the wind. It seems that when the barometric minimum increases in intensity the winds drive the ice fields toward the nucleus of the depression and thus cause dangerous ice pressures.'

The practical result, Filchner argued, was that in the Weddell Sea the ice can be compressed into ever more fantastic shapes and contortions, threatening ships unfortunate enough to be caught in their grip. The *Deutschland* avoided being crushed—others would not be so lucky.

It was in the broader field of oceanography that the Germans arguably made their biggest contribution to Antarctic science. The *Deutschland* probed below the surface from the start, making frequent measurements of the different properties of ocean water down through the Atlantic and across a range of depths. The observations resulted in a tome of data describing and mapping the changes in temperature, salinity, density and dissolved oxygen through the Atlantic Ocean, from 80°N to 78°S—a most impressive achievement.

From Buenos Aires, Brennecke reported: 'the main result of our serial sections is the demonstration of a deep current in about 1500 m to about 3000 m of depth which comes from the North Atlantic toward the south and because of its high temperature and high salt content passes between the overlying and underlying layers' and 'a northward moving current at about 1000 m (demonstrated through the salinity minimum)'. The latter, he argued, was identical to that found by *HMS Challenger* and the *Gauss*, and most probably originated at about 50°S, where it sank and headed north.

Brennecke's great insight, however, was made later, on the

continental shelf of the Weddell Sea, where he discovered that the water had very similar properties at all depths. He realised that the intense winter cooling of the surface produced such prodigious quantities of sea ice that large amounts of dissolved salt were being concentrated down below. The result, Brennecke argued, was that the density became great enough to cause the water to sink off the shelf and flow northwards along the sea bottom.

The upshot of all the *Deutschland*'s measurements was the knowledge that there were four alternating ocean layers in the Atlantic, transporting warmer and colder water south and north respectively, with the Weddell Sea playing a central role. While crossing the Southern Ocean around South Georgia, Brennecke had also noted there was a sudden drop in the saltiness of the surface waters flowing north. The German oceanographer did not realise it, but he had just discovered the Antarctic Convergence. At around 50°S, it is probably the most reliable boundary for defining the start of the Antarctic region and the distinctive cold, frigid waters to the south. All the key elements of the Atlantic Ocean circulation system had been found.

Here was the first substantial evidence that the world's oceans were circulating, replenishing nutrient levels in the south, and the Antarctic was in the thick of it. But it would be a decade before the German oceanographer Wilhelm Meinardus would pull everything together and show how important these observations were in understanding the bigger picture. The new continent was not as isolated as had been thought. Unfortunately for Brennecke, he never saw his results completely worked up, dying in 1924.

And yet, for all his innovative research on the *Deutschland* expedition, Brennecke was not a pleasant chap, at least according to Filchner. The German leader later remarked in *Exposé*, 'the arrogant Brennecke maliciously annotated my notices on the blackboard in the mess... he announced, talking down to me: "If you need advice and instruction please feel free. I represent rigorous science on board!'"

On their return to Germany, Brennecke wrote to Amundsen when he heard the Norwegian had invited Filchner to join him on an attempt on the North Geographic Pole. 'When Amundsen visited me in Berlin,' Filchner recorded, 'he gave me Brennecke's letter to read then threw it into the fire with the words: "You Germans always have to foul your own nest! It is a pity for Brennecke that he should stoop to such denunciations, since I know better than that schemer who you are!"' With the onset of World War I, Filchner's chance to go with Amundsen to the Arctic disappeared.

Although the fallout from the expedition threatened to overwhelm its good work, the Germans undoubtedly revealed a tremendous amount about a largely unknown part of Antarctica. Filchner might not have reached the South Geographic Pole but he showed the first of many phantom Antarctic lands to be exactly what it was, a mirage, and discovered the southern limit of the Weddell Sea. More importantly, his expedition proved that the Antarctic played a major role in the circulation of the world's oceans.

But it was the final expedition of 1912 that, spurning the South Geographic Pole, aimed for the first complete scientific study of this new continent, and showed the way forward for Antarctic research. The Australasian Antarctic Expedition, led by Douglas Mawson and championed by Ernest Shackleton and Edgeworth David, would both bring home a wealth of data and become famous for its adventures.

German Antarctic Expedition member Albert Kling
three thousand metres above the seabed, 1912. By Ernst Müller.
Reproduced from Wilhelm Filchner's *Zum Sechsten Erdteil* (1922).

CHAPTER 7

ICE-COLD IN DENISON

Douglas Mawson and the Australasian
Antarctic Expedition, 1911–1913

---

*The 'race' is over: ergo the work of exploration is done. No more foolish
mistake could be made, and none more disastrous in its consequences.*

SIR ERNEST SHACKLETON (1874–1922)

Returning to Australia a national hero in April 1909, Douglas
Mawson soon resolved to go back south. But he felt the South
Geographic Pole was a highly dubious proposition in scientific terms. Instead, the 27-year-old opted to lead a team to a
largely unknown part of Antarctica south of his newly federated homeland.

After Robert Scott's failed attempt to recruit Mawson in
London in late 1909, Ernest Shackleton became excited by
Mawson's ideas and proposed an alternative arrangement.
Mawson recalled: 'Shackleton came in early to the office one
morning and said to me, "I have decided to go to the coast west
of Cape Adare and you are to be Chief Scientist. I hope you will
agree to this. I can get the money and that will be your trouble
were you taking it yourself." I was rather taken aback. Apparently he had fully realised the value of the expedition and now
wished to run it.'

It was tempting. Shackleton was offering to support the whole shebang. Mawson agreed, and visited possible supporters with him, extolling the virtues of scientific research and mineral exploration in the south. They soon had a commitment of more than £10,000.

Shackleton could not leave get-rich-quick schemes alone, though, and he soon directed his efforts towards other endeavours. While waiting on Shackleton to chase down further Antarctic funding, Mawson was dispatched with a former *Nimrod* colleague, John King Davis, to investigate Hungarian gold mines for a possible Shackleton investment. The mines proved a non-starter—and, more worryingly for Mawson, no further money had been secured for the expedition south.

By May 1910 Shackleton had gone quiet on Antarctica. Frustrated, Mawson challenged the Anglo-Irishman about his intentions. An agreement was reached: if Shackleton would not lead the expedition, it would fall to the Australian. Reassured, Mawson returned home and informed the press he was going south—but whether Shackleton was joining him remained unclear. 'In desperation,' Mawson remembered, 'I cabled early December asking if he had decided to go in charge of the expedition, if not I would. He cabled that he could not go but would support me.'

The timetable for getting to Antarctica in 1912 was now very tight. 'It was then so late,' the new leader wrote, 'that I decided to put the matter before the Australasian Association for the Advancement of Science at the Sydney meeting, 7th Jan. 1911.' There, Mawson appealed to people's growing sense of nationhood: on Australia's doorstep was a vast new southern continent waiting to be discovered. This was an opportunity to follow up the success of Shackleton's British Antarctic Expedition with a largely Australian and New Zealand team.

The call was warmly received. The president of the

association was especially supportive, wrapping up Mawson's appeal with the words: 'because we are part of the British nation, which has always taken such a leading part in geographical discovery, and because we happen to be that section of the British nation which rests nearest to the proposed field of investigation, it is surely—if I may use an Australian phrase which is rather expressive—it is surely "up to us" to assist.'

A committee was swiftly formed, headed by Mawson's old mentor Edgeworth David, and an announcement made in the national press. Extolling the valuable fishing and mineral potential in the Antarctic, whose exploitation was apparently 'less formidable than the exploiting of the goldfields of Alaska', the statement also stressed the scientific value of an expedition, particularly in meteorology—'for it is from the icy regions to the west and south that we may look for an extension of our knowledge of Australia's weather and of our power of forecasting it; and who shall estimate the value of such knowledge in a country like ours?'

The promise of riches was a drawcard. Mawson wrote to Scott about economic resources, advising him that 'Australia will be the gainer should anything eventuate', while at a citizen's meeting in the Sydney Town Hall, David described Antarctica as 'a new El Dorado'. It was an age-old balancing act, refined by Shackleton and now perfected by the Australians: dangling profit alongside science.

Funds began to flow in, including a commitment from the prime minister, Andrew Fisher. But the expedition finances remained in a parlous state. Until now, Mawson had restrained himself from making a public call for support in Britain, for fear of Scott accusing him of being 'a usurper of funds'. Now needing a massive investment, Mawson returned to London in early 1911 to raise capital. The Australian was shocked to find the money apparently already secured with Shackleton had vanished into the Anglo-Irishman's shadowy finances. Mawson never really forgave Shackleton. Years later he would write, 'when it comes to the moral side of things S. [Shackleton] and I part brass rags, as they say in the navy.'

Things were now pretty desperate. 'Mrs Scott had asked me to live at her house in London if it would assist me in any way—although very friendly on her part, still the Scottites resented me asking for subscriptions in England...I pointed out however that I really did not intend calling for money from English people. I wanted to see wealthy Australians in London. Now however that things were going badly I told her that I anticipated having to call through the press for aid. I gave her one month grace, so that she could make a public appeal before me.'

Shackleton stepped forward and honoured his agreement to support Mawson. Weaving his magic, he convinced the newspaper baron Lord Northcliffe to agree to a free appeal in the *Daily Mail* for the proposed Australasian Antarctic Expedition. Not everyone was pleased. Despite Mawson's offer to Kathleen Scott, Sir Clements Markham was particularly angry and wrote to the newspapers, arguing any money should go to Scott's British expedition, known to be short of funds. But the old man's call was not enough to dampen enthusiasm for the new endeavour. Shackleton's name secured nearly £10,000, alongside a cornucopia of donated supplies—condensed milk, chocolate, gramophone records and enough tobacco for the men 'to smoke to their hearts' content'—helping defray the money pledged earlier and then mysteriously lost. The expedition looked like it now had a chance.

———— ✦ ————

Mawson's effort was born of Shackleton's British Antarctic Expedition. Perhaps inevitably, his Australasian Antarctic

Expedition—AAE, as it became known—used many of the same members, suppliers and equipment. In addition to Shackleton and David supporting the effort at home, John King Davis and Frank Wild agreed to join Mawson in the south. Davis had become a firm friend of Mawson's during the previous expedition, nursing him through frequent bouts of seasickness and saving him from a crevasse after the young Australian's now-famous journey to the South Magnetic Pole.

Mawson in turn had been greatly impressed with Davis's skill as a navigator and captain. In the final phase of the British expedition Shackleton had given Davis command of the *Nimrod* and ordered him to return the vessel to Britain—a journey of eight thousand kilometres—during midwinter. Not only did Davis bring the ship and crew home safely; he also disproved the existence of several islands marked on navigational charts of the time. It was a remarkable effort, and proof to Mawson that Davis was more than capable of being his second-in-command. Wild too had demonstrated ability in the Antarctic, with an incredible feat of endurance during the southern journey with Shackleton. The AAE needed all the experience it could get; most of the other men taking part had none at all.

Mawson had also learned a few of Shackleton's tricks when it came to finances. An old Dundee wooden whaling vessel, the *Aurora*, was identified as the expedition ship. It needed modifying, including reinforcing the bow with steel plates to handle the sea ice, but it would do. Because funds were short Mawson 'had to buy the *Aurora* without even having the money to purchase her. Materials which required time in preparation had been ordered and bought—we could not turn back. Already Capt. J.K. Davis and I had made a solemn compact that we would go come what may, even had we to go in a cutter with no equipment. We felt sure that even should we not succeed by this latter procedure, our example would not be lost on the Britishers of the future.' And it was not just the ship—a large part of the expedition's inventory was bought on credit. It was becoming an Anglo-Saxon exploration tradition.

A focus of the Australian effort was to be Cape Adare, Borchgrevink's former base on the north coast of Victoria Land. Mawson had been deeply frustrated by Scott's lack of interest, and at the time wrote, 'This area is crying out for investigation. It offers the greatest range of rocky coastline anywhere obtainable on the Antarctic Continent...it is here a connection must one-time have been effected with Australia...In my opinion it is the pick of the Antarctic for scientific investigation and I deplore Capt. Scott's inability to include part of it in his programme.'

Shortly after, Scott reconsidered. In early May 1910 he wrote to David, who was in Sydney: 'My idea has always been to try for the South Pole a second season if it is not possible to get there in one; and should the main object of the Expedition be achieved during the first season I have wished to transfer the station to the west of Cape North for the second season. Such a transference would, I think, be quite possible, though it would not be possible to go far beyond Adelie Land.'

Just a couple of weeks later Scott's mind was made up, and he reiterated the prospect of visiting Cape Adare in the outline of his expedition to the Royal Geographic Society. These plans were brought forward dramatically when the *Terra Nova* discovered the *Fram* in the Bay of Whales and took what then became the British Northern Party to Cape Adare. Mawson was furious. In the Australian's eyes, Scott had stolen his idea and, after Mawson's fallout with Shackleton, Scott's actions seemed hypocritical. Others were not so sure. Scott's former engineer, Skelton, wrote to the British leader at the time, 'Don't take any notice of what those other people say about that being Mawson's ground because you have a prior right to the whole of it, and anyway Shackleton and his friends can't talk about what is right.'

Calmed by Kathleen Scott, Mawson presented his proposed Antarctic expedition to the Royal Geographical Society in April 1911. It was breathtaking in scale: 'to accomplish a complete geographical and magnetic survey between Cape Adare and Gaussberg, a distance of over 2000 miles.' Mawson reminded the audience that 'it had been our intention of dropping a few men at Cape Adare, for that is the easiest and most accessible landing on the Antarctic continent. The facilities there afforded of coal and stores left by Borchgrevink's expedition would have further simplified matters...In the light of recent events'—a thinly veiled reference to Scott's switch to Cape Adare—'this must be eliminated from our programme.'

The plan was modified, but still unparalleled in vision: four expedition bases spread out along a near-unknown Antarctic coastline. This was not a return to old ground; it was a complete scientific exploration of what many suspected to be an entirely new continent, lying in the 'Australian quadrant'. With Scott taking Cape Adare, Mawson's expedition was becoming more daring. Multiple sledging parties were to head into the Antarctic hinterland, investigating almost all fields of science, including biology, glaciology, magnetism and meteorology, backed up by the first wireless link to Australia.

In tandem with the work on the ice, the *Aurora*, under Davis's command, would traverse the Southern Ocean collecting ocean and biological samples alongside depth soundings. Mawson was in no doubt about the importance of his mission: 'The early glimpses of the Antarctic continent, and its history, illustrate how little is yet revealed of the wealth of scientific data locked up within its icy ramparts, and calls for the united efforts of scientific bodies throughout the world to banish this ignorance, which stands as a reproach in this enlightened twentieth century.' Not averse to striking a nationalistic note, he reminded the audience that it was his intention to claim the region for the Empire. Here, he made clear, stood a worthy successor to Shackleton.

The expedition would have the largest number of scientists of any Antarctic expedition to date. Scott had ten science graduates and professionals in a cohort of thirty-three men; Mawson had nineteen in his complement of thirty-one, covering the breadth of scientific endeavour.

Magnetism would be a feature of the extensive observation program. Although Shackleton's British team claimed to have reached the South Magnetic Pole area, there were mutterings they might have fallen short; David and Mawson were unsure. Charles Chree, director of the Kew Observatory, wrote to David and said that, regardless, 'Every one, I am sure, appreciates the truly heroic quest made by you & Dr Mawson...We want a little poetry and adventure in science to show to the public that scientific men are not machines.' Mawson was determined to resolve the issue, preferably without heroics. He needed the expedition to approach the South Magnetic Pole from another direction and to be led by an expert. Just as Amundsen had, Mawson approached the Terrestrial Magnetism department at the Carnegie Institute for advice. After some deliberation they suggested Eric Webb, a trained magnetic observer, who after a five-month secondment at the Institute joined Mawson in Australia.

Mawson was all too aware that scientific results in themselves could not compete against what David had called the 'microbe of sport'. It was important to follow Shackleton's example and engage people with a strong visual record of the expedition: the BAE had shown just how powerful photographs were for scientific work and in exciting the public. Fate would deliver the expedition Frank Hurley, then a little-known photographer based in Sydney. Hurley had purchased a Kodak box brownie camera when he was seventeen and by his early twenties was running a postcard business in Sydney.

At twenty-five Hurley cornered Mawson in a train compartment and talked non-stop through the journey. His enthusiasm was infectious. Three days later Hurley was hired and charged with a wider remit than that of his day job: he was to keep a film record of the expedition's exploits. Unfamiliar with this new technology, called a cinematograph, he learned to operate the hand-cranked movie camera in just a few days. The expedition now had a dedicated professional photographer who would go on to repeatedly put himself in danger for the best possible shot, and who scribbled above his Antarctic work bench 'Near enough is not good enough.'

With stores and staff appointed, financing once again became the priority. After Mawson's presentation, the Royal Geographical Society marked their approval by contributing £500—the same as was given to Scott—while the promise of shares in future mineral discoveries helped secure thousands more pounds from investors. Several of the Australian state governments chipped in, offering a total of £18,500, while the federal government matched the funds provided to Shackleton, £5000—followed up later with a further £5000—but New Zealand controversially declined. Significantly, the British government also chipped in £2000. With loans and grants, Mawson could count on £39,000. Although considerably short of the £48,000 target, he had his expedition—and it was all arranged in just one year.

To maintain public interest in the enterprise—and keep funds flowing—Mawson looked to Scott's motorised sledges for supporting work on the ice. After reviewing the designs of the vehicles, however, he regretfully concluded they would not do. Instead, Mawson thought flight might be a better money-spinner. It was a shrewd move. Only ten years before, the

Wright Brothers had famously made the first powered flight; the technology had advanced swiftly since then, and with it public excitement about the possibilities of air travel.

Scott's wife, Kathleen, was an enthusiast and encouraged Mawson to take a plane for reconnaissance purposes. An unimpressed Skelton wrote to Scott in 1911: 'Mawson is apparently taking an airplane with him and a soldier called Watkins to fly in it,—really it is very silly,—wonderful flights have been made this year,—but we haven't got anywhere near the so-called conquest of the air yet, even in Europe, and going up in the Antarctic seems to me to be only asking for trouble.'

Negotiating with the manufacturer Vickers, Mawson acquired a single-winged two-seater with skis for landing on ice for under £1000, on credit. The pilot Hugh Evelyn Watkins told *Flight* magazine, 'it is doubtful if the airplane will be used for the final dash to the Pole, as it would have to surmount the great ice barrier.' Although Mawson had no designs on the South Geographic Pole, the magazine ended on the exasperated note: 'What hope is there of surmounting it if it could not be done by aeroplane?' Regardless, the plane was shipped to Australia, with much fanfare.

Wild wrote of this episode in his unpublished memoirs: 'Like almost all British explorers, Mawson had found a great difficulty in raising the necessary funds for his expedition…and he had planned to use the aeroplane to assist in this. For this purpose a huge marquee was erected on the race course, thousands of invitations sent out, and a sufficiency of refreshments of every kind provided for the guests. The Governor of South Australia promised to attend with his family, and to open the proceedings by taking the first of a series of short flights which would be given during the day at a charge of £5 a trip.'

The plane was checked over and all appeared well. Watkins and Wild took the opportunity for one last test flight the next morning:

The plane took off all right and had climbed to 500 ft when in making a turn it suddenly side slipped. We were almost down before Watkins got the plane straightened out, and the sensation was far from pleasant. We climbed again to about 150 feet when the plane put its nose down and dived. We were then over the centre of the race course and as the earth rushed at us, all my past life did not panorama before me. I felt no fear, just had time to think 'Frank old boy your days of exploration are done,' when we struck, and the plane fell over on its back on top of us. A heavy weight was on my chest and I could hardly breathe but was fully conscious. One leg was touching a hot cylinder and I was drenched in oil and petrol and in horrible dread that the machine would burst into flames. I lay it seemed a very long time when I heard Watkins grunt and then gasp out 'Poor old bus, she's jiggered up!'

The plane was a write-off and the event had to be cancelled. Mawson was unimpressed and blamed Watkins for the accident, 'as he had been very late at the Naval and Military Club the night before'. Although the plane could no longer fly, the engine and body were salvaged and shipped to Antarctica to be used as an 'air tractor'. In the *Sydney Morning Herald*, Watkins was said to be 'keenly disappointed': this was the first time he had ever had a serious accident. He returned to England and promptly had another crash. When the war came the Royal Flying Corp decided to overlook him for service.

With much excitement, the residents of the island state of Tasmania turned out in droves to farewell the heavily laden *Aurora* when it headed south from Hobart, on 2 December 1911. It had been an extraordinary year. Mawson had somehow managed to raise the necessary funds; appoint a team of scientists, engineers and ship's crew; buy and provision a vessel; and obtain enough equipment and supplies to sustain a scientific expedition in the field for fourteen months.

Remarkably the original plan, as put to the RGS, remained largely intact. There was one small exception: one of the bases would now be established on remote, subantarctic Macquarie Island, so it could operate as a relay station for Antarctic wireless messages and undertake scientific study. And because Macquarie Island fell under the jurisdiction of the Tasmanian state government, permission had to be obtained to work there; worryingly for Mawson, this was granted just five days before the *Aurora* left Hobart. Refusal would have thrown the whole expedition into chaos.

Weathering a violent gale south of Tasmania, the *Aurora* sighted Macquarie Island in nine days. Almost immediately the men saw a beached sealing vessel. The *Clyde* had been wrecked on a reef after a particularly bad storm and the sealers on board had been stranded for months with barrels of oil collected from fur and elephant seals on the island. The shipwrecked men were waiting to be rescued when the *Aurora* arrived—and Mawson was not one to pass up an opportunity to offset his costs. He negotiated their repatriation to Australia on a second, smaller expedition vessel that was returning to Tasmania. All the men had to do was pay for the cost of the charter.

Negotiations complete, a wireless mast was quickly erected on the island, and on a promontory at the northern end expedition members unloaded enough building materials, supplies and scientific equipment to support five men over the next year. Davis had some doubts about the leader of the group, the meteorologist George Ainsworth. On arrival Davis suggested that, in selecting the site of the base, 'it would be well to ask the islanders their opinion as having lived on the island they would probably know the sheltered spots. This idea was ridiculed by this gentleman who informed me with great dignity that what Ferrel—some meteorologist who had never been to the island—said was good enough for him. Well I am glad I shall not be with Ainsworth—he is an ass.'

But at least Mawson was reassured that this phase of the expedition was complete. The rest of the Australasian expedition could push on south.

The omens were good as the *Aurora* went south from Macquarie Island. For the first couple of days the sun came out and there was only a light northerly wind, allowing the men a well-earned break after two punishing weeks building the base on Macquarie Island. It was time to consider what might lie ahead, off the map. Some questioned whether there was even any land between Cape Adare and von Drygalski's Kaiser Wilhelm II Land.

The little known about the region was almost entirely based on reports made more than seventy years earlier. When Ross had found his path to the South Magnetic Pole checked by the mountains of Victoria Land, French and American fleets were exploring the icy seas to the west, south of Australia. The French were led by Jules Sébastien César Dumont D'Urville, who headed south from Hobart in 1839 and, after weaving his way around numerous tabular bergs, came across land.

Setting foot on a small island at what he called Pointe Géologie, D'Urville raised the flag and claimed the area for France. For the first time a piece of Antarctica was named after love, with the French leader bestowing the title Adelie Land, 'to perpetuate...my deep and lasting gratitude to my devoted wife'. After a brief stay collecting geological samples and a few unfortunate penguins, the French left, only to come across an American expedition led by the controversial Charles Wilkes.

If there were a prize for an Antarctic expedition with the poorest preparation and lowest morale, Wilkes's effort would be a strong contender. His ships were ill equipped for the icy conditions and, though he claimed to have a scientific agenda, Wilkes went out of his way to lose as many of the expedition scientists as possible before heading south. When the French and American ships met one another, they kept going—in opposite directions. After the encounter the Americans completed an impressive 1700-kilometre voyage, much of it through dangerous pack ice surrounding what we now know to be the eastern Antarctic. On returning home Wilkes confidently proclaimed he had discovered a continent in the south and, perhaps not unreasonably, expected to be welcomed as a hero. Instead, the American found himself mired in controversy, his reliability as an observer questioned, his leadership disputed.

D'Urville wrote of their meeting in the south, 'I would have been glad to give our co-explorers the results of our researches…it seems the Americans were far from sharing these feelings.' Wilkes in turn accused the French of fleeing. Tragically, D'Urville and his wife died in a train accident shortly after the Frenchman's triumphant homecoming, abruptly ending the argument. But, finding the French asserting they had landed on what was now thought to be a continent on 19 January 1840, Wilkes contended he had done so a few days before.

Complaints came thick and fast, and not merely from the French. Wilkes's claims of other land sightings were dogged by seemingly contradictory reports from those on the expedition, and the men had not appreciated his old-fashioned, tough leadership—119 of the 342 dying, deserting or discharged during the voyage. Wilkes found himself court martialled, charged with unbecoming behaviour, including handing out illegal punishment, and accused of 'deliberate and wilful falsehood'. He escaped with a reprimand but continued to flirt with disaster, notoriously nearly dragging Britain into the American Civil War when he hauled Confederate officers off a British vessel.

For want of an alternative guide, Wilkes's alleged observations formed a cornerstone of the Australasian plan—even though Ross was known to have sailed over land that Wilkes had mapped and Scott's *Discovery* had shown many of the so-called landfalls were false. As the *Aurora* approached the frozen coastline, Mawson was all too aware he was relying on observations similar to those Ross and Scott had disproved.

Sighting the first bergs on 29 December 1911 the crew was told to be vigilant, watching for icy hazards while scanning the horizon for land. It was a frustrating time: for Davis, the ship was continually threatened; for Mawson, the supposed land remained obstinately hidden. Since D'Urville had landed on Adelie Land no one else had been back, while Wilkes's finds seemed non-existent.

Before departing Australia, Mawson had become engaged to Paquita Delprat, the daughter of a mining engineer in Broken Hill, and among his numerous letters of affection he wrote to her of his frustration with Wilkes's claims of finding an Antarctic coastline: 'We met heavy impenetrable pack in several directions and failed to break through to the land. Much of this disappointment and trouble I find today are due to an undue reliance I had placed in the accounts of Commander Wilkes who made explorations here in 1840. His accounts are largely erroneous and misleading.'

Mawson had expected to find land by the beginning of January. The plan had been to establish the main base of operations as close as possible to the South Magnetic Pole, allowing the scientists to complement the measurements Mawson had made in 1909. With no land in sight the *Aurora* was forced west, away from the magnetic meridian. And the further west the vessel went, the less the chance of raising Macquarie Island on the wireless system. They had to make landfall, and soon.

'During the afternoon of January 6,' Mawson recorded, 'an ice cliff loomed up ahead, extending to the horizon in both directions. This proved to be an immense barrier tongue— afterwards named the Mertz glacier—pushing 60 miles out to sea from a great ice-capped land. This land, along which we steamed during the next two days, had never before been seen. Its continuity with Adelie Land was subsequently proved.' After cautiously working their way around the glacier over the next two days, the men of the *Aurora* discovered a small rocky outcrop and bay alive with penguins and seals. They had found a site for their first base.

'As a station for scientific investigations,' Mawson wrote, 'it offered a wider field than the casual observer would have imagined.' But the timetable was slipping and the scientific program had to be rationalised. With a shortage of coastline suitable for landing, and having been forced so far west, Mawson decided to combine two of the bases into one, making this his Winter Quarters. Uninspired by D'Urville's romantic streak or his own recent engagement, he named the new promontory Cape Denison after one of the expedition backers, Sir Hugh Denison, and their anchorage Commonwealth Bay in tribute to the recently federated Australia.

Almost as soon as they decided to establish the base a storm blew up, sweeping the rocky outcrops free of snow and sending newly formed pack ice far out to sea. The storm blasted the men on shore for two days as they huddled together in tents, while

Davis fought desperately to keep the *Aurora* off the rocks. With the winds finally subsiding, the men worked at a frenzied pace, taking ashore all the building material they needed for two huts, along with scientific equipment and stores for eighteen men, the former aircraft, one wireless mast, twenty-nine dogs and twenty-three tonnes of coal for fuel.

They had to erect the huts quickly: the place seemed to be a magnet for storms. The wind would pick up suddenly, often with no warning at all, threatening the expedition. The churning sea surface tested Davis's captaincy skills to the limit as he was frequently called upon to save the *Aurora* from being dashed against nearby reefs. For the men on shore conditions were equally wretched. The high winds, dangerous for those walking outside, seemed to drive the temperature lower. Although the concept of wind chill was yet to be developed, the men were all too aware of its effects. The expedition biologist, Charles Laseron, later remarked, 'the landing of the stores seemed interminable, as all of us were bitterly cold and miserable.'

The supplies were unloaded in eleven days and, after a further eleven, the wooden huts were habitable. The Winter Quarters were complete, to everyone's great relief. After brief handshakes and cries of farewell, the *Aurora* headed west. Time was perilously short: Davis had to get Frank Wild's Western Party established before the onset of winter.

Mawson had asked that Wild be set down 'not nearer than a couple of hundred miles, and preferably about 500 miles distant'. Obstacle after obstacle frustrated efforts to land the men, though, and Davis was exhausted. Through the fog and mist, the coastline appeared to be made of steep ice cliffs and shelves.

Heading further west, 'new land was sighted—icy slopes rising from the sea, similar to those of Adelie Land, but of greater elevation.' Soundings of the sea depth showed they were in shallow water and must be close to land. Now more sympathetic to their American predecessor, the men called this discovery Wilkes Land, to 'commemorate the name of a navigator whose daring was never in question, though his judgment as to the actuality of *terra firma* was unreliable'. But they could not get close enough to land. The *Aurora* pushed on, more in hope than promise.

Three weeks after leaving Mawson, the *Aurora* was 2400 kilometres west of Cape Denison when the ship suddenly came across a vast glacier tongue. Twenty-five metres high, this river of ice seemed to tower over the vessel and disappear far out to sea. It took two days to circumnavigate.

The glacier was not land—but things were desperate, and at any moment the *Aurora* might become trapped by sea ice. Wild had to be dropped off as soon as possible if his men were to remain in Antarctica and do the work intended. And here they were in a relatively sheltered spot.

Davis talked to Wild about whether the glacier might suffice, 'which seems to me the only alternative just at present, I think it would be a risky business but would prefer it to going back. I feel pretty sure that if we do find land here it will be inaccessible.' The spot did not enthuse Davis: 'It is certainly a cheerless place, no sun all day, nothing but snow and gloom.' In the end Wild decided there was no choice. The base commander wrote a letter confirming it was his decision alone—and, worryingly, stated that he felt as safe as Amundsen did on the Great Ice Barrier.

With the decision made, the ship's company swung into action. Supplies and equipment were quickly unloaded and moved to the top of the ice cliff using a flying fox, before being dragged by sledge to the site of their wooden hut, some six hundred metres from the edge. It was far from ideal. The base was set on what we now know to be floating ice, three times the distance from Cape Denison than Mawson had wanted and with a coastline nearly thirty kilometres away.

Davis was not known for his optimism—he was frequently referred to as Gloomy Davis, though not to his face—but his diary shows a more personable side, with genuine concern for the men and ship in an unknown, hostile environment. Feeling he had been harsh towards Wild's men on one occasion, Davis remonstrated with himself the next day, 'Since I wrote up my log yesterday evening I have recovered my temper. I was irritated then and I feel differently about the party as they have behaved in a very generous manner...I feel that it was very nice of them as I have hardly been friendly to anyone this last month with the constant worry and anxiety let alone the repeated disappointment. However it was very pleasant to feel that the party appreciate the fact that we have done our best for them.'

When the *Aurora* left, on 21 February, Davis recorded his worries in his diary: 'Was this an ice-shelf, attached to the land, on which we were leaving them? Or would it, and they, have "gone to sea" before the arrival of the "Aurora" next year?'

With two bases now established on the Antarctic continent—of sorts—and one on Macquarie Island, Davis was eager to get his ship and crew out of danger and back to Hobart. He was desperately short of fuel, yet managed to make the 4300-kilometre journey, arriving with just nine tonnes of coal to spare. The *Aurora* straggled into Hobart on 12 March 1912 to find the *Fram* at anchor: Amundsen had beaten Scott to the South Geographic Pole.

Davis's role was not only to safely deliver men and equipment to disparate, troublesome locations: Mawson had also entrusted him with overseeing a major part of the scientific program. After restocking the *Aurora* and making necessary repairs, the expedition's second-in-command was to undertake an extensive oceanographic survey of the Southern Ocean, taking depth soundings, and collecting biological and water samples.

Davis was keen; like Mawson, he was scathing of the attempt on the South Geographical Pole. Writing to William Speirs Bruce, a kindred spirit, Davis remarked: 'I hope to hear that you are going away with a Scottish Expedition before long. If Scott or Amundsen reach the Pole, people will perhaps realise that nothing much can be learnt from this sort of thing and be more willing to help really useful work.' During the Australasian Antarctic Expedition, Davis would take the *Aurora* to Antarctica three times and the subantarctic twice more, charting new territory.

Travelling the wild Southern Ocean may not have been the most glamorous of roles, but taking soundings and trawling its depths could crack the great scientific conundrum Mawson had raised with David years before: had there been a land bridge between Australia and Antarctica in the past? By 1912 scientists appreciated that, on geological timescales, mountains could be thrown up and oceans created—a process described as diastrophism—but how such large upheavals in the past came about was often the subject of outlandish conjecture.

One rather eccentric possibility was put forward by Osmond Fisher, at the end of the nineteenth century: the Earth had rotated too quickly during its early formation, causing it to split and form the moon, leaving the Pacific Ocean as a scar on the surface. Fisher speculated that, as a result of this massive rupture, the granite crust left behind experienced tremendous pressures and fractured, forming continents and causing massive amounts of volcanic activity that created the world's mountains. It was an imaginative idea, but no one seems to have taken it seriously.

The American Frank Bursley Taylor put forward an alternative concept in 1908, suggesting that the continents were formed by 'huge landslides from the polar regions towards the equator'. Granite and other continental rocks could flow, and in doing so formed mountains, leaving ocean basins behind. To explain why the continents moved out from the pole, Taylor pointed to the gravitational pull of the moon and associated tides dragging rock equatorwards. But the forces required were so vast they would have stopped the planet rotating millions of years ago. Taylor's idea that continents could move horizontally as well as vertically was too left-field for most, and was largely forgotten.

Instead, the most widely accepted view explaining the surface of our planet was contraction theory, the brainchild of the American geologist James Dwight Dana. During 1873 he published a series of influential papers outlining the principle, which was based on the well-known fact that miners found it considerably warmer deeper underground, consistent with the idea that the planet had started as a molten ball of rock and cooled over time. Being a liquid, it was reasoned, the hot interior should contract relatively more than the solid surface, shrinking as it did so. Over time the cooler exterior would then collapse into the newly formed space, creating folds and faults in the rocks—'just as an apple wrinkles owing to the loss of more moisture from the interior than from the rind', as one textbook of the time put it.

Edward Suess, the great Austrian geologist, described it less eloquently as 'the collapse of the Earth is what we are seeing,' and used the sinking of the Earth's crust as the premise for an explanation of earthquakes. By the time the expeditions were heading south for 1912 a large part of the scientific community had embraced contraction theory. It was an elegant idea, and it was completely wrong.

An Earth cooling quickly in its early history implied tremendous subsequent upheavals. These upheavals, some scientists argued, could have created or destroyed the purported land bridges, now considered the most likely explanation of the similar geology and life forms scattered across the southern hemisphere. As Mawson declared to the Royal Geographical Society in 1914, 'Rumours of the existence of wingless parrots and other continental forms of life indicated that perhaps Macquarie island was the last remaining summit of a vast sunken southern land. Other evidence also suggested that probably at one time such a land existed uniting Australia with the Antarctic Continent.'

During the expedition the wireless operator on Macquarie Island, Arthur Sawyer, repeatedly noted earthquakes in his diary, which suggested that the same process underway in the past continued into 1912. The evidence seemed to support an early separation of the southern continents, and not all at the same time. 'New Zealand, though possessing many of the features of Antarctic flora and fauna, never received a marsupial population, and its final separation is thereby allocated to the early Tertiary times,' Mawson reasoned. 'Australia, then separated by the formation of Bass strait, and more recently Tasmania and South America, have become isolated by the engulfment, due to diastrophism, of the land bridges connecting both with the Antarctic continent.' Davis just had to take the *Aurora* across the Southern Ocean and take depth soundings of the seabed to find the evidence required.

As he was to the German expedition, Bruce was extraordinarily generous to the Australasian effort, providing advice and lending equipment from his own ship, the *Scotia*. The most important piece of kit was a Lucas sounding machine, set up on the forecastle head. When a site was chosen, the vessel was stopped and one or more sinker weights were dropped over the side. The weights were attached to a long metal wire, which was fed out from a central drum until the line went limp, indicating the seabed had been reached. The genius of the Lucas machine was that the wire passed over a measuring wheel which, with its spring brake system, meant it could provide accurate and rapid measurements to an impressive depth of eleven thousand metres.

The AAE targeted key areas in the ocean, including the mysterious Royal Company's Islands, a group supposedly southwest of Tasmania and perhaps marking the high point of a subterranean land long since drowned. Davis had previously attempted to find them as part of Shackleton's *Nimrod* expedition, but with no success. Again, there was 'No appearance of land!' and the Lucas machine indicated no hint of anything resembling a sunken land bridge.

Moving on to Macquarie Island, Davis was not surprised to learn that all had not been well among the team there. Ainsworth's high-handed leadership grated with the other men and several times it had nearly led to blows. The much-needed supplies from the *Aurora* gave a welcome relief and broke the strained atmosphere, albeit temporarily. Davis continued his search of the seabed but found the island shelf dropped away quickly in all directions. Frustratingly, there did not appear to be a vast submerged land anywhere.

Then, on 15 November 1912, Davis remarked in his diary, 'Blowing a fresh breeze this morning at 5 am when we got a sounding of 792 Fathoms [around fifteen hundred metres] and rock—this was a surprise, I imagined the weights had slipped off somehow so putting more on sounded again, this time got 794 Fathoms so I think we may claim to have made a very interesting discovery, there is evidently a submerged ridge here which I hope we shall be able to trace for some distance.'

Davis was hopeful: it was 'a most curious confirmation of the theory of a land connection between Australia and the Antarctic'. But his excitement proved premature. The shallow depths did not continue across the ocean but rather appeared to mark an isolated plateau. Later reporting his findings, including what became known as the Mill Rise—since renamed the South Tasman Rise—to the RGS, Davis left others to speculate about whether he had discovered a remnant of the long-sought land bridge.

———•———

In Adelie Land it had soon become obvious that the storms experienced during the establishment of the Winter Quarters were not unusual. No one had ever reported anything like it. The Norwegian explorer Borchgrevink had written of 'frightful winds' at Cape Adare, commonly experiencing speeds of more than sixty kilometres an hour, but Cape Denison appeared considerably worse.

Anemometers were critical to the team's scientific work, and they frequently could not cope with the conditions: high winds would often rip the spinning cups off, while the extremely low temperature often meant they seized up. To try to understand just how strong the winds were at the highest speeds, Mawson built what became known as the puffometer, an ingenious device set up on a pole from which a small aluminium ball would seemingly dance in the air. The ball was connected to a spring, the pull on which was a measure of the wind strength. Each tug was recorded on carbonised paper housed in a small wooden box that could be retrieved under more hospitable conditions.

In the highest wind speeds the puffometer was 'left out for an hour at a time, and separate gusts up to one hundred and fifty and one hundred and eighty miles [240 and 280 kilometres] per

hour were commonly indicated', providing a unique measure
of what was happening outside. Longer-term wind speeds
averaged a staggering seventy kilometres per hour, with temperatures around -14°C, equivalent to -40°C with wind chill added.
During the winter one twelve-hour period had a wind-speed
average of 143 kilometres per hour, hurricane in strength, which
Laseron later described as an 'icy inferno'. The Australian and
New Zealand team had established their base in the windiest
place on the planet.

They still had to operate outside, and the high winds often
resulted in a characteristic gait, the men walking at a jaunty
angle into the wind. Journeys to collect scientific data under
such conditions were fraught with danger. The Stephenson
screen housing the thermometers and barometers was a particular hazard, set on a local high point to the east of the living
quarters. Remarkable footage shot by Hurley shows observers
frequently being thrown to the ground, often onto surrounding
rocks. When conditions were too poor, 'little could be done
except keep the self-recording instruments in order,' and during
so-called calmer times it was not uncommon for the paper
records to be 'carried off by the wind'.

When going to put the puffometer up one day, Mawson was
surprised to find that 'the wind picked me up clear of the ground
and dashed myself and the instrument on some rocks several
yards away. The latter was badly injured, but thick clothing
saved me from serious injury.' No one was safe.

Of all the scientific observations made at Cape Denison, arguably the most important in Mawson's eyes were the magnetic
readings. Needing a large flat area and to be free of any influ-
ence from the wireless masts or metal in other huts, the

Magnetograph House was built four hundred metres from the living quarters, the furthest away of the scientific sites.

To make the measurements Eric Webb and his assistant—whoever had drawn the short straw—would first have to negotiate the conditions outside. Snowdrifts, a constant threat, could produce large dumps in just an hour, preventing the use of guide ropes, while high winds threatened to blow the men towards open water. During the long winter night the effects were exacerbated. The two men were often found going out on their hands and knees, following a set course with their heads down, until they reached a distinctive rocky ridge, over which they would clamber to the Magnetograph House.

But the wind could sometimes help. Webb wryly commented, 'If the Magnetograph House had been advertised, it would have been described as "two minutes from the Hut." This can easily be understood, for the magnetician after leaving home is speedily blown over a few hillocks and sastrugi, and, coming to an ice-flat about one hundred and fifty yards wide, swiftly slides over it, alighting at the snow-packed door of his house.'

Day in, day out, regardless of the conditions, measurements were made. Inside the small wooden hut the observer would grope his way forward through the darkness, as Webb later reminisced, 'to a large box almost concealing the feeble glimmer of a lamp. The lamp is the source of the light, projected on to small mirrors attached to the magnetic needles of three variometers. A ray of light is reflected from the mirrors for several feet on to a slit, past which revolves sensitized photographic paper folded on a drum moving by clockwork. The slightest movements of the suspended needles are greatly magnified, and, when the paper is removed and developed in a dark-room, a series of intricate curves denoting declination, horizontal intensity and vertical force, are exquisitely traced.'

Webb struggled to fit in with many colleagues on the expedition. His superior professional air tended to wind many up, including Mawson, who at one point found he was being challenged over the value of his 1909 magnetic measurements. Mawson was so concerned about the younger man's ability to work in a close-knit sledging team that he seriously considered holding Webb back from the attempt on the South Magnetic Pole.

While scientific observations continued through the winter months of 1912, Mawson mapped out the research program for the approaching summer. Leaving behind a small group at the Winter Quarters, parties of men were to be sent out east, south and west to tackle all manner of scientific and geographical questions.

In the meantime there was no escaping the daily domestic chores, and not everyone lived up to Mawson's expectations. The Australian leader and Leslie Whetter, a New Zealand doctor on the team, had one of the more extreme run-ins. After a particularly disappointing attempt at cooking by Whetter, Mawson scribbled on a piece of paper: 'at dinner, the soup was badly burnt…not fit to eat, no bread and the pudding tapioca a damned disgrace, only tapioca and butter—and nothing else.' Then the New Zealander failed to dig the snow out from around the hut. Mawson challenged him—why had he joined the expedition?

Whetter: 'Not to do such kind of work!'

Mawson: 'You're a bloody fool to come on the expedition if that was the case.'

Whetter: 'Bloody fool yourself! I won't be caught on another.'

Mawson later wrote, 'According to his own words he came

on the expedition so as to have a quiet time for study—I believe he came also for his health. This is a criminal matter.' Luckily, things calmed down soon after.

The growing sense of isolation through the winter was only exacerbated by the disappointing wireless results. Hopes had been high that the wireless stations would allow the bases to communicate, while also liaising with the *Aurora* over future needs and allowing weather reports to be broadcast to the Meteorological Office at Hobart. But the radio mast at Cape Denison was so badly battered by the strong winds that it was unclear whether any messages were getting out at all. Kites, tins and even one of the plane's propellers were used as alternative ways to keep the aerial in the air, but without much success.

The occasional message from Antarctica did reach Macquarie Island. One sent in May was particularly enigmatic: 'We are sorry for poor Laseron.' Spirits must have been high at Cape Denison and the message was most probably sent as a prank, its sender not believing it would get through. But it was one of the few that did and its receiver, thinking the message was reporting Laseron's death, diligently sent it on to Tasmania. Fortunately, nothing was announced until its content could be confirmed and, when enquiries duly came, the biologist was at a loss to know what the fuss was about.

With the arrival of the summer sun in July there was a noticeable improvement in morale. It was a welcome relief to the men to know that they would shortly be getting away from Cape Denison and into a landscape they had only briefly explored. Mawson was excited, but he was also keenly aware the wind would be a constant companion on the ice and feared what it might do to his teams. The expeditionary groups readied themselves: clothing was checked and double-checked, and sails were devised for the sledges to make travelling easier.

Mawson was leading the Far Eastern Party, journeying over the plateau towards Victoria Land with the aim of connecting Cape Denison to the western discoveries of Borchgrevink, Scott and Shackleton. Accompanying Mawson was Xavier Mertz, a Swiss champion ski runner, and Belgrave Ninnis, a young British Royal Fusilier officer who had originally been hired by Shackleton. Strikingly young-looking for his twenty-three years, Ninnis soon earned the nickname Cherub. In contrast, Mertz's first name caused problems for his English-speaking colleagues, who ended up calling him the ominous-sounding X, though he was a favourite in the hut. To cover the distances involved the expedition's dogs would be essential, and Mertz and Ninnis had looked after them since London, making the two men obvious companions for Mawson.

The Far Eastern party set out on 10 November 1912, initially making great progress. The dogs covered the ground quickly, and the team collected geological samples, noted the weather and mapped the route. But on 13 December, Mertz considered they were in a dangerous place: 'At 4 pm we entered a height with crevasses...after there was a nice flat area ahead on which we walked until 12 pm. At 8 pm it cracked a few times underneath us. The snow masses must have broken their vaulting. The noise was like distant cannon fire. My comrades were frightened because they have never heard avalanches going off.'

The next day tragedy struck. Mertz, who was leading the three men, turned to find Ninnis was no longer bringing up the rear. Searching along the way they had come Mawson made a shocking discovery: an enormous crack had opened up across their path, and the British officer had disappeared down it. That evening Mertz wrote, 'Dear old Ninnis, he is dead. This change was so rapid I almost can't believe it...150 feet [forty-five metres] down in a crevasse we could see the back part of Ninnis' sledge. [They could hear a dog whining.] No other noise was recognisable...Ninnis must have died immediately...We lowered a rope with a weight and it struck the dog we could see but this one did not move anymore so it was obviously also dead.'

Ninnis's death might have been avoided. Had the Briton worn skis instead of finnesko boots, his weight would have been more evenly distributed and the snow bridge covering the crevasse would most probably have held.

They had a 'bare one a half week's man food' and it had taken them thirty-five days to reach their current location. Mawson ruefully reflected that Mertz had 'suffered the loss of his Burberry trousers: as a substitute he used henceforth an extra pair of woollen under trousers that happened to be saved. The six dogs remaining were the poorest of the pack, for the best preserved animals had been drafted into the rear team, as it was thought that the risk lay in front.' Now, more than five hundred kilometres out from base and not expected back for a month, the two explorers turned their backs on the icy grave and looked to home. There seemed little prospect of rescue.

The lack of supplies meant the men were forced to eat their way through the few remaining dogs. Mertz was a vegetarian and the tough, smelly dog meat was particularly repulsive to him. On 29 December he wrote, 'Ginger, the last beloved dog, was killed and the meat was sliced. We cooked a part of it. In the tent it started to rain if the Primus was used for more than an hour....The tent is too small, only one person can move, the other one has to sit huddled in one corner...This morning I rose one hour early to cook the dog meat because if you don't do this it is uneatable.'

As they trudged on, both men suffered from constant lethargy and dizziness. Mawson's companion was deteriorating more quickly, with bouts of dysentry, loss of skin, depression and, finally, insanity. The cause of this rapid decline appears to have been vitamin A poisoning, most probably brought on from eating dog livers, which contain toxic levels of the vitamin. The last line in Mertz's diary reads: 'The dog meat does not seem to agree with me because yesterday I was feeling a little bit queasy.' In a final bout of madness the poor man bit one of his fingers off and then fell asleep, never to wake up.

The loss hit Mawson hard and, because of an ever-strengthening wind, the Australian was forced to stay by the grave for three days. During this time he fell into despair. 'As there is little chance of my reaching human aid alive I greatly regret my inability to set out the coast line as surveyed for the 300 miles we travelled and the notes on glaciers and ice formations, etc.— the most of which latter is of course committed to my head.' He was a scientist to the core. Two days later Mawson pulled himself together and pushed on, wanting to do the 'utmost to the last for Paquita's and supporters' and members of expedition's sakes'.

Mawson gave the position of Mertz's resting place in his diary. If he died, too, at least both men might be found and receive a proper burial. There has been a suggestion that the Australian may have turned to cannibalism, but this seems highly unlikely, given the effort he made to advertise what would have been a dreadfully macabre scene. Mawson trimmed back the amount he was dragging: the sledge was cut in half; photographs were left behind; and the last of the dog meat was cooked, saving precious weight in kerosene. Drinking water would now be obtained from snow left in a container to melt on the sledge top.

Over the next two weeks Mawson steered his way back to base using navigation pages ripped out of *Hints to Travellers* and the *Nautical Almanac*. Physically and mentally exhausted, he reflected in his diary that his body was rotting but 'Providence'—God—was with him. On 17 January, halfway across the southern end of what became known as the Mertz Glacier, Mawson fell five metres down a crevasse. Fortunately, he was connected by a rope to the sledge, now wedged in the opposing wall of ice.

Expecting the sledge to follow him at any moment, he 'thought of the food left uneaten in the sledge—and, as the sledge stopped without coming down, I thought of Providence again giving me a chance. The chance looked very small as the rope had sawed into the overhanging lid, my finger ends all damaged, myself weak...With the feeling that Providence was helping me I made a great struggle, half getting out, then slipping back again several times, but at last just did it. Then I felt grateful to Providence...who has so many times already helped me.' Mawson considered suicide during the ordeal, but worried he would 'fall on some ledge and linger in misery'. The climb back to the surface took four and a half hours.

Mawson struggled on, but not before he constructed a rope ladder to haul himself out of future crevasses. He was suffering various maladies, brought on by physical exertion, lack of food and acute vitamin A poisoning from the dog livers, and—the most jaw-dropping complaint of all—he was regularly strapping the soles of his feet back on with lanolin cream. His diary entries at this time are shocking but restrained: 'Both my hands have shed the skin in large sheets, very tender and it is a great nuisance.' Others hint at a dark humour: 'For the last 2 days my hair has been falling out in handfuls and rivals the reindeer hair from the moulting bag for nuisance in all food preparations.'

He continued, despite his afflictions, to keep weather records. Every day he noted the wind strength and direction, sometimes interpreting what this meant for the local landscape. Just a day after falling—again—into a crevasse that nearly claimed his life, he commented: 'The wind died down as the morning advanced...It is quite apparent now that the direction of the wind is affected by the glacier valley. Here in the centre of the valley a night wind flows down it and on each side the winds are deflected into it.' No doubt the routine helped him cope.

Two weeks late and forty-seven kilometres from base camp, Mawson stumbled upon a small snow cairn that had been erected just a few hours earlier by a team of three—led by Archibald McLean, the chief expedition doctor—out from Cape Denison. In it he found supplies and a note dated 29 January 1913 giving the location, and news of the safe return of all parties and the arrival of the *Aurora* a fortnight before. It was a remarkable stroke of good fortune—a link to home, a promise of life, an affirmation of hope. He scanned the horizon: no one was in sight.

Mawson was terribly weak by now. Hope was one thing, but he had little energy in reserve to catch up with the three men. His diary entry for the day is a classic understatement: 'What a pity I did not catch McLean's party this morning.' With renewed vigour, however, Mawson pushed on and three days later reached the depot known as Aladdin's Cave, an ice cave at the top of the glacier overlooking Cape Denison. Inside was a wealth of supplies, including oranges and a pineapple—quite a sight for someone who had not eaten fresh fruit for a year.

Resting overnight and then preparing crampons for a safe descent, he was hit by a week-long storm. When the wind finally eased a little Mawson decided to risk an attempt. He staggered down to Cape Denison, three months after his departure, and was greeted by smoke on the horizon. The *Aurora* had sailed that morning.

———•———

When the *Aurora* returned to Commonwealth Bay, Davis soon became concerned about the Far Eastern Party. Searching

Mawson's correspondence he found hurriedly written instructions that the men were intending to be back by 15 January 1913. They were long overdue.

Davis took immediate control of the situation. The *Aurora* sailed along the coast searching for signs of life; signals were fired; a large kite was flown to attract attention. Nothing. Sending McLean's team out towards Mawson's last known position, he ruminated on board, 'I am worn out with the constant worry and anxiety...The search party will have had a very bad time. I hope they are safe. It must be hell on the slope. This weather it is bad enough under the cliff.'

By 8 February he could wait no longer. Wild's team was at risk on the ice shelf and no word had been received by wireless, meaning they could already be in trouble. And, unlike those at Cape Denison, Wild's party had no ready access to wildlife to tide them over for another year. Davis's responsibility was clear. Winter was fast approaching and he had to go. Supplies were left at Cape Denison with six volunteers, along with a promise to return next year.

Almost as soon as the *Aurora* left the bay an urgent message arrived: 'To Capt Davis, Aurora. Arrived safely at hut. Mertz & Ninnis dead. Return & pick up all hands. Sgd Dr Mawson'. With the conditions rapidly worsening, Davis tried to get his vessel back into Commonwealth Bay, but to no avail.

'Why did they recall us?' Davis fumed in his diary. 'It simply means that we are going to lose Wild for the sake of taking off a party who are in perfect safety...I am just worn out and a heap of nerves.' Mawson had shelter, food and companionship for another year; Wild and his men were a different matter altogether. Davis had to make the hardest decision of all: he turned the *Aurora* west, and left his leader and friend behind.

Mawson would have to spend another winter in Antarctica. On the day of his return to Cape Denison he wrote in his diary,

'My internals overthrown—legs swollen, etc'; and, several days on, 'My legs have now swollen very much.' A few weeks later he acknowledged the psychological effects of the experience for the first time: 'I find my nerves are in a very serious state, and from the feeling I have in the base of my head I [have the] suspicion that I may go off my rocker very soon. My nerves have evidently had a very great shock. Too much writing today brought this on. I shall take more exercise and less study, hoping for a beneficial turn.'

Weakness, headaches, nervous symptoms, sleep disturbance and urinary problems are all symptoms of chronic vitamin A intoxication. Mawson was dangerously unwell and in urgent need of company—he often followed one of the other men around just to be near someone. He had experienced a series of disasters befitting a Hollywood script. The Everest and Antarctic veteran Sir Edmund Hilary later described it as 'the greatest survival story in the history of exploration'.

The greatest, true—but the cost was high: two dead and, for Mawson, serious illness and another year away from loved ones. On the ice a cross was erected with a plaque acknowledging 'the supreme sacrifice made by Lieut. B.E.S. Ninnis and Dr. X. Mertz, in the course of science'.

During his enforced second winter in Antarctica, Mawson learned what the other sledging teams had achieved. Most importantly, Robert Bage had led the Southern Party towards the South Magnetic Pole, along with Webb and Hurley. As they pushed ever further south the men took measurements at every camp and found the compass became more sluggish, just as Edgeworth David had noted in 1909; but, spectacularly, there were also enormous swings in the needle, in one instance shifting 90° across just twenty kilometres of travel. A wealth of data had been obtained, but the needle stubbornly held off the vertical.

Slowed by bad weather and limited food supplies, the men were forced to turn back when the greatest angle of dip sat at 89°43'. Webb wrote in his diary, 'So near yet so far.' Desperate for a Christmas celebration on the return journey, the men concocted a vicious alcoholic beverage 'by boiling 5 raisins in a little of our primus methylated spirit. A drink known as "Tangle-foot" and the recipe of one Bob Bage. It was as distasteful as its appearance, and could only be drunk in gulps by holding the nose and breath.' Their resolve stiffened, the men staggered on. They barely made it. One more day of bad weather and they most probably would have perished. The party had turned back from its furthest south at the last possible moment. In spite of this, Bage stayed the second year and continued the magnetic measurements at Cape Denison.

The other groups had also made significant inroads. The Western Party had given up on the air tractor after it failed fourteen kilometres out from base, but the men had pushed on to discover the first meteorite in Antarctica. The remaining teams had mapped hundreds of kilometres of coastline, collecting geological samples and taking weather observations as they went.

Davis's work with the *Aurora* in the Southern Ocean raised more questions than it answered, but the ship had successfully collected Wild's men in the west and returned to Australia with all on board. Davis was relieved to find the wireless system had never been operational: hence the silence. Cut off, the Far Western Party had succeeded in charting 650 kilometres of coastline, including reaching Kaiser Wilhelm II Land. Alongside these efforts they had made continuous weather and magnetic observations through the year. The Far Western

Party's contributions were especially significant: a picture of Antarctica, continent-wide in scope, was taking shape.

While Mawson had been away the winds at Cape Denison weakened, and a more sturdy wireless mast was erected. With news that a team was staying behind at Cape Denison, the men on Macquarie Island agreed to remain in place as well, allowing messages to be properly relayed between Antarctica and Australia, as originally intended. At last the Adelie Land wireless was working as planned. Mawson could now contact the rest of the world, including his fiancé, Paquita, who was waiting desperately for news. For the first time, an Antarctic explorer could communicate with home in real time.

Many of the men loathed their time on the ice and vowed never to return. The air-tractor engineer Frank Bickerton expressed a common sentiment when he remarked of his sledging journey: 'This is a dismal rotten country. To think that Regents Street, the New Forest, Bedford River and Dartmoor are in the same world as this hole. Thank goodness they are as far away as it is possible to get.' And, later: 'These present conditions are nearly enough to cure a man of a desire to poke his nose into the odd corners of the earth.' Webb observed, 'It is doubtful whether later generations, even of Antarctic explorers, can imagine the physical and psychological discipline imposed...It was a different world.'

In the late 1890s de Gerlache's Belgian expedition imploded while overwintering for the first time in Antarctica. And yet, before 1912, there had been little research into the psychological effects of close confinement with no natural light. Most expeditions followed Shackleton's philosophy of keeping busy. Scott was fully aware of what the return of the summer sun meant for his men, remarking in July 1911, 'I am glad that the light is coming, for more than one reason. The gale and consequent inaction not only affected the ponies...the return of the light should cure all ailments physical and mental.' For most, time spent in Antarctica was a learning experience, one that they never forgot; but for one man on the Australasian expedition, it would change his life.

Sydney Jeffryes came south with the *Aurora* as a replacement wireless operator for the Cape Denison base. He was pivotal in telling the world what had happened to Mawson and the rest of his team. Over time, though, there was a noticeable change in his character. Sometimes Jeffryes would behave erratically, concerned people were talking about him; other times he seemed fine. Things changed for the worse on 7 July 1913, as Mawson recorded in his diary:

> Last night Jeffryes at the table suddenly asked Madigan to go into the next room (to fight) as he believed that something had been said against him—nothing whatever had...This morning after breakfast Madigan was filling his lamp with kerosene in the gangway and Jeffryes went out, pushing him. Asked him to fight again, danced round in a towering rage, struck Madigan, rough and tumble. Madigan got a clinch on him, then I had to speak to him and others. McLean thinks [Jeffryes] is a bit off his head. I think his touchy temperament is being very hard tested with bad weather and indoor life. A case of polar depression. I trust it will go now.

McLean had worked in a mental hospital for a while and spotted worrying symptoms in Jeffryes. By 10 August, Mawson was at a loss, scribbling: 'What can be done with him [Jeffryes] I can't imagine, for if I try to get him to keep up to scratch, his miserable temperament is likely to cause trouble in sending [wireless messages]. He takes the crystal out of the setting each evening so that nobody else can use the [wireless] instruments.

I certainly feel like skinning him, but will wait another day and see how things go.'

Things reached a head on 3 September, when Jeffreys was caught hammering out a message very quickly. It was so fast that the rest of the team could not read what was sent. When challenged, Jeffryes admitted he was transmitting in Mawson's name: 'Five men not well probably Jeffryes and I may have to leave the hut.' Bickerton had some wireless skills and Mawson asked him to send a message to Macquarie Island, advising that Jeffryes was insane. On his return to Australia, Jeffryes was placed in a mental asylum, where he remained until his death.

For all its challenges, wireless operation indirectly opened up another area of research. Because radio messages follow a straight line through the atmosphere, they cannot follow the curved surface of the Earth. Instead, they are reflected off a region of the upper atmosphere known as the ionosphere, more than sixty kilometres above the surface. Here the thin air works like a mirror, reflecting any message and allowing it to travel vast distances over the horizon. Mawson used this to great effect, sending messages from Antarctica, but he soon saw there was a relationship between what could be seen in the atmosphere and the quality of the messages being sent and received.

It had been known for some time that the eerie light displays of the Aurora Australis over Antarctica affected the Earth's magnetic field. But now it seemed to Mawson that they might also affect the wireless signals. The relationship was not clear-cut: somehow the shape, colours and length of the display conspired to disrupt broadcasts.

Even though Mawson had suffered greatly during the previous summer, he was intrigued by the irregular poor radio reception in Antarctica and suspected it was more than just new technology struggling with the windy conditions. The line would go dead when there was bad static, and this coincided with the light displays of the aurora.

During Shackleton's *Nimrod* expedition Mawson had spotted that the aurora took place at the same time as interruptions to telegraph services across Australia, suggesting the overhead lights may be linked to electrical currents in the atmosphere. On the Australasian expedition detailed descriptions of the frequency and type of aurora were made, and the first reasonable photograph of a display in the south—with a ten-second exposure—was taken.

It was an area of research ripe for analysis, but Mawson was frustrated in his attempts to study it properly. Jeffryes and Bickerton were not interested. 'I can't get him [Jeffryes] or Bickerton to take the subject up scientifically,' an infuriated Mawson wrote. 'If I were choosing another staff I would get specialists for each branch, true scientists capable of assisting with sledging.'

Working out what created the aurora was a major line of scientific enquiry in the early twentieth century. Pioneering work in the 1880s and 1890s had showed that some kind of discharge emanated from the sun during times when there were large numbers of spots on its surface. Shortly after, it was found that something similar to an aurora could be mimicked in the lab by exposing a magnet to electrons in a vacuum.

On board the *Terra Nova*, Simpson and Wright came close to putting it all together by measuring the changing electrical charge of air molecules as they travelled south, and deduced that something was originating from outside the Earth to cause this effect. But it was only in 1911 that a brave soul flew in a balloon to a frighteningly high five thousand metres and found a stream of high-energy electrically charged particles were striking the upper atmosphere from the sun and outer space. Cosmic rays had been discovered.

We now know that an aurora is caused by cosmic rays funnelled into the Earth's magnetic field above the geomagnetic poles, those marking the theoretical magnetic axis of our planet. Colliding with oxygen and nitrogen molecules in the upper atmosphere the rays produce the luminous streams of light we know as aurora. When the sun is particularly active the flow of charged particles increases massively, causing a visual treat that disrupts the ionosphere. But the first report of a polar radio blackout caused by auroral activity would not come until 1966. Mawson had again been ahead of the game.

Back in civilisation Davis and Edgeworth David worked financial miracles—even returning to London—and somehow found the extra money to support the expedition for another year. It was not enough to cover all the costs, but at least it meant Mawson and his men could be brought home. The *Aurora* returned to Cape Denison in December 1913 and a relieved team left the Winter Quarters.

Even with the prospect of returning to Australia, Mawson could not leave research alone. Insisting they head west, he convinced his long-suffering captain to return to Wild's base and Drygalski's winter position of 1902, undertaking soundings as they went.

Davis was exhausted from the strain and Mawson started to suspect he had pushed the captain too far. On 21 January, '4 pm: suggest sounding to Capt Davis who has turned in since 2 pm... However, now a case of sleepy bad temper: "Christ Almighty, leave me alone, look after your own business," etc which nevertheless is best for me to waive. It is with great difficulty that one assumes the tactful position.'

They turned north for home soon after.

Heading to London in 1914 Mawson received a knighthood and worked hard at finishing a book on the expedition for a general readership. *The Home of the Blizzard* was published by Heinemann a year later. Reviews were positive, with the *Observer* remarking, 'Nothing could better prove the contention that, though the explorer's quest is knowledge, the world's test is heroism. This record of the Mawson Expedition answers both demands.' The British media could not resist a dig at Amundsen: 'In this respect of comparisons, it is fair to say that Sir Douglas deferred to Captain Scott's wishes in framing his programme, and thus avoided that un-English form of competition which has stripped Amundsen of half his laurels.'

Scientific communication was key. When Frank Hurley returned to Australia on the *Aurora*, in 1912, the public were enthralled. Around 2500 photographs, some in colour, and hundreds of metres of film were shown around the country. Images of expedition members, the sweeping landscape and blizzards of Commonwealth Bay, and the obligatory penguins captivated audiences. An hour of silent but stunning film footage under the same title as Mawson's book brought the public ever closer to visiting Antarctica. It was the basis of one of the first— and most successful—documentary films. The Australians were telling a story of epic proportions and Antarctic science was in the lead role.

In London, Mawson reported to the RGS. The new president, Douglas Freshfield, who had just taken over from Lord Curzon, remarked in his introduction: 'All men of science will confirm what I say, that there has been no Antarctic expedition the results of which, geological, glaciological, or in the way of throwing light on the past history of our planet, have been richer than that of which we are going to hear an account.' Mawson was only thirty-two, but his contribution ranked among the greatest the RGS had witnessed.

When Mawson showed images taken by Hurley of their Antarctic home and its local inhabitants, the president was glowing in his praise: 'We are told that geography has connections with every other science. We have seen in what an extraordinary way, with the aid of photography, it can throw light on zoology. One does not expect, when taken to the Antarctic Regions, to go there for the sake of seeing life; but I think to-night we have seen to the full the bird-life of the Antarctic brought before us in a most wonderfully vivid way. We owe our thanks, not only to Dr. Mawson, but to the very able photographer, or photographers, who have secured for us the pictures.'

The weather observations paid handsome dividends. When Mawson had first suggested his expedition, newspaper wags produced cartoons depicting Antarcticasas a new health resort. But once the wireless system was fully operational, daily coded reports immediately began to improve weather predictions across the region. Although initially disbelieved by some, film footage in *Home of the Blizzard* and tests on the instruments provided irrefutable proof that Cape Denison suffered from massive blasts of cold air that poured off the plateau, frequently hurricane in strength.

There had been other successes as well. While not opening the floodgates to mining companies, the expedition produced the first discovery of gold in Antarctica, with significant finds of silver and copper. The newspapers declared it to be a development of great economic value.

Magnetic measurements proved to be a greater challenge. The huge amount of data, and the onset of World War I, caused significant delays. Webb went to fight and, although he continued to correspond with Mawson, the data was worked up by twelve young female students in University College, Christ-church, New Zealand, who became known as 'the magnetic ladies of Canterbury College' and 'the Mawson club'.

The results were a revelation. Between April and October 1912 the Australasian and British Antarctic observations had been made at exactly the same time. The data showed the hori-zontal part of the magnetic field had an effect over a far greater area than first expected, and this explained the exasperating sluggishness of the compasses that the sledging parties had complained of in 1909 and 1912. Although neither group had achieved a true vertical alignment, all was not lost. Enough data had been collected to get the most accurate fix yet for the South Magnetic Pole: the results allowed a best estimate of 71°10'S 150°43'E. Bage, Hurley and Webb had turned back 113 kilo-metres short. The average position meant the pole probably lay about 130 kilometres northwest of that reached by David, Mawson and Mackay.

And still the pole continues to move. Since Ross's stab at its location, in 1841, the pole has migrated at an average rate of nine kilometres a year. Mawson's expedition data was forcing Antarctica to give up its secrets—and with them, clues to the workings of our planet.

———•———

On his return from Antarctica, Mawson faced a debt of £7000, despite David's and Davis's best efforts. The sales of *Home of the Blizzard* were disappointing, badly hit by the war, and the publisher remarked that he hoped things would improve once the public's love of reading about 'blood and bloodshed' had passed.

'Had I perished, possibly an appeal would have brought forth funds,' Mawson observed. 'As I survived, there is a debt and the publication account to face and I trust this appeal will

not be in vain.' Funds came in slowly, but he was plagued with
the debt for years afterwards. To make matters worse, Vickers
complained that it had not been paid the hundreds of pounds
owed for the plane. Mawson had to plead poverty, asking that
the craft might be considered a donation to the expedition. No
doubt thanks to booming military sales during World War I,
the debt was written off.

Slowly Mawson collected funding to publish the expedition's
scientific reports. The sums involved were almost pathetic:
£50 here, £100 there. With the help of the New South Wales
state government the reports were published over the following
decades. But in return, scientific samples, diaries and gear from
the expedition had to be delivered from South Australia, where
Mawson lived. He was forced to agree, though he was reticent.
There were times when Mawson loathed the effort involved,
sometimes describing the process of raising funds and cajoling
authors as 'tedious' in his introductions to the reports. By 1947
the job was finally done: twenty-two volumes made up of eighty-
nine individual scientific reports, describing for the first time
in glorious detail the excitement of discovering a whole new part
of Antarctica.

The Australasian expedition was of a scale never previously
attempted: three bases, thirty-one land-based members, seven
major sledging journeys and a full oceanographic program.
Mawson's venture gave the world its first complete scientific
snapshot of a new continent. The men had explored a vast
stretch of eastern Antarctica; discovered new bays, mountains
and glaciers; and linked up areas that had previously been
discovered only in isolation. The scientific volumes described
Antarctica's violent and extreme weather, its flourishing plant
and animal life, the ocean's fickleness.

The polar historian Gordon Hayes wrote a glowing assess-
ment in 1928: 'Mawson's Expedition, judged by the magnitude

both of its scale and of its achievements, was the greatest and most consummate expedition that ever sailed for Antarctica... Its excellence lay in its design, its scope and its executive success; and [in its origin and conduct] by scientists of administrative ability...Mawson's was the first British Expedition which had clearly passed beyond the novitiate stage in Antarctic exploration, previously so painfully evident.'

But perhaps the highest praise came from Frank Hurley, who succinctly summed up the Australasian effort: 'Shackleton grafted science on to exploration—Mawson added exploring to science.'

The first recognisable photograph of an auroral display in the south, with a ten-second exposure, 1912. By Frank Hurley. Courtesy of the Mitchell Library, State Library of New South Wales, Sydney (36856).

CHAPTER 8

MARTYRS TO GONDWANALAND
The Cost of Scientific Exploration

Something hidden. Go and find it. Go and look behind the Ranges—
Something lost behind the Ranges. Lost and waiting for you. Go!
RUDYARD KIPLING (1865–1936)

On 11 February 1913 England woke to the *Daily Mail* headline 'Death of Captain Scott. Lost with four comrades. The Pole reached. Disaster on the return.' Just a day before, the press had reported that Scott was back in New Zealand; the Royal Geographical Society had even prepared a telegram congratulating him on his success. The palpable sense of anticipation and excitement now turned to despondence.

A few days later a hastily organised memorial service was held in St Paul's Cathedral, London. The numbers attending were staggering, exceeding those at the service for the 1500 lives lost on the *Titanic* in the same year. 'The presence of the king,' *The Times* declared, 'conveyed a symbolism without which any ceremony expressive of national sentiment would have been inadequate.' The Empire grieved.

The details of what had happened in Antarctica appeared contradictory. The five men had last been seen heading confidently towards the South Geographic Pole. They were well provisioned, and fit and strong. What had happened did not make sense—but the latest reports from Antarctica had a frightening ring of truth.

These accounts described a team returning from the pole in deteriorating weather conditions, the likes of which had never been seen before. Pushing on in the bitter cold the expedition had continued its scientific program, making observations and collecting geological samples as it travelled back to the Cape Evans base. And yet the journey proved fatal.

Petty Officer Edgar Evans (not to be confused with Scott's deputy, Teddy Evans) was the first to die, apparently from the effects of concussion at the base of the Beardmore Glacier. Later, suffering from frostbite and exhaustion, and recognising his ever-slowing pace was threatening the others, Captain Oates famously walked out into a blizzard with the words, 'I am just going outside and may be some time.' Struggling forward with limited food and fuel, in plummeting temperatures, the remaining three men continued their trek to base.

In late March 1912 a nine-day blizzard pinned down Scott, Wilson and Bowers in their tent. There would be no escape. All three wrote messages for loved ones until the end, which came sometime around 29 March. Scott's diary reads: 'Every day we have been ready to start for our depot 11 miles away, but outside the door of the tent it remains a scene of whirling drift. I do not think we can hope for any better things now we are getting weaker, of course, and the end cannot be far. It seems a pity, but I do not think I can write more. R. Scott. For God's sake look after our people.'

They died disappointed men, 150 days out from base and a mere eighteen kilometres from salvation at One Ton Depot.

In his 'Message to the Public', Scott wrote one of the finest short pieces of English prose:

We took risks, we knew we took them; things have come out against us, and therefore we have no cause for complaint, but bow to the will of Providence, determined still to do our best to the last. But if we have been willing to give our lives to this enterprise, which is for the honour of our country, I appeal to our countrymen to see that those who depend on us are properly cared for. Had we lived, I should have had a tale to tell of hardihood, endurance, and courage of my companions which would have stirred the heart of every Englishman. These rough notes and our dead bodies must tell the tale, but surely, surely, a great rich country like ours will see that those who are dependent on us are properly cared for.

Scott wrote to his 'wife'—a word he later struck out and changed to 'widow'—and said of their two-year-old son, Peter: 'Make the boy interested in natural history if you can; it is better than games.'

On 12 November a search party from Cape Evans came across the frozen remains of the three men. Apsley Cherry-Garrard later wrote, 'We have found them—to say it has been a ghastly day cannot express it—it is too bad for words.' But Cherry was amazed: 'We have everything—records, diaries, etc. They have among other things several rolls of photographs, a meteorological log kept up to 13 March, considering all things, a great many geological samples. And they have stuck to everything. It is magnificent that men in such case should go on pulling everything that they have died to gain.' With the papers and samples collected, the tent was collapsed over the men and, after a failed search for Oates's body, the search team returned to base.

Scott's death with his men was a defining moment early in the twentieth century, not least for those connected to Antarctic exploration. Sir Clements Markham eulogised in his diary: 'There has passed away, if it is really true, a very exceptionally noble Englishman. What struck me most was his chivalrous generosity in dealing with contemptible self-seekers such as Shackleton and Amundsen. Very rarely have so many great qualities been combined in one man. Perhaps the greatest was that which won him the love of all who served under him.'

Overseas, the shock was no less. Roald Amundsen was quoted as saying, on hearing the news, 'horrible, horrible'; while Count Okuma, Nobu Shirase's public champion, wrote, 'Scott rests forever in that frozen realm, and his great spirit watches for all eternity over the Antarctic's icy wastes.'

Lord Curzon reflected: 'Arm-chair geographers were sometimes disposed to complain that the days of adventure and risk in exploration were over. The last year gave the melancholy lie to such fireside fallacies. The toll of human life was still demanded, and was still cheerfully paid. Should the day ever arise when it was not, then indeed might geographical societies shut their doors and hand over their work to an educational bureau of the State.' The loss of life counted for something.

———•———

In the aftermath of Scott's death there was serious soul-searching. Markham searched for a scapegoat. On 8 March he wrote to Fridtjof Nansen, describing Amundsen's actions as 'not honorable'. He explained: 'I allude to the proceeding of Amundsen in making a rush to the South Pole, to forestall Captain Scott, and scamper back for the reward. I do not think that it can be justified....The only possible excuse would be that the route was entirely different: but even then the secrecy would be dishonorable.'

Nansen did not agree. Responding politely, the great polar explorer said he considered that anywhere was up for grabs, and no one had a prior right to geographical science. 'I took

naturally a keen interest in his [Scott's] expedition, and I was
very sorry that he would not listen to my advice or take plenty
of good well broken dogs and turned to them and not to ponies,
which I never considered much fit for polar work of that kind.
He took some dogs though but had he done what I would have
had him do, we should still have had him around us.'

Markham remained unconvinced about Amundsen but felt
Nansen was right about the ponies, and commented, 'I opposed
the south pole but Scott was smitten by it. I have always felt
that the rushes to the poles to please the newspapers and rake in
money has been the curse of polar discovery.'

Others celebrated the work of the *Terra Nova* expedition.
Rudmose Brown, a member of Bruce's *Scotia* party, wrote, 'Great
as the disaster has been, England is immeasurably the richer for
it in tradition and inspiration. Luck was against him it is true,
but without in the smallest degree minimising the heroic efforts
of these men, it may be possible to indicate some contributory
cause...In time all these scientific results will be appreciated. At
present it is difficult to think of anything except the fate of the
southern party, and the lesson in simple manliness that is has
given to the nation.'

In Germany, Wilhelm Filchner was full of praise for the
British leader: 'Scott achieved his aim...The scientific notes and
observations that have been saved promise to yield a valuable
contribution to our knowledge of the Antarctic, in the exploration of which Great Britain has taken a prominent part. This
fresh sacrifice will be painfully felt beyond the Channel and
throughout the world.'

The RGS led calls for donations to meet Scott's final wishes.
Money was urgently needed to support the families left behind,
and to commemorate the death of Scott and his men through
memorials and the publication of scientific results. Before,
funding had proved difficult; now, money—government and

private—poured in, doubling the amount raised by the expedition. Clock towers were raised, streets renamed and monuments erected. Statues crafted by Scott's widow, Kathleen, were placed in London's Waterloo Place and Christchurch, New Zealand—sadly, the latter figure was badly damaged during the February 2011 earthquake. In Madame Tussauds, a wax model of Scott was put alongside one of Shackleton, remaining on display there until the 1960s.

Some eighty official scientific reports were produced from the *Terra Nova* expedition. Eight volumes on zoology were published, along with others on the aurora, botany, cartography, geology, glaciology, gravity and magnetism. All spoke of scientific insights gathered from a mysterious landscape, and many would lay the foundations for future polar scientific work. On the biological front alone, of the more than two thousand different species of plants and animals collected, more than four hundred were completely new to science. Unlike the aftermath of the *Discovery* expedition, there would be little criticism. The effort directed to developing a full scientific program had paid enormous dividends.

On a memorial cross erected to the dead men near their base in Antarctica, the departing expedition members inscribed a short quote from Alfred Lord Tennyson's 'Ulysses': 'To strive, to seek, to find, and not to yield.' Robert Scott achieved his aim.

———•———

Arguably some of the most significant scientific reports to come out of the expedition were the three volumes on meteorology. After leaving on the *Terra Nova* at the end of the Antarctic summer of 1912, George Simpson had diligently spent the next seven years working up the weather observations taken on the ice. His analysis was groundbreaking. All data had value—including that taken by the different sledging teams and during Amundsen's expedition. The result was a stunningly comprehensive study of Antarctic weather as seen from the Great Ice Barrier and plateau, allowing the Briton to explore the role weather conditions played in Scott's death.

Simpson showed, for instance, that there was indeed a high-pressure system sitting over the Antarctic continent, fed by air flowing south from warmer climes in the upper atmosphere. Today we know that by the time this air reaches the southern continent it has been intensely chilled, falling to temperatures below -80°C, and sinks. This cold air—katabatic, or downhill, wind—periodically pours off the central plateau towards the coast, like air spilling out of an open refrigerator door.

What precipitated the fatally long storm Scott and his men experienced was not certain, but Simpson was amazed at how well connected Antarctica was with the rest of the world, writing, 'This connexion between the pressure departures over the Antarctic and surrounding regions is most interesting and still more important. It appears that the Antarctic is one of the great "centres of action" of the world and further investigation is imperatively demanded.'

In 1912 the global climate was tumultuous. Exceptionally harsh droughts were experienced in Australia and Indonesia; heavy rain and flooding crippled parts of North America; in the North Atlantic high numbers of icebergs were spotted, sinking the *Titanic* two weeks after Scott and his men died. The world was feeling the effects of a massive upheaval in the tropical Pacific. Known as El Niño, this weather event occurs once in every five to eight years, when the warm western waters migrate out into the centre of the ocean. Weakening trade winds set off a cascade of change around the world—including Antarctica. El Niño had not been recognised when Simpson was analysing his data, but we now know that at the end of the summer and through the winter the Ross Sea region is particularly vulnerable to its effects, through a peculiarity of geography.

It is important to realise that within the westerly winds that dominate the mid-to-high latitudes of the south, the air can also spin, creating areas of spiralling low pressure that migrate around the ocean. It is these lows in what is known as the circumpolar trough—often spanning several hundred kilometres—that can swing in towards the Antarctic coastline. In an El Niño year, the lows tend to sit for longer over the eastern Ross Sea during autumn and winter.

Because air flows around southern hemisphere lows in a clockwise direction, these strategically placed pressure systems encourage katabatic winds to whip off the plateau and down to the Ross Ice Shelf, where they are funnelled west, and then north by the mountains of Victoria Land. This created unusually cold conditions in the western half of the Great Ice Barrier when Scott and his men were attempting to get back to Cape Evans.

In March 1912 the British team found the summer was ending far sooner than expected. During their attempt to get back to base the struggling party was hit by a succession of blizzards that pushed temperatures more than 10°C lower than normal. This is just what we would expect during an El Niño. Simpson wrote, 'There can be no doubt that the weather played a predominating part in the disaster, and...was the immediate cause of the final catastrophe,' and concluded: 'the Barrier could be traversed many times without again encountering such low temperatures so early in the year.' Recent scholarly investigation, most notably by Susan Solomon in her fascinating book *The Coldest March*, has shown that 1912 was exceptionally cold, even in the context of modern weather data.

The work done on Mawson's expedition supported the British interpretation. Weaving in the Australasian expedition's results, the New Zealand meteorologist Edward Kidson was able to build on Simpson's work and produce daily weather maps that spanned the Antarctic to the tropics. The new continent was not nearly as meteorologically isolated as had been thought. Kidson showed that the changes in atmospheric pressure recorded by the different expedition barometers of 1912 were tracking the seemingly endless procession of lows from west to east.

During 1913 Frank Wild claimed in *The Times* that 'from March 21 for a period of nine days we were kept in camp by the same blizzard which proved fatal to Scott and his gallant companions'. At one level he was right. Kidson's work indicated that the successive low pressure systems were all linked. As Wild and his men were pinned down by a blizzard, the same low-pressure system was sweeping inexorably east towards the Ross Sea, keeping the British team trapped. Antarctica's weather danced to the changes offshore. Scott really was in the wrong place at the wrong time.

On a cold evening in January 1914 a long procession of people converged on the plush red-brick premises of the Royal Geographical Society, in central London's Kensington Gore. The society had just moved into its new home and was leaving behind the controversy that had inadvertently kick-started the explosion of work in the south. Female fellows were now openly welcomed, and the RGS was tackling the twentieth century with confidence. It was a fresh start for all.

This particular January night was unusually busy. Held on the eve of World War I, the meeting was not about the geopolitics of the region. Instead, lodging their heavy outdoor clothing at the cloakroom, the audience members had come to hear a speech by one of the scientific heavyweights of the era, 'Prof' Edgeworth David.

David was here to show how the research of 1912 had spectacularly advanced the world's knowledge of Antarctica. It seemed fitting that he provide this overview. Although he had not been south for five years, David had maintained contact with many of the expeditions, helping them to interpret their results and weaving these into his own findings from Shackleton's *Nimrod* expedition.

Over the next hour David gave a dizzying survey of what had been discovered in the new continent and the research questions that remained. Where things were hazy he intuitively suggested hypotheses, many of which would be confirmed decades later. There was no one better informed.

In his posthumously published book, *The Lands of Silence*, Markham declared that the 'great object of Antarctic exploration is to discover the outline of the Antarctic continent, and to study the physiography so far as the great ice-cap will admit of such researches'. The year 1912 was a watershed in this regard. The exploratory work had gleaned an understanding of what lay south.

Not only were new coastlines found, David remarked: others that had confounded explorers for years were finally dismissed. The Australasian expedition, with Davis captaining the *Aurora*, had proved that the Company Islands were a mirage, while in the Weddell Sea, Filchner had escaped the bullets of the *Deutschland* crew to show that Morrell Land was most likely a figment of an eccentric American sealer's imagination.

Mawson likened Antarctic exploration to discovering missing parts of a huge and complicated jigsaw. Thanks to the exploits of five teams in an amazing short burst, several large pieces of the puzzle were unearthed and the picture started to make sense.

Often sustained by sheer willpower, the teams had worked against the odds to show the great white continent was not just a vast wilderness. Some 8500 kilometres of the coast had been mapped on oceanographic cruises. As a result of these efforts the Antarctic coastline looked to be 22,500 kilometres long—an estimate not far off the eighteen thousand kilometres that today we know it to be. And where sledging parties had gone inland, vast tracts of previously unknown ground had been discovered. Mawson's expedition alone explored 3200 kilometres, while Amundsen covered 2800 and Scott a further 460.

One huge uncertainty before 1912 had been how the continent's mountain chains linked up—if they linked up at all. From Amundsen's descriptions and photographs, the Beacon Sandstone first described in Victoria Land seemed to extend to the Axel Heiberg Glacier, which the Norwegian had climbed to reach the plateau. Unfortunately, at the other end of the continent, Filchner had fallen short of a suite of rock samples from Prinz Luitpold Land. David was disappointed, because this would have conclusively shown whether the new coastline joined the mountains Amundsen had seen carrying over the horizon.

There was a strong reason for supposing they did. The wholly different geology of the Andes tended to support Amundsen's observations that this mountain range continued towards Prinz Luitpold Land, a staggering distance of 3500 kilometres, making it one of the longest mountain ranges in the world.

If the mountains of Victoria Land did indeed cut across the continent, the question remained whether the barriers of the Ross and Weddell seas linked up, cutting Antarctica in two. The Japanese expedition looked south from King Edward VII Land and saw high ground that implied the presence of land; Amundsen suggested there might also be mountains to the northeast of his point of ascent, which he called Carmen Land.

If these were real—though because of the known refraction of the air in this part of the world, they might have been hundreds of kilometres away—there could not be a wide strait, David argued. Filchner's Luitpold Land, at the southernmost part of the Weddell Sea, lent support to the idea. At best there was a narrow strait. Decades later, David's supposition was proved correct.

———————•—•———————

After the expeditions of 1912 there was a backlash against the bewildering array of names being given to different parts of Antarctica. People were getting tired of the landscape being named after monarchs and rich benefactors. Today naming is strictly controlled and many of the locations in Antarctica have been retitled. Although individual mountains have largely kept the titles bequeathed to them, the chain that cuts a swathe across the continent now goes by the name of the Transantarctic Mountains, while the Antarctic Andes are best known as the Antarctic Peninsula.

With this rationalisation, there was also a recognition that the word 'barrier' did not do justice to the extraordinary features found in the Ross and Weddell seas. During 1912 the Australasian team discovered a similar floating formation on the east Antarctic coastline. This find was given a more accurate term, and named after the Anglo-Irishman who had supported the Australasian effort: the Shackleton Ice Shelf. It would be some years before the Great Ice Barrier became known as the Ross Ice Shelf. But the work undertaken by the British and Norwegian teams did show that this enormous feature was essentially flat and rose only very slightly towards the Transantarctic Mountains.

Shirase's team had found the only significant amounts of rock debris in the barrier ice near the coast of King Edward VII Land and close to numerous outlet glaciers, giving a strong clue about its formation. David astutely realised that the ice shelf must be shaped by a combination of factors: ice flowing in from surrounding glaciers and snow falling from above, melting at the base and calving into the Ross Sea.

The timescale involved was vast. The British calculated the barrier's movement was somewhere in the order of 460 metres each year, not far off today's estimate of a metre a day. And, thanks to the mapping efforts of 1912, the Ross Ice Shelf was shown to be equivalent in size to France, allowing David to calculate that it took some twelve hundred years for 'ice at the apex...to travel to the sea cliff'.

But it was by crossing the crevasse-torn ice shelf that the most significant discoveries about this ancient landscape were made. Shackleton found a succession of different rock types exposed in the mountainsides at the top of the Beardmore Glacier, at a spot known as Buckley Island. Thanks to detailed work by Scott and his team, it was realised that Mawson had found the same sequence of rocks some 2250 kilometres away. Although finding an identical geological pattern in two different locations, albeit over a huge distance, was not in itself thrilling, one part of the sequence excited considerable comment: coal.

In 1912 it was well known that the existence of coal spoke of forested swamps in the past. Based on the plant remains the Antarctic coal contained it was evident there were parallels to those found in other parts of the world during a geological period of luxuriant plant growth known as the Permian, more than 250 million years ago. This geological link helped David, an expert on Australian coal, to decipher the geological history of Antarctica.

The mere presence of coal posed a tricky question: how did vestiges of ancient forests come to be found at the Beardmore Glacier? As David remarked, 'We are thus confronted with the extraordinary problem of trees, probably coniferous, flourishing with 5° of the South Pole itself in a zone which is now, in winter-time, more or less in complete darkness for five months in the year.'

Prophetically, David asked: 'Could this coal-flora have flourished, even under warmer conditions, with the Beardmore glacier situated in its present relation to the South Pole, so that the flora would have been in darkness for five months of the year? If not, has the Pole shifted, or has Buckley Island shifted in regard to its present distance from the Pole?'

<hr />

The answer to why coal was in Antarctica lay within the sixteen kilograms of samples Scott and his team had collected and dragged to their deaths. With the publication of *Scott's Last Expedition*, a collection of the British leader's journals, the public learned that on discovering the dead men the search party 'recovered all their gear and dug out the sledge with their belongings on it. Amongst these were 35 lb. of very important geological specimens which had been collected on the moraines of the Beardmore Glacier; at Doctor Wilson's request they had stuck to these up to the very end, even when disaster stared them in the face and they knew that the specimens were so much weight added to what they had to pull.'

The remaining expedition members immediately saw their scientific value. The geologist Griffith Taylor remarked that the 'specimens brought back by the Polar Party from Mt. Buckley contain impressions of fossil plants of late Palaeozoic age, some of which a cursory inspection identifies as occurring in other parts of the world. When fully examined, they will assuredly prove to be of the highest geological importance', while his colleague Frank Debenham argued that their preservation would allow people to 'settle a long-standing controversy between geologists as to the nature of the former union between

Antarctica and Australasia'. But what precisely the specimens were was not widely known.

Buckley Island—or Mount Buckley, as it is sometimes referred to—is a nunatak atop the Beardmore Glacier. It was here, on the return from the pole, that Edward Wilson found the coal deposits reported by Shackleton. The men spent the afternoon of 8 February 1912 and some of the following morning under the cliff face. Searching among the jumble of rocks they scanned the surface for samples, splitting promising-looking blocks of stone in the search for elusive fossils while the eagle-eyed Wilson made detailed notes. On close inspection some were found to contain the clear impression of ancient leaves.

Today these delicate samples are carefully preserved in London's Natural History Museum, locked away in small cardboard boxes, hidden among a global collection that has been gathered over centuries. It is hard to believe these small rocks, several centimetres across and rough-edged, are the same ones that caught Wilson's eye all those years ago. The scientist described them as 'dark blackish slaty, shaly or coaly matter, some exceedingly hard, some splitting easily, and some breaking vertically into blocks', where 'the best leaf-impressions and the most obvious were in the rotten lumps of weathered coal which split up easily to sheaf-knife and hammer. Every layer of these gave abundant vegetable remains. Most of the bigger leaves were like beech leaves in shape and venation, in size a little smaller than British beech, and the venation were much more abundant and finer in character, but distinctly beech-like.' The romance of their effort was not lost on Markham, who commented: 'There is no more glorious and more touching event in the whole range of polar history.'

At the time of David's 1914 talk in London, work on these fossils was nearing completion at the University of Cambridge.

Working on the precious samples, Albert Seward, a professor of botany, reported in the first of several natural-history accounts from the expedition that some of the fossils were *Glossopteris*, the ubiquitous Gondwanaland flora that David had referred to in his Dunedin talk a decade before. Seward wrote: 'the discovery of *Glossopteris* on the Buckley Island moraine supplies what is needed to bring hypothesis within the range of established fact.'

Here was proof that Antarctica had not only been warmer in the past: it had somehow been linked to South America, India and Australia at the centre of Gondwanaland. If the botanist Marie Stopes had been influential in encouraging Scott and his team to collect them after their heady night of dancing years before, it was serendipity indeed.

The simplest explanation for how *Glossopteris* came to be in Antarctica was through one of the hypothesised land bridges connecting the southern continents. In the oceans, however, the much-sought evidence had remained elusive. As part of the Australasian effort the expedition ship *Aurora* had made several vast sweeps of the Southern Ocean, taking soundings for water depth and trawling the sea for biological evidence of an ancient link. Even though Mawson was keen to find proof, he was not convinced by what they had found. The most promising was the Mill Rise, which Davis had discovered south of Tasmania, but this was an isolated plateau and did not span nearly enough of the ocean to make the case.

David did not give up on the idea of a land bridge, and contacted Teddy Evans and the crew of the *Terra Nova* about making depth soundings in a different sector of the ocean to the Australasian party. Shortly before the British set off to collect Scott and his men, David wrote to Evans: 'King Edward Land and the land found by Amundsen and Lieutenant Shirase southwards from King Edward Land shows that the land probably consists of some very large and low islands, forming an almost continuous land mass, at the foot of the Antarctic Andes further south, in fact an island group analogous to that of the Palmer Archipelago and of the South Shetlands. There should be sunken islands to the north of King Edward VII Land and you might be lucky enough to locate some of these or the submarine Plateau on which they rest.'

He was convinced that 'there is no part of the ocean more intensely interesting scientifically than that which lies between the South end of New Zealand and the Ross Sea.' The measurements were made, but there was no sign of a land bridge there either. So how did *Glossopteris* come to be in Antarctica?

Bold new scientific ideas were coming to the fore as the Antarctic expeditions returned home. Alongside reports proving the existence of the atom and the discovery of a possible fossilised human species in England, a little-known German scientist called Alfred Wegener was suggesting something more controversial: the world's continents formed part of an enormous jigsaw.

By 1912 Wegener was publishing scientific papers on his solution to the confusing observation that distinctive fossils were found across many continents. Later developed in a landmark book called *The Origin of Continents and Oceans*, his ideas were not published in English until 1924, delaying their discussion among the wider scientific community. Wegener proposed that you did not need drowned land bridges to account for similar geological formations in disparate locations. Instead, everything could be resolved if the continents had ploughed their way through the oceans—which Wegener described as displacement theory—changing their location on the surface.

Gondwanaland had been one massive supercontinent and,

instead of parts sinking into the world's oceans, it had split and the continents drifted apart from one another during the Jurassic period, which began around 161 million years ago. If the thinking was correct, it meant the Antarctic coal was no longer in the location where it had formed: Gondwanaland had torn apart and created the world we see today.

Not everyone in the scientific community welcomed this theory. Critics were scathing, largely because there was no evidence for how Wegener envisaged the continents moved across the surface. Comments such as 'German pseudo-science' and 'purely fantastic' indicate the depth of feeling. It was not until the 1960s that Wegener's ideas became widely accepted, once it was recognised that it wasn't the continents that moved per se but the plates on which they sit and float. Plate tectonics was able to explain how new continents and oceans were created, destroyed or rubbed along uncomfortably together.

Ironically, a focus of the Australasian effort, Macquarie Island, is now known to lie on the eastern boundary of the Indo-Australian Pacific Plate, explaining the frequent earthquakes experienced by Mawson's men. It was not enough, however, to convince the Australian leader, who remained distinctly cold to the idea, though David did come round to the concept. More importantly, though, continental drift suddenly made it possible to argue that the Antarctic coal measures had formed in lower latitudes and then moved on. But was this the whole story?

During a long spell in our planet's history, 299 to 251 million years ago, *Glossopteris* dominated the Gondwanan scenery. But it was not the only thing growing in the landscape. The diversity of Antarctic vegetation found alongside *Glossopteris* was relatively low, implying cooler conditions. More significantly, associated deposits were found to contain magnetic particles that sit close to vertical—the same principle behind dipping compasses—proving Antarctica was close to the magnetic pole at the time of *Glossopteris* and the formation of coal. It appeared that Antarctica had not been that far north, after all: at least, not far enough to avoid several months of twenty-four-hour darkness each year. And yet, given the large size of *Glossopteris*, it must have been relatively warm.

A strong clue to how this was so is provided by a remarkable living fossil, the Chinese deciduous tree ginkgo, or *Ginkgo biloba*. Fossils of this plant have been found in Antarctic rocks dating back to the Cretaceous period, some one hundred million years ago. Although this was after the time of *Glossopteris*, we know greenhouse gas levels were at similarly high levels. Concentrations of air-breathing stomata on fossil leaves provide a first-order estimate of the amount of carbon dioxide in the atmosphere. The greater the concentration of gas, the more efficiently the plant photosynthesises and the fewer stomata it needs. By nourishing the plants at different levels of carbon dioxide the relationship can be quantified, and the results make fascinating reading. Compared to today's level of 396 parts per million and rising, estimates for the time ginkgo was flourishing in Antarctica suggest it was around eight hundred parts per million. The Earth was in the grip of an extreme greenhouse effect.

The corresponding high temperatures meant there were no icecaps. Instead, the landscape was dominated by rainforest and inhabited by a wealth of wildlife. By growing ginkgo seedlings in blacked-out greenhouses with high levels of carbon dioxide, scientists at the University of Sheffield, in England, have been able to test whether the tree was capable of withstanding complete darkness for months on end. Although the ginkgo plants used up precious food reserves during winter, they could more than compensate for this by photosynthesising during the twenty-four hours of summer daylight. So long as carbon dioxide levels remained high, the forests of Antarctica could not only survive in the dark but thrive.

With the ceaseless shuffling of plates on the surface, Gond-wanaland's time was limited. Huge flows of lavas dating back to the Jurassic period are preserved within the Transantarctic Mountains, testament to the massive forces Alfred Wegener envisaged. By the late Cretaceous, some eighty million years ago, the last hanger-on, New Zealand, finally split from the West Antarctic. The supercontinent was no more. The rifting continues today: the Mount Erebus volcano in the Ross Sea is a visible sign of the process that began all those years ago. Satellite data collected since the 1980s shows how perceptive Wegener was. The crust still carries the physical scarring that marks the break-up of Gondwanaland, and the links between Antarctica and the other southern continents. It is a spectacular confirmation of the German's idea of a 'flight from the poles'.

The end of Gondwanaland had global repercussions. The opening up of the Drake Passage and Scotia Sea around thirty million years ago brought one of the world's great ocean currents, the Antarctic Circumpolar Current, into being. Although this Antarctic current sustains abundant life in the Southern Ocean—including South Georgia and other subant-arctic islands—it isolated the southern continent from the rest of the planet. Temperatures in Antarctica dropped precipitously and the vast ice sheets we see today began to grow. With the accompanying cooling there were massive evolutionary changes. For those left behind on the keystone continent of Gondwana-land, the future would prove considerably challenging.

The scientists of 1912 were only just starting to grapple with some of these issues. Although Wilson got the primitiveness of emperor penguins wrong, he was correct in thinking that they offer a significant insight into the origin of modern birds. With

the discovery in 1953 of deoxyribonucleic acid—usually shortened to DNA—scientists realised that the evolution of species
is accompanied by changes in their genetic make-up. When
two species arise from a common ancestor and go off on their
own evolutionary pathways, differences in DNA accumulate.
The changes in the genetic composition of a species are like the
hands of a clock, each change equating to the tick of a molecular
timepiece. These accumulating ticks can be used to calculate
when a species evolved. The critical thing is to find out the rate
at which genetic mutations take place.

This is where penguins come in. Penguins have arguably
the best fossil record of modern birds around the Cretaceous–
Tertiary boundary, sixty-five million years ago, a period best
known for the extinction of the dinosaurs. The earliest fossil
penguin evidence has been found in New Zealand, and dates
back sixty-two million years, shortly—geologically speaking—
after the separation of Gondwanaland. These early fossils
provide an important fixed point in time, not just for calibrating
the rate of changes in penguins but across the whole genetic
tree of birds, allowing major junctures to be dated.

The results are fascinating, not least because the popular
early theory that penguins evolved from the extinction of the
dinosaurs is wrong. There almost certainly was a dinosaur relative to birds. However, the genetic code shows that modern
birds had a last common ancestor long before the end of the
Cretaceous, with penguins separating from their next nearest
living relative, the stork, around seventy-one million years
ago—long before dinosaurs became extinct. As Antarctica
became cloaked in ice, species of penguins moved out along the
circumpolar current to the subantarctic islands, and from there
to other southern landmasses, reaching as far north as the Gala-
pagos Islands a trifling four million years ago. For the penguins
that stayed behind, the continent became a lot quieter.

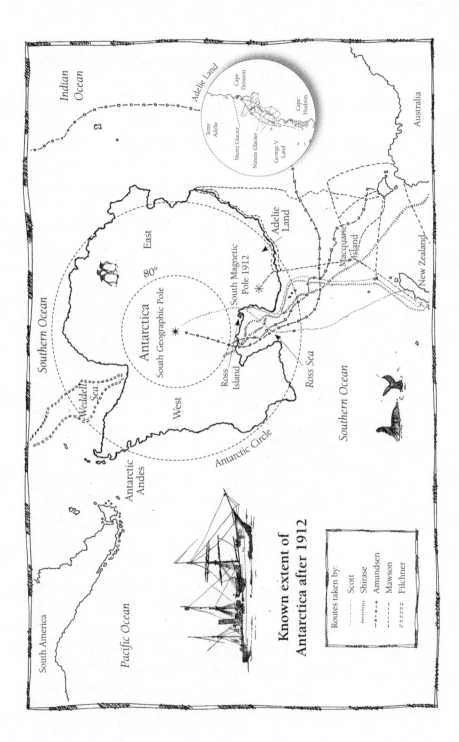

Indian Ocean

Adelie Land

Cape Denison

Terre Adelie

Mertz Glacier

Ninnis Glacier

Cape Hudson

George V Land

Australia

East Antarctica

80°

South Magnetic Pole 1912

Adelie Land

Macquarie Island

New Zealand

Southern Ocean

Antarctica

South Geographic Pole

Ross Island

Ross Sea

Weddell Sea

West

Antarctic Circle

Southern Ocean

Antarctic Andes

Pacific Ocean

South America

Known extent of Antarctica after 1912

Routes taken by:

.... Scott

—···— Shirase

—·—·— Amundsen

————— Mawson

– – – – Filchner

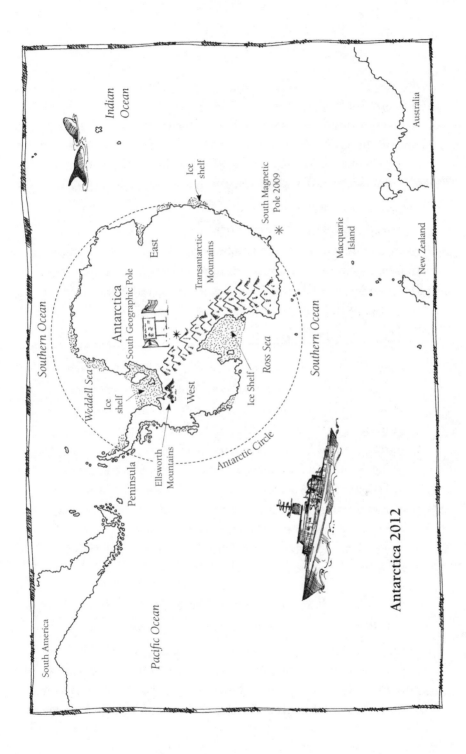

Antarctica 2012

After the exploration work of 1912 Antarctica went from being an inaccessible land described in fantastical stories to being part of the real world. Before, the information gleaned had been sporadic. Now there were careful observations and hard data. A common misconception—as pervasive as the tall tales— that Antarctica was just a land of white nothingness had been disproved, and with this the world's perception changed irrevocably. The southern continent was a staggeringly complex landscape—and now there were more questions than answers. The expeditions of 1912 had shown the way, and it was only the beginning of the scientific work.

The Times reported:

> Now that the South Pole has been reached geographers will be free to carry on the investigations of this huge continent without any unpleasant element of rivalry, such as has existed hitherto in both ends of the earth. The expedition which started last year from Australia under Dr Mawson is the type of expedition that is to be encouraged in the future; and it is to be hoped that Dr Mawson's example will be followed by other explorers until the whole contour of this Antarctic Continent is mapped and such knowledge of its geographical, meteorological, biological and other conditions acquired as will satisfy the demands of science.

Mawson and Scott inspired fierce loyalty. From their efforts there emerged scientists dedicated to Antarctic affairs, who established research organisations and institutions that persist today. Debenham and Priestley helped found the British Scott Polar Research Institute in 1920; in Australia, Mawson succeeded in establishing the Australian National Antarctic

Research Expeditions, the forerunner of today's Australian Antarctic Division.

This enthusiasm for the south extended to protecting the continent itself, through the Antarctic Treaty. Enacted in 1961, this international agreement is now supported by forty-five signatories, and puts all territorial claims south of 60° on hold while preserving a nuclear- and mining-free Antarctic for future generations. The continent is now dedicated to science and exploration—a fitting tribute to those who undertook pioneering work and lost their lives on the ice.

By the first decade of the twentieth century rapid industrialisation was engendering a new form of confidence. The romance of civilised explorers battling against brute nature to unearth its hidden secrets captured a collective mood. And it was not entirely positive: this new swagger found articulation in the global power game of World War I.

The scientific explorations of 1912 proved an inspiration for the European youth of the day. Tales of ripping yarns and daring feats preached the value of self-sacrifice for the greater good. Poems drawing comparisons between the conflicts at Gallipoli and Flanders with the expeditions in Antarctica became widely known, while Ponting's original film of Scott's expedition, *The Great White Silence*, was shown to more than one hundred thousand officers and men of the British Army, with the photographer lecturing daily in London through most of 1914. The British tragedy in Antarctica struck a poignant note.

World War I resulted in the deaths of tens of millions of soldiers and civilians. Within these statistics lie the men to whom Shackleton dedicated his book *South*: those 'who fell in the white warfare of the south and on the red fields of France and Flanders'. The Japanese declared for the Allies but it does not appear any of Shirase's men died during the fighting, while Norway remained neutral.

Of the other expeditions, however, one in ten of those who had served in and survived the extremes of the Antarctic did not live to see 1919. Many were mentioned in dispatches. Filchner's expedition lost two men to the war and Scott's three, while Mawson's two team members included Robert Bage who, after surviving a second winter in Antarctica, died during the first fortnight of the Australian campaign at Gallipoli. It was a terrible waste of life.

And it wasn't just men who were victims. The war suddenly created a large market for explosives—in particular, glycerine, a by-product of whale-oil production. Antarctica's natural resources were tapped, ensuring the continent joined the modern world.

———◆———

The first meeting of the British Association for the Advancement of Science in Australia was held on the verge of the conflict, in August 1914. The German scientist Friedrich Albert Penck was en route when war was declared. David defended Penck in the same way he had Shirase and his men in Sydney, speaking highly of the German and vouching for him while in Australia. The sentiment was not reciprocated; it seems Penck did spy for Germany during his visit, taking photos of harbour defences in the New South Wales city of Newcastle.

David went on to volunteer for the war effort, though he was fifty-eight, and became a major in the Australian Mining Corps—better known as The Tunnellers—which he helped establish; his geological expertise proved crucial to the Allies efforts, most notably at the Battle of Messines in 1917, for which he later received the Distinguished Service Order. It was yet another remarkable achievement in a remarkable career.

Ernest Shackleton went on to lead the Imperial Trans-Antarctic Expedition, hoping to cross the great continent for the first time, but met a similar fate to Filchner. Before he could make land, his ship, the *Endurance*, became locked in the Weddell Sea ice during 1915 and iconic images taken by Frank Hurley, fresh from his Antarctic mission with Mawson, immortalised the expedition as the vessel sank.

Shackleton led his men through the ice floes to reach Elephant Island at the tip of the Antarctic Peninsula. Leaving most of the men under the leadership of Frank Wild, he proceeded to sail the thirteen hundred kilometres to South Georgia in a tiny boat. Becoming the first to cross the island's mountains, he then raised the alarm at a whaling station and returned to Elephant Island to find everyone alive. Yet again Shackleton lived up to his towering reputation.

During an expedition to the Antarctic in 1922, again with Wild, the great man died of a heart attack. He was only forty-seven. At his wife's request, Shackleton's body was buried at Grytviken in South Georgia, where today his grave looks over the cruise ships that visit the island.

Roald Amundsen returned north after celebrating his success at reaching the South Geographic Pole. But his dream of doing the same in the Arctic was frustrated. The *Fram* was badly rotted after its travels, so Amundsen had to build a new ship to drift over the pole—and the attempt failed, with the vessel missing the location. Amundsen later flew over the North Geographic Pole in the airship *Norge*, but after falling out with his brother Leon he struggled with money and was later declared bankrupt. Amundsen returned north yet again—in 1928, to help find a lost explorer—but was sadly lost over the ice, dying aged fifty-five.

Nobu Shirase lived a considerably longer time, in relative poverty, spending most of his life paying off the cost of the Japanese expedition. Finally clear of debt he lived for a further decade, barely surviving on an army pension, and died in 1946, at the age of eighty-five. It was a shocking way to treat a man who claimed, with some justification, to have 'kindled the latent fire in the hearts of the Japanese'.

In Germany, after World War I, Wilhelm Filchner helped the Kaiser flee to the Netherlands. He never went south again but continued his work in Nepal and Tibet, spending World War II in India, where he made public his anti-Nazi feelings. Filchner died in Zurich in 1957, aged eighty.

Douglas Mawson went on to marry his love, Paquita Delprat, with John King Davis as his best man, and then served in the war as an army major. He later returned to Antarctica as part of the British, Australian and New Zealand Antarctic Research Expedition, where he explored vast sections of the continental coastline. He was appointed professor of geology at the University of Adelaide in 1920 and died in 1958, aged seventy-six, the last of the great leaders from the Heroic Era of Exploration.

And the man who started it all? Sir Clements Markham died in an unpleasant way that was anything but heroic. In 1916 he was overcome by smoke from a candle that set fire to his hammock. He was eighty-five, and had defended Scott's efforts over all others to his last day.

The centenary of 1912 is an opportunity to celebrate scientific exploration in the south. No group encapsulates the spirit more than Robert Scott and his South Pole party. Unfortunately, their deaths overshadowed their expedition's great work—and arguably much of that achieved by the other teams.

Heroic tales of sacrifice and endurance in the face of extreme hardship became the main story, to the detriment of almost everything else.

When I started this project I had no desire to add to the commentary on the deaths of Scott and his men. There are many wonderful books on the events surrounding this journey and all give a more comprehensive view of them than I could hope to. But, during my research, I stumbled across a new part of the story, with implications for the way we honour the men's memory and, more generally, how science is communicated to people outside the profession.

Scott's fellow explorers were at a loss to explain what had gone wrong. How could one of the best-provisioned expeditions in Antarctica have ended so badly? When told of Scott's death, Shackleton was incredulous: 'I cannot believe it is true. It is inconceivable that an expedition so well equipped as Captain Scott's could perish before a blizzard.' There is no doubt that the weather played a major role, but might something else have contributed?

With the news of the tragedy, rumours circulated that the full story had not been told: that something else had happened on the ice, something that was being quietly ignored. Apsley Cherry-Garrard was convinced of it. Writing in his diary in January 1914 Cherry reports that he went to Lincoln's Inn Fields for a meeting with the expedition's solicitor, Arthur Ferrar, who was also Cherry's own legal advisor. The response was swift. 'They would not listen,' Ferrar insisted when Cherry said he wanted to go before the Antarctic Committee handling the expedition in Britain. 'They will say you are overstrained. You see, there must be no scandal.'

'The Committee,' Cherry noted in the margin of his journal, 'meant to hush up everything. I was to be sacrificed.' Nothing was ever proven and Cherry's concerns were put down to paranoia. But the speculation persisted. To try to understand why, I went in May 2011 to view some of Lord Curzon's papers held by the British Library.

The first clue was in a short set of notes: seven pages that had been buried in a file for nearly a century. They shed light on a chain of events that was precipitated in April 1913 by Lady Kathleen Scott's arrival in London from New Zealand, returning after news of her husband's death. During the month-long voyage Lady Scott had pored over her late husband's diary and correspondence. Arriving in London on 14 April, she immediately contacted Lord Curzon, in his role as president of the Royal Geographical Society, and arranged a meeting in two days' time.

Curzon made the meeting notes after what appears to have been a wide-ranging discussion over Lady Scott's findings. The deaths of all five men were discussed. Oates, it was claimed, most probably took opium before leaving the tent to commit suicide. But the meeting began, unsurprisingly, with talk of her late husband: 'Scotts words in his Diary on exhaustion of food & fuel in depots on his return. He spoke in reference of "lack of thoughtfulness & even of generosity". It appears Lieut Evans – down with Scurvy – and the 2 men with him must on return journey have entered & consumed more than their share.'

This must have come as a shock to Curzon. Had one of the returning parties, led no less by the expedition's second-in-command, taken more than their fair share of supplies? Scott's Antarctic venture was seen in some quarters as the society's expedition. If Teddy Evans was even remotely suspected of being complicit in Scott's death, the RGS might be asked some very difficult questions, particularly as he had since assumed the leadership of the expedition.

Curzon immediately initiated an inquiry, asking several senior RGS members if they would discreetly help him investigate the matter. Most were supportive, but he received a confidential note of caution from Admiral Lewis Beaumont:

As you have seen and talked to Lady Scott you now know that
Evans had lost Scott's confidence to a great extent and that
he will be dependent upon what Lady Scott gives him, out of
the Diaries and Journals, for the building up of his paper. I
think your idea of having an informal meeting of those you
name…a very good one—the important point, to my mind,
being the necessity of deciding what attitude the Society
should take with regard to your questions (a) & (b) that is:- the
exhaustion of the supplies of food & fuel—and the conduct of
the relief parties. I am not in favour of the informal meeting
becoming a Committee of Enquiry—because for the Society
to be on sure ground it would have to probe very deep and
would have probably to disapprove of what was done in many
particulars—it would be different if good could come of the
enquiry, but I fear nothing but controversy would come of it.

Curzon was not so sure—but things changed a few days
later, when he met Edward Wilson's widow.

His notes continue with the subsequent meeting he held
with Mrs Oriana Wilson. It records an unknown part of
the expedition's story: 'Mrs Wilson told me later there was a
passage in her husbands diary which spoke of the "inexplicable"
shortage of fuel & pemmican on the return journey, relating to
depots which had not been touched by Meares and which could
only refer to an unauthorised subtraction by one or other of the
returning parties. This passage however she proposes to show
to no one and to keep secret. C.'

Scott's dog driver, Cecil Meares, was known to have removed
extra supplies from one of the supply dumps, the Mount Hooper
Depot. Halfway back across the barrier in 1912, Meares was
starving. He had travelled the entire ice shelf on the outward
journey, and the extra two weeks meant he and his dogs were
desperately short of food. Taking the bare minimum, he left a
letter telling the others of his actions.

However, it was not Meares's removal of the food that Wilson was referring to. The returning South Pole team did not reach Mount Hooper until 10 March, eleven days after Wilson's last journal entry. The shortage of food must have been else-where. But the published version of Wilson's diary makes no mention of a shortage of fuel or of pemmican.

To check Curzon's claims, I was fortunate to view Wilson's original journal at the British Library. The small dark hardback book contains remarkably light writing in pencil. Dates are jotted in the margins and the accompanying text is of varying length before the entries end abruptly, on 27 February 1912. All the material aligns with the published version, but the latter fails to convey a vital characteristic of the journal. Before 11 February, each line is filled with jottings; not one is wasted. After this date there are gaps in the text, with some entries missing entirely.

The key date seems to be 24 February, when the returning party reached the Southern Barrier Depot. Scott was horrified to find there was a large fuel shortage, and could not account for it. It appears there was natural leakage through the lids: something Amundsen avoided by soldering all his tins. In the published version of his diaries Wilson not only fails to mention the fuel shortage in the relevant entry; he does not even remark upon the team having reached the all-important depot. In the original diary there are gaps in the text: the final statement of the day, 'Fat pony hoosh', is a separate entry from the rest of the text; half a line, clear of text, precedes it, followed by a blank two and a half lines before the next day's entry.

Whether someone has rubbed out text is unclear, but the gaps in the diary entry for 24 February correlate with Curzon's notes. It suggests that one or more individuals did indeed take more than their fair share of food. And this was not the first time. On its return the South Pole team found a full day's biscuit allowance missing in the Upper Glacier Depot on

7 February, and both Scott and Wilson remarked upon this in their diaries.

Determining nutritional needs for working in polar environments was not an exact science in 1912. Past efforts—most of them operating near sea level—were the principal guide in expedition planning. Low temperatures and high altitudes are massive energy drains when dragging sledges for days on end. As a result, the estimated five thousand or so calories Scott had allowed for each man every day—reasonable for traversing the Ross Ice Shelf—was far too low on the Antarctic Plateau. Contemporary estimates suggest the men probably needed somewhere around double that amount. Scott and his men were starving long before they died. So a shortage of food was the last thing they needed, particularly as—regardless of fuel supplies—the pemmican could have been eaten cold.

The evidence pointed towards Evans's team as the guilty party. And Lord Curzon could not risk the story getting out. Scott and his companions had been declared heroes. To suggest that one of the returning teams—albeit suffering scurvy—had helped themselves to more than their share of food, contributing to the men's deaths, would have changed everything. The deaths would no longer be mere 'bad luck' but in part due to others' need for self-preservation: not in the spirit of selfless Antarctic exploration. Survivors' lives would be tainted and reputations—not least of the RGS, so closely aligned with the expedition—would be damaged.

Lady Scott's comments had sparked concern, and Mrs Wilson had made the accusation explicit. But there was little appetite for public scandal. Curzon appears to have shut down the inquiry—after 24 April 1913, there were no further references to it.

Newspaper reports expressed suspicions from the start. The *Daily Chronicle* interviewed Teddy Evans shortly after the *Terra Nova* reached New Zealand and remarked that the new expedition leader became reticent when asked about shortages on the ice, commenting, 'I think you had better not touch upon it.' Some RGS fellows privately expressed fears that more had happened on the ice than was publicly known. On the expedition, Cherry despised the Welshman: 'I should like to see that man branded the traitor and liar he is,' he wrote in his diary, and, later, 'It would be an everlasting shame, if the story of this Expedition were told by the one big failure in it.' By the end of July 1913 Evans had been removed from the official leadership of the expedition.

Of the returning Last Supporting Party, only William Lashly's sledging diary has been published, the most popular version apparently reproduced in full within Cherry's *The Worst Journey in the World*, some ten years after the events they describe. Although Lashly would later insist their contents were true, the entries appear to have been significantly embellished. Curiously, the original diary entries give no detail on how much food the three men took from the allegedly impoverished depots, despite the definite statements in Cherry's version; and Evans's scurvy—a possible justification for taking extra food—is not commented on until the men were halfway across the Ross Ice Shelf, eight days after that given in the popular version when the men were still descending the Beardmore Glacier. There is nothing in Lashly's diary to refute Lord Curzon's notes.

If Wilson's diary entry for the 24 February was partially rubbed out, the most likely candidate is his widow. Oriana Wilson is known to have destroyed some of her husband's correspondence and, given the record of the conversation with Lord Curzon, she probably always intended to remove the offending statements. But Wilson's and Lashly's diaries were not the only expedition accounts altered.

For some years it has been well known that a number of changes were made to Scott's diary before it was published in 1913. Temperature readings were sometimes altered, derogatory comments about individuals removed. The latter is easy to understand. But some of Scott's text from the final part of the journey was also changed, seemingly to make the ending more dramatic—as if it was not dramatic enough already.

On 17 January, Wilson wrote at Polheim, 'we start for home and shall do our utmost to get back in time to send the news home.' Curiously, in Scott's published diary there was a similar statement but it was altered, completely changing the meaning. Here the entry read, 'Now for the run home and a desperate struggle. I wonder if we can do it,' implying Scott was not sure he would be able to get his team home. Although the reader would have known the ending before they began the book, this published version is odd: if Scott thought they might die, he would not have wasted the best part of a day fossicking for geological samples at Buckley Island.

The actual passage for 17 January reads: 'Now for the run home and a desperate struggle *to get the news through first. I wonder if we can do it.'* (The emphasis is mine.) The edited version gives a completely different view of Scott's thoughts and, unfortunately, continues to misguide people. Yet you still see the edited version trotted out, time and again.

What both Wilson and Scott were saying is: we need to get back to base before the *Terra Nova* leaves, so we can tell the world we reached the pole; in the meantime we are staying in Antarctica to continue the scientific work. For the two men the pole was the means to an end: it was the science that mattered. Communicating their success was essential to attracting the precious funding that would support their research efforts.

It is a shame that the complete, correct text in the sledging diaries is not better known. The nature of the British explorers' deaths and the editing of their final words has for too long created a fixation on the 'race', rather than the bigger story of how the five expeditions of the era worked towards understanding what made Antarctica tick.

By focusing on the race we do these men a disservice. Scott and his men died for science. I hope that, after a century, we can get the balance right and remember the pioneering work they did. It was all about the science—and it is time we remembered them for that.

POSTSCRIPT

Give me ex-Antarcticists, unsoured and with their
ideals intact: they could sweep the world.

APSLEY CHERRY-GARRARD (1886–1959)

With all the celebrations and mourning over the heroics and losses of 1912, the public lost sight of the huge increase in Antarctic knowledge attained. And yet the stories from this time continue to be re-evaluated, and to inspire. Even though we have never been more familiar with this frigid environment, Antarctica remains exciting, otherworldly. If you are fortunate enough to visit it, the vastness, the sense of scale, the brightness, the merging vista of ice and sky, the silence: they are all a blitz on the senses that cannot be experienced anywhere else. For some people, this sparks a need to beat records made by great past explorers and adventurers; for others, to spend long periods at the bottom end of the world, away from families and friends, making scientific measurements to better understand our planet.

The Antarctic continues to offer scientific insights. Mawson's work from one hundred years ago shows the Southern Ocean is warming at an ever-increasing rate; Filchner's observations

demonstrate that the glaciers on South Georgia have spectacularly retreated; and Scott's collections are providing valuable
insights into the changing biology and carbon cycle of the
Antarctic. Some of these samples have even forced change in
global regulations. Penguin skins collected during the torturous
Cape Crozier trip by Wilson, Bowers and Cherry in 1911
showed beyond doubt that by the 1960s the pesticide DDT
had even reached as pristine an environment as the Antarctic,
leading to a worldwide ban.

Even the endpoint of the so-called race, the South Geographic
Pole, long derided as having no scientific value, now has one:
the permanent American Amundsen–Scott South Pole Station
hosts IceCube, a multimillion-dollar research project funded
by the US, Sweden and Germany to investigate the nature of
matter itself. A cubic kilometre of ice holds one of the largest
instruments in the world, made up of more than five thousand
detectors, spread across eighty-six holes drilled down nearly 2.5
kilometres. The South Geographic Pole is an ideal location for
trying to detect elusive particles known as neutrinos. Electrically negative, with little mass, neutrinos are one of the building
blocks of atoms, created by the sun and supernovae. Most travel
through the Earth unimpeded, without any of us even being
aware of them. Occasionally, however, they interact with the
matter they pass through. Because of its location and the purity
of ice, IceCube can detect when a neutrino strikes a water mole-
cule by the small pulse of blue light created. From this, scientists
can identify the direction from which the neutrinos came and
how much energy they contain, giving insights into their origin
in the universe. Only a large detector is capable of picking up
these incredibly rare events. The explorers of 1912 would have
been impressed.

More importantly, 1912 tells us something special about
scientific exploration: how it was funded, undertaken and

communicated so effectively a century ago. I am not sure we manage this so well now. The distinction between science and exploration did not exist then as it does today. When you explored in 1912, you undertook science; the activities were essentially synonymous. And it excited the public. With the latest technology rolled out to help conquer new land came a groundswell of interest.

In 1912 people made history happen when governments were not keen to fully fund an Antarctic venture. Anyone could help their favourite explorer out with a little contribution; small companies, as sponsors, could get their products in the pages of newspapers whether or not an expedition was successful; business people could have a new discovery in Antarctica named after them, buying a slice of immortality. It was an amazing time in which the radical suddenly seemed possible.

It was, too, the dawn of the modern science documentary. All the expeditions of 1912 took film with them, and only the whereabouts of the German movie is unknown. The other expeditions embraced film as a new way of communicating the spoils of their discoveries to an eager public.

Books and newspaper reports also helped. As early as 1830 the founding members of the new Royal Geographic Society recognised that 'a vast store of geographic information existed in Great Britain, yet it is so scattered and dispersed, either in large books that are not generally accessible, or in the bureaus of the public departments, or in the possession of private individuals, as to be nearly unavailable to the public.' The new society, and its journal, meant new ideas were accessible to anyone with a passing interest in the subject. Newspaper barons' money helped get projects started and guaranteed full news coverage, almost instantly. Even if you were not backed by one of the main players in the industry, an expedition south could garner front-page coverage and help raise funds.

When expedition parties returned home, their stories were written and the books published almost immediately, with science incorporated in the tales. Only later were formal scientific reports written up. The money for exploration depended on capturing the public mood, and speed of delivery was everything. The public craved rattling tales, which meant the authors would sometimes step outside their comfort zones. Cherry wrote tellingly after his return: 'When I went South, I never meant to write a book: I rather despised those who did so as being of an inferior brand to those who did things and said nothing about them.' But the expedition changed his mind: 'every one who has been through such an extraordinary experience has much to say and ought to say it.' Even Mawson, a scientist first and foremost, started work on *The Home of the Blizzard* during his enforced winter stay in the south. These early books provided the masses with great entertainment, combining tragedy, excitement, discovery and comradeship.

Returning a hero, however, was sometimes as hazardous as being on the ice. Tales of crew members being mobbed and trophies being taken from expedition vessels were common. Sometimes samples were requested and, if not made available, carried off. As Shackleton's *Nimrod* expedition made its way back, some entrepreneurial sailors decided to collect rocks from the New Zealand shore and sell them as Antarctic souvenirs, making tens of pounds a week from sales.

For the expedition leaders, there never seemed to be enough money. As Thomas Huxley put it, 'Science in England does everything—but pay. You may earn praise but not pudding.' So much depended on success, and often pre-expedition hyperbole was needed to enthuse the public.

Not everyone liked the way expeditions were pitched, though. Mawson's second-in-command, Davis, commented: 'Recent expeditions have had to beg for funds. Really useful work has too often been sacrificed to the purely spectacular. The explorer, who is handicapped by debt, may be tempted to stimulate the public with sensational feats: the temptation is difficult to resist—or justify. To the explorer who has not the money to provide good equipment of every kind, my advice is "Keep out of the Antarctic!"'

Amundsen was of a similar mind, declaring in *The South Pole* that previous claimants of geographical quests were often guilty of 'romancing rather too bare-facedly'. But we should remember that Heinemann withdrew an offer to publish the Norwegian's book over fears about his ability to communicate the excitement of what he had achieved. No matter how high-minded you wanted to be, spinning a yarn was essential in plugging an idea.

———•———

Over time scientific funding was centralised and the public lost sight of what was happening. Governments required outputs, boxes had to be ticked, and communication switched to telling other scientists the results—the story is the same in so many professions. Narratives describing the excitement of scientific exploration became the exception rather than the norm.

Edgeworth David was on to something when he joined Shackleton in 1907: science can compete with sport when working in extreme environments. As David wrote in 1904, 'Has she [science] not taught men to be fearless in the pursuit of truth—taught them to sacrifice all for the truth?' Although there was little scientific value at the time in making an attempt on the South Geographic Pole, the public loved the thought of the challenge. They wanted to take part as much as possible, supporting the different expeditions in many different ways.

At the time of David's London lecture in 1914 Shackleton was working towards his Imperial Trans-Antarctic Expedition, and he made a perceptive point:

> A lot of people say 'Don't go and do spectacular things,' but deep down in the hearts of everyone who goes to the South Pole is the desire to do something which is of interest to their country. When I went out before we intended to reach the South Pole. We didn't do it. Every expedition that has gone out has done so in order to get as near the South Pole as possible. The last thing to be done in the Antarctic is try and cross the continent. This may not be actually scientific. There is sentiment attached to it. Sentiment has been the ruling force in every great work that has ever been done, and I shall be sorry when the day comes when science is divorced from sentiment or sentiment from science.

It was this philosophy—this ability to see science, adventure and communication as one—that drew people to Shackleton's projects.

I fear we've since taken a wrong turn. The scientific work continues to be done, but we don't tell the story in the same way anymore. Scientists have to explain their work to the public; to inspire, to enthuse; to demonstrate the relevance of what they do. In a time of austerity, it is no longer good enough to take public money, keep busy and hide out of sight. The important thing we can learn from 1912 is that scientific work should get the public excited. I don't believe the public has lost interest, but as a scientist I do wonder whether we could do better. Scientists largely communicate with one another through journals few people can afford or understand. As research has become more focused, the language has become more obscure. Research articles are often so specialised that only those in the immediate field can understand what they are about. I believe we can learn from 1912, and try a different approach to reawaken the public passion for scientific discovery and exploration.

Perhaps surprisingly, not all the world has been explored. Although atlases proudly display our planet's coastlines, there still remain some parts of the globe untouched by humans. Some of these 'unexplored regions' are found in Antarctica; others await discovery in places like Greenland, the Amazon, tropical Africa, New Guinea and under the sea. And it's important. Science and exploration can come together again and make a contribution. It's not just about putting features on a map: it's about understanding how the planet works. And as our planet faces ever-greater challenges, exploration of different environments can play an important role in helping to enthuse people about the planet.

We can learn from the discovery of Antarctica at the turn of the previous century and recapture the spirit of the age. We can exploit the expanding range of media to get the public in the field, physically and virtually. As the centenary of this amazing year is celebrated, we can take stock of how the world was electrified by scientific exploration in 1912 and use these lessons to rouse the next generation, to work on the challenges of the future together.

Institutions make wonderful efforts, developing interactive websites and writing fine press releases; but there is not enough of it—and, at a time when people are blitzed with information, scientists must speak over the noise and talk directly to them.

Getting people engaged can only help. As David said in Dunedin in 1904, 'Science expects every man to learn in the simple way a child learns the great lessons of the universe… she wants him to learn well so that he may live well; to learn well by experiment rather than wholly through the experience of others, so that he may be self reliant and think for himself.

Thinking of this kind brings discoveries, and the discoveries of science uplift humanity.'

Scientists might help out at a local school, or describe expeditionary work using instant messaging, or upload fieldwork footage to the web. Aspiring scientists can follow these activities or, if adventurous, join an international expedition organised by groups like Earthwatch Worldwide or Raleigh International that allows people to get directly involved. There is so much to do—and so much more that can be done.

It's 17 January 2012 and I'm standing among a good-natured crowd at the South Geographic Pole. Despite it being a fresh -35°C, spirits are high. Even one hundred years on, it's not difficult to imagine what it must have been like when Scott and his men reached this very spot. Away from the research station, the brilliant blue sky frames the seemingly endless white of the Antarctic Plateau, throwing our presence into stark relief. It's a tremendous privilege to be here: to celebrate the centenary of the great scientific expedition's arrival.

Although we're in one of the remotest places on the planet, a large number of the brightly attired throng are tourists, pilgrims to this special place. When asked why they have come, all confess to being inspired by the events of a century ago. It's the spirit of adventure that's attracted them. Scott remarked on this before setting out for the pole: 'We are all adventurers here.'

This is the central lesson from a century ago: scientific exploration still plays a vital role, not only in what we can learn about the world but in how we communicate the importance of that learning. We have to be passionate about its value and, like the expeditions of 1912, reach out.

APPENDIX

Lord Curzon's Notes

Key sections of Lord Curzon's handwritten notes from his meetings with Lady Scott (opposite) and Oriana Wilson (overleaf), April 1913. © British Library Board (MSS EUR/F112/51). A transcript of the text follows.

Lady Scott
~~Ma~~ April 16.13
Scotts words in his
Diary on exhaustion
of food & fuel
in depots on
his return.
He spoke in reference
of "lack of thoughtful
ness & even of
generosity".
It appears Lieut
Evans – down with
Scurvy – and the 2
men with him must
on return journey
have entered &

consumed more than
their share...

Mrs Wilson told me
later there was a
passage in her
husbands diary
which spoke of

the 'inexplicable'
shortage of fuel &
pemmican on the
return journey,
relating to
depots which
had not been
touched by Meares
and which
could only refer

to an unau
thorised subtraction
by one or other
of the returning
parties.
This passage
however she
proposes to show
to no one and
to keep secret.
                    C.

Lord Scott

1, CARLTON HOUSE TERRACE,
S.W.

~~The~~ April 16 ·17

Scott's words in his
diary on exhaustion
of food & fuel
in depot on
his return

He spoke in one place
of "lack of thoughtful
ness and even of
generosity."

It appears that
Evans — down with
Scurvy — and the 2
men with him must
on return journey
have consumed
~~more than~~

consumed more than
their share.

Mrs Wilson told me
later there was a
passage in her
husbands diary
which spoke of

the inexplicable
shortage of fuel &
kerosene on the
return journey.
Relatively ?
depots which
had not been
touched by means
and which
? only after

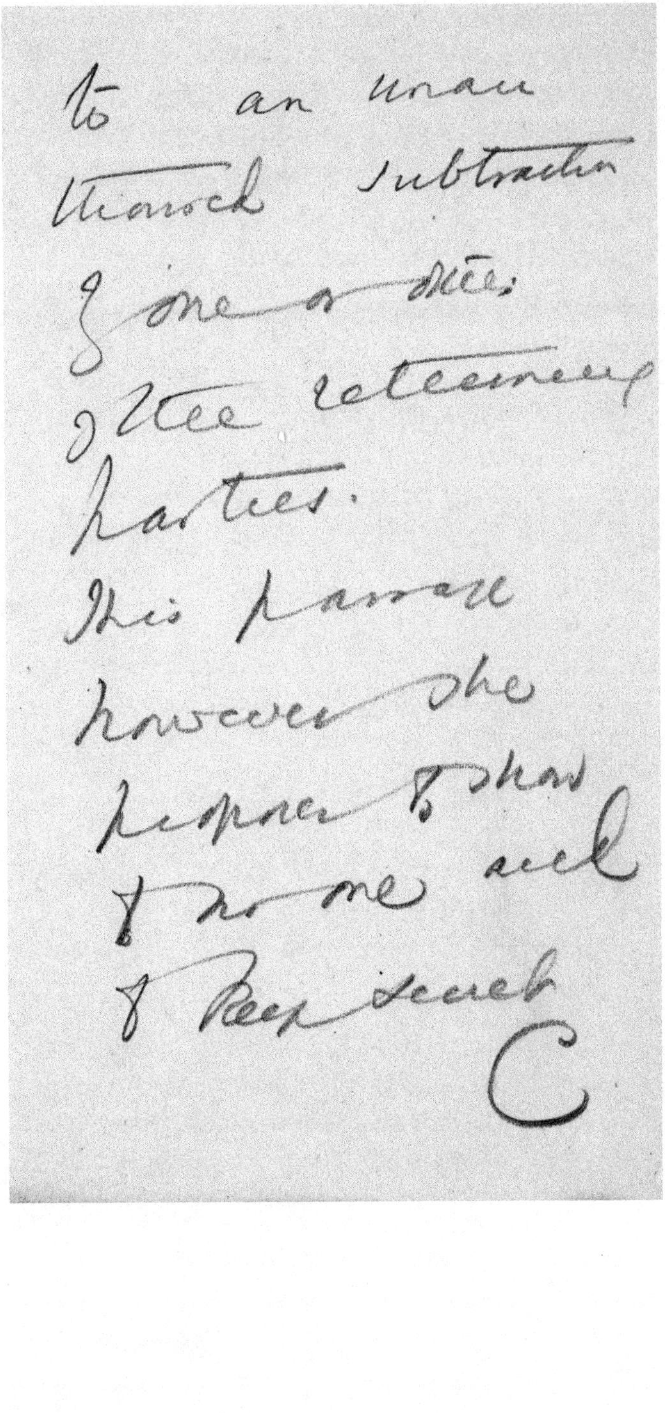
to an unau
thorised subtraction
of one or other
of the interested
parties.
This passage
however she
happens to show
to no one and
& keep secret
C

ACKNOWLEDGEMENTS

Writing a book has to be one of the most self-indulgent things anyone can do. It wouldn't be remotely possible without family, friends and colleagues being polite, feigning understanding, nodding at the right time, and giving me the time to talk endlessly about Antarctic exploration and science. It still surprises me just how many ideas come from talking about things. I owe you all a great deal: more than you will ever know.

Many people have patiently answered my questions, dug out files and helped me find my way about. Without the archives dedicated to preserving the documents relating to 1912, this book would never have happened. I'd particularly like to thank Naomi Boneham and Hilary Shibata at the Scott Polar Research Institute in Cambridge (UK); Mr Oyagi, Jun Kato and Ms Sasaki at the Shirase Antarctic Expedition Memorial Museum in Nikaho (Japan); Anne Melgård and Nina Korbu at the National Library in Oslo (Norway); Helmut Hornik at the Filchner Archive in Munich (Germany); Mark Pharaoh at the Mawson Archive in Adelaide (Australia); Peta Hayes, David Smith, Douglas Russell, Polly Parry and Paul Taylor at the Natural History Museum in London (UK); William Frame at the British Library in London; Frank Bowles at the Cambridge University Library; Kevin Leamon at the Mitchell

Library in Sydney (Australia); Jan Turner and David McNeill at the Royal Geographical Society in London; Verity Andrews at the University of Reading Special Collections Service (UK); Carol at the Nottingham Central Library (UK), for aiding research; Jane Britten and Libby Watters at the Woollahra Library in Sydney; and Vicki Farmery at the Tasmanian Museum and Art Gallery in Hobart (Australia). Their help made a huge difference.

A book on this subject and of this scope inevitably ends up being a journey of individual discovery. As part of my day job I was fortunate to work in the Antarctic in 2011 and 2012, and this had a tremendous impact on my understanding of the expeditions in the region one hundred years ago. Antarctic Logistics and Expeditions, the South Georgian government, and the British Antarctic Survey at King Edward Point were all incredibly supportive.

A host of other people also helped me find key facts or assisted me with equipment from 1912. Many thanks to Charlie Bird; Julia Collins at Madame Tussauds; Alan Cooper at the University of Adelaide; Nicholas Cox at the British Antarctic Survey; Richard Dennison at Orana Films; Bryony Dixon at the British Film Institute; Chris Fogwill and Charlotte Cook at the University of New South Wales; Brenda, Martin and Garth Franklin, who put up with me for months on end; Mark George; Stephen Haddelsey; Geir Hasle; Roland Huntford; Richard Jones at the University of Exeter; Matt McGlone at Landcare Research, New Zealand; Kathryn McLeod at the National Film and Sound Archive in Canberra; Greg Mortimer; John Murray; David Newton at the Honiton Clock Clinic; Billy Stevenson; Stephen Tredwin and Chris Turbitt at British Geological Survey; Tas van Ommen at the Australian Antarctic Division; Phil Wickham at the Bill Douglas Centre for the History of Cinema and Popular Culture, at the University of Exeter; and

Alan and Nikki Williams, whose humour and everlasting coffee supply kept me going.

Elaine Nipper prepared the fantastic maps—thanks for all your patience on these. Annegret Larsen, and Malin and Espen Hoiseth, kindly helped in translating sections of Wilhelm Filchner's, Xavier Mertz's and Hjalmar Johansen's diaries; without them I would have had little idea what I was reading. I'd also like to thank Bob and Irene Goard at Photantiques, and Ozzie Emery from Mittagong, Australia, who guided me in the use of early twentieth-century photography and which buttons to press; I wouldn't have known what I was doing without their help, and any shocking results are entirely my own responsibility!

I would like to thank the Bickerton, David, Davis, Mawson, Scott and Shackleton estates, for allowing me to quote from private correspondence. Crown copyright documents in the India Office Private Papers of the British Library appear by permission of the Controller of Her Majesty's Stationery Office. Sarah Strong granted me permission to cite documents held by the Royal Geographical Society. Lady Kennet kindly allowed me to view Lady Scott's diaries. And Mr William Krasilovsky kindly permitted me to quote from Robert W. Service's poem 'The Lure of Little Voices'.

Of course, if I have managed to get the wrong end of the stick on any matter it remains entirely my own fault. Every effort has been made to trace copyright owners, and I would be pleased to rectify any errors or omissions in future editions.

A particularly big thanks to my editor, David Winter, whose enthusiasm, endless patience and tireless good humour kept me focused and helped me to do justice to this incredible story. David, I owe you a few drinks for this one! Many thanks also to Michael Heyward, Rachel Shepheard, Anne Beilby and the other fantastic people at Text Publishing; Kay Peddle and Will

Sulkin at Bodley Head; and Jack Shoemaker at Counterpoint Press. I couldn't have done it without you.

Family is the backbone of any endeavour such as this. My parents, Cathy and Ian, were always enthusiastic. But most importantly my wife, Annette, and children, Cara and Robert, gave me everything I dared hope for: patience, encouragement and a judicious kick up the backside when it was needed.

This will be the last book for a while, I promise!

SOURCES

There is a wealth of books on early twentieth-century Antarctic exploration, and ever more manuscripts and articles are available online (many of them are out of print). In particular, the Ebook and Texts Archive (www.archive.org/details/texts) has an amazing range of works in high resolution.

1912 is intended to be as readable as possible, so I decided against using footnotes or endnotes. Fuller text references, linked to the relevant sources, can be found on my website (www.christurney.com).

Below, I have split the sources used into Books, Journal Articles and Reports, Newspaper and Magazine Articles, Films and Recordings, Unpublished Sources, and Websites, listed under the appropriate chapter. Apart from unpublished material, almost all of these works can be found in bookshops or libraries, or online. Institutions have brought some of the more precious film and sound recordings into the public domain, but there remains a lot of footage that can still only be accessed in certain archives around the world.

For Unpublished Sources, BL refers to the British Library (London); CUL is the Cambridge University Library (UK); MAC is the Mawson Antarctic Collection (Adelaide, Australia); ML is the Mitchell Library (Sydney, Australia); NB is the

National Library (Oslo, Norway); NFSA is the National Film and Sound Archive (Canberra, Australia); NLA is the National Library of Australia (Canberra); RGS is the Royal Geographic Society (London); SAEMM is the Shirase Antarctic Expedition Memorial Museum (Nikaho, Japan); SLV is the La Trobe Collection, State Library of Victoria (Melbourne, Australia); SPRI is the Scott Polar Research Institute (Cambridge, UK); and URL is the University of Reading Library (UK).

Some unpublished material was very lightly edited—primarily in punctuation—to ensure clarity.

I have endeavoured to contact the copyright holders of all unpublished material cited in the text. I apologise in advance for any omissions and would be delighted to add missing acknowledgements in future editions.

INTRODUCTION

Books

Fogg, G. E. 1992. *A History of Antarctic Science.* Cambridge University Press, Cambridge.

McGonigal, D., Woodworth, L. 2001. *Antarctica: The Complete Story.* Frances Lincoln, London.

MacPhee, R. D. E. 2010. *Race to the End: Amundsen, Scott and the Attainment of the South Pole.* Sterling Innovation, New York.

Wheeler, S. 1997. *Terra Incognita: Travels in Antarctica.* Vintage, London.

CHAPTER 1: LOOKING POLEWARDS

Books

Aughton, P. 2004. *Resolution: The Story of Captain Cook's Second Voyage of Discovery.* Weidenfeld & Nicolson, London.

Armitage, A. B. 1905. *Two Years in the Antarctic: Being a Narrative of the British National Antarctic Expedition.* Edward Arnold, London.

Borchgrevink, C. E. 1901. *First on the Antarctic Continent: Being an Account of the British Antarctic Expedition 1898–1900*. George Newnes, London.

Carpenter, K. J. 1986. *The History of Scurvy and Vitamin C*. Cambridge University Press, Cambridge.

Cook, F. A. 1900. *Through the First Antarctic Night 1898–1899: A Narrative of the Voyage of the 'Belgica' Among Newly Discovered Lands and Over an Unknown Sea About the South Pole*. Doubleday & McClure, New York.

Galton, F. 1878. *Hints to Travellers*. Edward Stanton, London.

de Gerlache, A. 1998. *Voyage of the Belgica: Fifteen Months in the Antarctic*. Erskine Press and Bluntisham Books, Norwich.

Lloyd, C., Coulter, J. 1963. *Medicine and the Navy, 1200–1900. Vol. IV (1815–1900)*. Livingstone, Edinburgh.

Markham, C. R. 1921. *The Lands of Silence: A History of Arctic and Antarctic Exploration*. Cambridge University Press, Cambridge.

Mawer, G. A. 2006. *South by Northwest: The Magnetic Crusade and the Contest for Antarctica*. Wakefield Press, Kent Town.

Murgatroyd, S. 2002. *The Dig Tree*. Text Publishing, Melbourne.

Murray, G. 1901. *The Antarctic Manual: For the Use of the Expedition of 1901*. Royal Geographic Society, London.

Scott, R. F. 1905. *The Voyage of the Discovery*. Smith, Elder & Co., London.

Speak, P. 2003. *William Speirs Bruce: Polar Explorer and Scottish Nationalist*. National Museums of Scotland, Edinburgh.

Stafford, R. A. 2002. *Scientist of Empire: Sir Roderick Murchison, Scientific Exploration and Victorian Imperialism*. Cambridge University Press, Cambridge.

Wilson, E. 1966. *Diary of the Discovery Expedition to the Antarctic Regions 1901–1904*. Blandford Press, London.

Journal Articles and Reports

Anonymous. 1830. Prospectus of the Royal Geographical Society. *Journal of the Royal Geographical Society* 1: vii–xii.

Bell, M., McEwan, C. 1996. The admission of women fellows to the Royal Geographical Society, 1892–1914: The controversy and the outcome. *Geographical Journal* 162: 295-312.

Fogg, G. E. 2005. A century of Antarctic science: Planning and serendipity. *Archives of Natural History* 32: 129–143.

Gregory, J. W. 1901. The work of the National Antarctic Expedition. *Nature* 63: 609–612.

Hamilton, R. V. 1906. Review: Antarctic exploration. *Geographical Journal* 27: 76–82.

Hinks, A. R. 1941. Antarctica discovered: A reply. *Geographical Review* 31: 491-498.

Lee, I. 1913. The voyages of Captain William Smith and others to the South Shetlands. *Geographical Journal* 42: 365–370.

McConnell, A. 2005. Surveying terrestrial magnetism in time and space. *Archives of Natural History* 32: 346–360.

Murray, J. 1913. Notes on the Antarctic soundings of the 'Aurora'. *Geographical Journal* 42: 362–364.

Murray, J. 1898. The scientific advantages of an Antarctic expedition. *Proceedings of the Royal Society of London* 62: 424–451.

Murray, J. 1894. The renewal of Antarctic exploration. *Geographical Journal* 3: 1–27.

von Neumayer, G. 1906. Recent Antarctic expeditions: Their results. *Geographical Journal* 27: 259–265.

Poulton, E. B. 1901. The National Antarctic Expedition. *Nature* 64: 83–86.

Rice, A. L. 2005. Discovery at sea: A heady mix of scientists, ships and sailors. *Archives of Natural History* 32: 177-191.

Richards, P. 2002. Inflation: The value of the pound 1750–2001. UK House of Commons Library, Research Paper 02/44, 22.

Newspaper and Magazine Articles

Curzon, G. N. 1893. Ladies and the Royal Geographical Society. *The Times* 31 May: 11.

Mullay, A. J. 2009. James Weddell and a debt of £245. *History Scotland* 9: 35–38.

Unpublished Sources

Letter from C. Markham to Lord Curzon, 9 November 1911. BL MSS EUR/F112/51.

CHAPTER 2: AN AUDACIOUS PLAN

Books

Branagan, D. 2005. *TW Edgeworth David: A Life*. National Library of Australia, Canberra.

Daly, R. W. 2009. *The Shackleton Letters: Behind the Scenes of the Nimrod Expedition*. Erskine Press, Norwich.

Darwin, C. 2006. *More Letters of Charles Darwin: Volume II*. Echo Library, Teddington.

Darwin, C. 1859. *The Origin of Species*. Penguin, London (republished 1985).

Drivenes, E.-A., Jølle, H. D. 2006. *Into the Ice: The History of Norway and the Polar Regions*. Glydendal Akademisk, Oslo.

Herbert, W. 1989. *The Noose of Laurels: The Discovery of the North Pole*. Hodder & Stoughton, London.

Hooker, J. D. 1844. *The Botany of the Antarctic Voyage of H. M. Discovery Ships Erebus and Terror in the Years 1839–1843: Flora Antarctica*. Reeve Brothers, London.

Huntford, R. 2009. *Nansen: The Explorer as Hero*. Abacus, London.

Huntford, R. 1996. *Shackleton*. Abacus, London.

Jackson, F. G. 1899. *A Thousand Days in the Arctic*. Harper & Brothers, London.

Mill, H. R. 1905. *The Siege of the South Pole*. F. A. Stokes Company, New York.

Mills, L. 2008. *Men of Ice: The Lives of Alister Forbes Mackay (1878–1914) and Cecil Henry Meares (1877–1937)*. Caedmon of Whitby, Whitby.

Nansen, F. 1898. *Farthest North. Being the Record of a Voyage of Exploration of the Ship Fram 1893–96 and of a Fifteen Months' Sleigh Journey by Dr. Nansen and Lieut. Johansen. With an Appendix by O. Sverdrup, Captain of the Fram (In Two Volumes)*. George Newnes, London.

Nield, T. 2007. *Supercontinent: Ten Billion Years in the Life of Our Planet*. Granta Books, London.

Ortmann, A. E. 1902. *Tertiary Invertebrates*. Princeton University, New York.

Riffenburgh, B. 2004. *Nimrod: Ernest Shackleton and the Extraordinary Story of the 1907–09 British Antarctic Expedition.* Bloomsbury, London.

Shackleton, E. H. 1909. *The Heart of the Antarctic: Being the Story of the British Antarctic Expedition 1907–1909 (In Two Volumes).* William Heinemann, London.

Suess, E. 1885. *Das Antlitz der Erde.* F Tempsky, Vienna.

Journal Articles and Reports

David, T. W. E., Priestley, R. E. 1914. *British Antarctic Expedition 1907 – Under the Command of Sir E. H. Shackleton, C. V. O. Reports of the Scientific Investigations: Geology.* William Heinemann, London.

David, E. 1913. Notes by Prof. Edgeworth David. *Nature* 91: 651.

David, T. W. E. 1904. The aims and ideals of Australian science. *Australasian Association for the Advancement of Science* (Dunedin, New Zealand): 1–43.

Ferrar, H. T. 1907. *Report on the Field Geology of the Region Explored During the 'Discovery' Antarctic Expedition.* 1901–05 National Antarctic Expedition, London, 1 (Geology).

F. G. D. 1910. The proposed Scottish National Antarctic Expedition of 1911. *Nature* 83: 101–102.

Read, W. J. 1856. On the applications of photography. *Sutton's Photographic Notes* 6 March: 130.

Shackleton, E. 1907. A new British Antarctic expedition. *Geographical Journal* 29: 329–332.

Shackleton, E. 1904. Life in the Antarctic. *Pearson's Magazine* XVII: 307–322.

Newspaper and Magazine Articles

Anonymous. 1910. The dash for the South Pole. *Penny Illustrated Paper* 30 April: 552.

Anonymous. 1910. South Pole rivals: Friendly messages across the Atlantic. *Manchester Guardian* 12 February: 9.

Anonymous. 1909. Peary to seek South Pole? Mailboat from Labrador reports he and Bartlett are going. *New York Times* 16 September: 1.

Anonymous. 1909. Commander Peary and the North Pole: Messages from the explorer. *The Times* 7 September: 3.

Anonymous. 1909. The North Pole: Dr. Cook describes his journey. *Manchester Guardian* 3 September: 7.

Anonymous. 1909. News from the Nimrod: Landing of Macquarie Island. *Sydney Morning Herald* 10 July: 13.

Anonymous. 1909. Mr Shackleton on his expedition: Presentation of medals by the prince. *The Times* 29 June: 10.

Anonymous. 1909. Mr Shackleton's Return. *The Times* 16 June: 11.

Anonymous. 1909. Mr. Shackleton in London. *The Times* 16 June: 10.

Anonymous. 1909. Nimrod's future work: Shackleton's scheme. *Sydney Morning Herald* 24 April: 13.

Anonymous. 1909. The explorers: Mr. Mawson in Sydney. *Sydney Morning Herald* 17 April: 13.

Anonymous. 1909. The Scottish Antarctic Expedition: Dr. Bruce's Plans. *The Times* 2 April: 23.

Anonymous. 1909. South Pole discoveries. Lieut. Shackleton's achievement. *Daily Mail* 25 March: 5.

Anonymous. 1909. Sir E. Shackleton on polar expeditions. *The Times* 7 January: 6.

Anonymous. 1908. Along Antarctic ice: Leaders' reported dissension. *Sydney Morning Herald* 13 April: 7.

Anonymous. 1907. New British expedition to the South Pole. *The Times* 12 February: 12.

Bernacchi, L. C. 1909. To the editor of *The Times*. *The Times* 6 September: 3.

Sprent, C. P. 1889. Antarctic Exploration. Mercury Office, Hobart.

Films and recordings

Shackleton, E. 1910. My South Polar Expedition. NFSA 562537. www.aso.gov.au/titles/spoken-word/my-south-polar-expedition

Unpublished sources

Correspondence of Antarctic Committee, Royal Geographical Society of Australasia, 1890s. ML MSS 7540/8.

Letter from T. W. E. David to A. Deakin (Australian Prime Minister), 10 December 1907. ML MSS. 3022/1 C73809.

Letter from T. W. E. David to E. Shackleton, 5 October 1909. ML MSS. 3022/1 C73809.

Letter from F. G. Jackson to A. Nansen, 8 April 1895. NB Brevs 36L.

Letter from F. G. Jackson to F. Nansen, 18 November 1892. NB Ms. fol. 1924: 2c3.

Letter from A. F. Mackay to Mr Mackay, 24 February 1909. ML DOC 3472.

C. Markham Journal, 15 November to 6 May 1913. RGS CRM/53.

Letter from D. Mawson to T. W. E. David, 28 September 1907. ML MSS. 3022/1 C73809.

Letter from R. Peary to Mr Reick, 27 November 1909. SPRI MS 761/11.

Letter from E. Shackleton to T. W. E. David, 8 February 1910. ML MSS. 3022/1 C73810.

Telegram from E. Shackleton to R. F. Scott, 4 March 1907. SPRI MS 25/2.

Letter from E. Shackleton to R. F. Scott, 18 February 1907. SPRI MS1537/2/14/8.

Letter from E. Shackleton to R. Skelton, 13 June 1907. SPRI MS 342/31.

Letter from R. Skelton to R. F. Scott, 8 October 1911. SPRI MS 342/14/9.

E. N. Webb. 1965. Magnetic Polar Journey 1912. ML MSS 6812.

CHAPTER 3: A NEW LAND

Books

Back, J. D. 1992. *The Quiet Land: The Diaries of Frank Debenham.* Bluntisham Books and Erskine Press, Bluntisham.

Briant, K. 1962. *Passionate Paradox: The Life of Marie Stopes.* W. W. Norton & Co., New York.

Bull, C., Wright, P. F. 1993. *Silas: The Antarctic Diaries and Memoir of Charles S. Wright.* Ohio State University Press, Columbus.

Cherry-Garrard, A. 2003. *The Worst Journey in the World.* Pimlico, London (originally published 1922).

Crane, D. 2006. *Scott of the Antarctic.* Harper Perennial, London.

Evans, E. R. G. R. 1921. *South with Scott*. Collins Clear-Type Press, London.

Fiennes, R. 2003. *Captain Scott*. Hodder & Stoughton, London.

Huntford, R. 2009. *Scott and Amundsen: Their Race to the South Pole*. Abacus, London.

Huxley, E. 1977. *Scott of the Antarctic*. Weidenfeld and Nicolson, London.

King, H. G. R. 1988. *The Wicked Mate: The Antarctic Diary of Victor Campbell*. Erskine Press and Bluntisham Books, Norwich.

Lee, G. 2008. *The People's Budget: An Edwardian Tragedy*. Shepheard-Walwyn, London.

Levick, G. M. 1914. *Antarctic Penguins: A Study of Their Habits*. McBride, Nast & Co., New York.

Scott, R. F. 2008. *Journals: Captain Scott's Last Expedition* (edited by M. Jones). Oxford University Press, Oxford.

Scott, R. F. 1913. *Scott's Last Expedition (In Two Volumes)*. Macmillan and Co., London.

Strange, C, Bashford, A. 2008. *Griffith Taylor: Visionary, Environmentalist, Explorer*. University of Toronto Press, Toronto.

Wilson, E. 1972. *Diary of the Terra Nova Expedition to the Antarctic 1910–1912*. Humanities Press, New York.

Journal Articles and Reports

Chree, C. 1908. Presidential address to the Physical Society of London, 14th February, 1908. *Proceedings of the Physical Society of London* XXI: xi–xxxii.

David, T. W. E., Smeeth, W. F., Schofield, J. A. 1895. Notes on Antarctic rocks collected by Mr C. E. Borchgrevink. *The Royal Society of New South Wales Journal* 29: 461–492.

Debenham, F. 1923. *Report on the Maps and Surveys: British (Terra Nova) Antarctic Expedition 1910–1913*. Harrison and Sons, London.

Lyons, H. G. 1924. *British (Terra Nova) Antarctic Expedition 1910–1913: Miscellaneous Data*. Harrison and Sons, London.

Markham, C. 1912. Antarctic discovery at the British Association. *Geographical Journal* 40: 541–546.

Royds, C. W. R. 1905. Meteorological observing in the Antarctic regions. *Quarterly Journal of the Royal Meteorological Society* 39: 1–14.

Scott, R. F. 1910. Plans of the British Antarctic Expedition, 1910. *Geographical Journal* 36: 11–20.

Scott, R. F. 1905. Results of the National Antarctic Expedition. 1. Geographical. *Geographical Journal* 25: 353–370.

von den Steinen, K. 1891. Allgemeines über die zoologische Thätigkeit und Beobachtungen über das Leben der Robben und Vögel aus Süd-Georgie. In *Die Internationale Polarforschung 1882–83. Die Deutschen Expeditionen und Ihre Ergebnisse.* (G. Neumayer, ed.) A. Asher & Co., Berlin, 194–279.

Walker, M. 2005. Antarctic meteorology and climatology: an unfolding story of discovery. *Archives of Natural History* 32: 316–333.

Wilson, E., Bowers, H. 2011. *A Tale for Our Generation: An Account of the 'Winter Journey'.* Australian Capital Equity, Perth.

Wilson, E. A. 1907. *Aves. National Antarctic Expedition, 1901–4, Natural History Vol. II, Zoology.* British Museum, London.

Newspaper and Magazine Articles

Anonymous. 1912. Captain Scott's comment on Amundsen. *Manchester Guardian* 5 April: 5.

Anonymous. 1912. South Pole quest achieved: Triumph of Captain Amundsen. *Manchester Guardian* 9 March: 9.

Anonymous. 1911. Captain Scott in the Antarctic. *Manchester Guardian* 7 November: 7.

Anonymous. 1910. Captain Scott's Wolseley sleighs. *Commercial Motor* 7 April: 96.

Anonymous. 1910. Antarctic expedition: Support for Captain Scott in Manchester. *Manchester Guardian* 17 February: 14.

Anonymous. 1910. Captain Scott in Manchester yesterday. *Manchester Guardian* 17 February: 5.

Anonymous. 1909. The British Antarctic Expedition: Problems of the South Pole. *The Times* 13 October: 12.

Anonymous. 1909. Captain Scott's Expedition. *The Times* 14 September: 8.

Turner, H. H. 1908. Antarctic weather. *Times Literary Settlement* 13 August: 258.

Wilson, E. A. 1912. British Antarctic Expedition. Report of the work. *The Times* 16 May: 5.

Films and Recordings

Ponting, H. G. 1924. *The Great White Silence*. British Film Institute (rereleased with new score 2011).

Ponting, H. G. 1912. *With Captain Scott at the South Pole*. NFSA 9730.

Unpublished Sources

Letter from V. Campbell to Miss V. Campbell, 17 August 1911. SPRI MS 1363/1.

Letter from L. Darwin to R. F. Scott, 31 June 1909. SPRI MS 145 3/72.

Letter from E. Evans to J. P. Irven, 5 July 1912. ML DOC 1468.

Letter from C. Markham to S. Keltie, 1 March 1912. RGS CB7 Box 3 of 3, File 2 of 9, 3/2.

Letter from R. Skelton to R. F. Scott, 31 March 1910. SPRI MS 342/14/5.

Letter from R. Skelton to R. F. Scott, 12 June 1907. SPRI MS 342/14/2.

Letter by R. Skelton regarding motorised sledge design, 11 June 1907. SPRI MS 342/10/1/5.

Scott, R. F. 1911. Proposed Plans for Southern Journey. SPRI MS MS 1453/28.

CHAPTER 4: OF REINDEER, PONIES AND AUTOMOBILES

Books

Amundsen, R. 1928. *My Life as an Explorer*. Doubleday, Doran & Co., Inc., New York.

Amundsen, R. 1912. *The South Pole: An Account of the Norwegian Antarctic Expedition in the 'Fram', 1910–1912*. John Murray, London.

Amundsen, R. 2010. *The Roald Amundsen Diaries: The South Pole Expedition 1910–12*. The Fram Museum, Oslo.

Amundsen, R. 1908. *'The North West Passage': Being the Record of a Voyage of Exploration of the Ship 'Gjoa' 1903–1907*. E.P. Dutton and Co., New York.

Bomann-Larsen, T. 2006. *Roald Amundsen.* Sutton Publishing, Stroud.

Bowman, W. E. 2001. *The Ascent of Rum Doodle.* Pimlico, London (originally published 1956).

Huntford, R. 2010. *Race to the South Pole: The Expedition Diaries of Scott and Amundsen.* Continuum, London.

Huntford, R. 2009. *Scott and Amundsen: Their Race to the South Pole.* Abacus, London.

Journal Articles and Reports

Amundsen, R. 1913. The Norwegian south polar expedition. *Scottish Geographical Journal* 29: 1–13.

Amundsen, R. 1912. Amundsen's expedition to the South Pole. *Bulletin of the American Geographical Society* 44: 822–838.

Barr, W. 1985. Aleksandr Stepanovich Kuchin: the Russian who went south with Amundsen. *Polar Record* 22: 401–412.

Brown, R. N. R. 1913. The South Pole: A review. *Scottish Geographical Journal* 29: 17–22.

Drewry, D. J., Huntford, R. 1979. Amundsen's route to the South Pole. *Polar Record* 19: 329–336.

Hann, J. 1909. Die meteorologischen ergebnisse der Englischen Antarktischen Expedition, 1901–4. *Meteorologische Zeitschrift* 26: 289–301.

Hinks, A. R. 1910. Notes on determination of position near the Poles. *Geographical Journal* 35: 299–303.

Mill, H. R. 1913. Review: Amundsen's 'South Pole': A review. *Geographical Journal* 41: 148–151.

Mohn, H. 1915. *Roald Amundsen's Antarctic Expedition Scientific Results: Meteorology.* Kommission Hos Jacob Dybwad, Kristiania, 78.

Rees, W. G. 1988. Polar mirages. *Polar Record* 24: 193–198.

Shackleton, E., Bruce, W. S. 1913. The Norwegian South Polar expedition: Discussion. *Geographical Journal* 41: 13–16.

Newspaper and Magazine Articles

Anonymous. 1912. Amundsen's success. Conclusive proof. Professor David's tribute. *Sydney Morning Herald* 4 April: 10.

Anonymous. 1912. Copyright test here interests England. *New York Times* 21 March: 4.

Anonymous. 1912. The Uncertain 'Pole': Margin of possible error in locating it. *Observer* 10 March: 9.

Anonymous. 1912. At random. *Observer* 10 March: 7.

Anonymous. 1912. The conquest of the South Pole. *The Times* 9 March: 8.

Anonymous. 1912. Captain Amundsen's achievement. *The Times* 9 March: 5.

Anonymous. 1912. The South Pole. *Manchester Guardian* 8 March: 8.

Anonymous. 1912. The South Pole discovered: Norwegian explorer reaches coveted goal. *Daily Chronicle* 8 March: 1.

Anonymous. 1911. South Pole explorations. *National Geographic* xxii: 406–409.

Anonymous. 1909. New polar expedition: Captain Amundsen's next attempt. *Manchester Guardian* 26 January: 8.

Coetzer, C. 2012. South Pole anniversary final week interview with Henry Worsley. *Explorersweb*, 27 March: www.explorersweb.com/polar/news.php?id=20700

Films and Recordings

Norsk Film Institut. 2010. *Roald Amundsens Sydpolsferd (1910–1912)* (DVD and accompanying book). Norsk Film Institut.

Unpublished Sources

Map of South Magnetic Pole and declination to South Pole. NB Brevs. 480A.

Lantern slides used as part of Roald Amundsen's 1912 'South Polar Expedition' lecture at the Royal Geographical Society. RGS LS/676.

Telegram from R. Amundsen to F. Nansen, 7 March 1912. NB Ms. fol. 1924:5,3.

R. Amundsen South Pole Observations. NB MS. 8° 1196:17.

Letter from R. Amundsen to O. O. Bjaaland, 8 September 1909. NB Brevs 812:3.

Letter from R. Amundsen to F. Cook, 3 September 1909. NB Brevs 812:3.

Letter from R. Amundsen to H. Edmonds, 22 July 1910. NB Brevs 812:3.

Letter from R. Amundsen to H. Edmonds, 13 September 1909. NB Brevs 812:3.

Letter from R. Amundsen to H. Edmonds, 31 August 1909. NB Brevs 812:3.

Letter from R. Amundsen to J. S. Keltie, 22 October 1910. NB Brevs 812:3.

Letter from R. Amundsen to F. Nansen, 22 August 1910. NB Ms. fol. 1924:5,3.

Letter from R. Amundsen to K. Prestrud, 8 September 1909. NB Brevs 812 3.

Letter from R. Amundsen to Mr. Reid (BAE Secretary), 16 February 1910. NB Brevs 812 3.

Letter from L. A. Bauer to R. Amundsen, 5 August 1910. NB Brevs. nr. 812:1.

Letter from L. A. Bauer to R. Amundsen, 6 December 1909. NB Brevs. nr. 812:1.

Letter from British Admiralty to L. Amundsen, 11 March 1909. NB Brevs. 812 2b.

Letter from W. S. Bruce to L. Amundsen, 13 December 1912. NB Brevs. 812:2i.

Lantern slide used as part of Edgeworth David's 1914 lecture at the Royal Geographical Society. 'Plan showing changes in the edge of the Ross Barrier near Amundsen's headquarters at the Bay of Whales since the time of Scott's Expedition in the "Discovery" in 1902. The outline of the Bay of Whales in 1911 is after Amundsen.' RGS LS/333.

Letter from H. M. W. Edmonds to R. Amundsen, 5 August 1909. NB Brevs. nr. 812:1.

Letter from H. M. W. Edmonds to R. Amundsen, 1 July 1910. NB Brevs. nr. 812:1.

Letter from W. Heinemann to F. Nansen, 18 March 1912. NB Ms. fol. 1924 5,3 Mars 1912.

Letter from W. Heinemann to F. Nansen, 9 March 1912. NB Ms. fol. 1924 5,3 Mars 1912.

Letter from F. G. Jackson to R. Amundsen, 18 April 1900. NB Brevs 812:1.

H. Johansen Diary. NB MS. 4° 2775:C5.

Letter from J. S. Keltie to L. Amundsen, 7 October 1912. NB Brevs 812:2i.

Letter from J. S. Keltie to L. Amundsen, 24 September 1912. NB Brevs 812:2i.

Letter from J. S. Keltie to R. Amundsen, 4 July 1912. NB Brevs 812:2i.

Letter from J. S. Keltie to L. Amundsen, 20 April 1912. NB Brevs. 812:2i.

Letter from J. S. Keltie to L. Amundsen, 9 October 1909. NB Brevs 812:2i.

Letter from J. S. Keltie to L. Amundsen, 28 July 1909. NB Brevs 812:2i.

Letter from J. S. Keltie to R. Amundsen, 12 October 1906. NB Brevs 812:2i.

Letter from C. Markham to S. Keltie, 1 March 1912. RGS CB7 Box 3 of 3, File 2 of 9, 3/2.

F. Nansen. Scientific Guidance for R. Amundsen, 1901. NB MS. 4° 2670.

Letter from E. Shackleton to L. Amundsen, 12 July 1911. NB Brevs. nr. 812:1.

E. Searle. *Tasmanian Views*. Photographs of Australia, Antarctica and the Pacific, 1911–1915. NLA 3044988.

CHAPTER 5: THE DASH PATROL

Books

Asahina, K. 1973. The Japanese Antarctic Expedition of 1911–12. *In Polar Human Biology: The Proceedings of the SCAR/IUPS/IUBS Symposium on Human Biology and Medicine in the Antarctic.* (O. G. Edholm and E. K. E. Gunderson, eds.) William Heinemann Medical Books, London, 8–14.

Shirase Antarctic Expedition Supporters' Association. 2011. *The Japanese South Polar Expedition of 1910–12: A Record of Antarctica (Translated into English by Lara Dagnell and Hilary Shibata).* Erskine Press and Bluntisham Books, Norwich (originally published in Japanese in 1913 by Nankyoku Tanken Koenkai, Tokyo).

Toshitaka, S. 2002. *Yamato Snow Plain in Antarctica: Shirase's Expedition Story.* Fukuinkan Shoten Publisher, Tokyo.

Journal Articles and Reports

Anonymous. 1911. Japanese Antarctic Expedition. *Scottish Geographical Journal* xxvii: 314–315.

Anonymous. 1911. Japanese Antarctic Expedition. *Scottish Geographical Journal* xxvii: 151–152.

Byrd, R. E., Saunders, H. E. 1933. The flight to Marie Byrd Land: With a description of the map. *Geographical Review* 23: 177–209.

Darwin, C. 1839. Note on a rock seen on an iceberg in 61°S. lat. *Journal of the Royal Geographical Society of London* 9: 526–528.

Hamre, I. 1933. The Japanese South Polar Expedition of 1911–1912: A little-known episode in Antarctic exploration. *Geographical Journal* 82: 411–423.

Stevenson III, W. R. 2011. Science, the South Pole, and the Japanese expedition of 1910–1912. *Endeavour* 35: 160–168.

Swan, R. A. 1955. Forgotten Antarctic venture: The first Japanese south polar expedition 1911–1912. *Walkabout Magazine* 21: 31–33.

Newspaper and Magazine Articles

Anonymous. 1912. Japanese explorers. Return to Sydney. *Sydney Morning Herald* 5 April: 8.

Anonymous. 1912. Japanese return. From Antarctica. *Sydney Morning Herald* 25 March: 9.

Anonymous. 1912. The race to the South Pole: News possible at any moment. *Manchester Guardian* 29 February: 5.

Anonymous. 1911. Japanese Bound South. *Daily Telegraph* 20 November: 9.

Anonymous. 1911. The Australian Antarctic Expedition—Departure of Dr. Mawson. *Town and Country Journal* 15 November 28.

Anonymous. 1911. Swore by Buddha they'd find South Pole but Jap expedition was miserable failure. *Tacoma Times* 28 August: 8.

Anonymous. 1911. Another dash for the Pole: Count Okuma to raise funds for second venture of Lieut. Shiraze. *Japan Times* 22 July: 762–763.

Anonymous. 1911. Spy mania. *Daily Telegraph* 16 May: 6.

Anonymous. 1911. Japanese espionage. *Clarence and Richmond Examiner* 16 May: 5.

Anonymous. 1911. The mysterious Japs: Vaucluse camp deserted. *Sun* 15 May: 1 and 5.

Anonymous. 1911. Antarctic fiasco: Why the Japanese expedition failed. *Observer* 7 May: 6.

Anonymous. 1910. The siege of the South Pole: A Japanese expedition. *Manchester Guardian* 7 June: 7.

Shirase, N. 1912. The first Japanese Polar Expedition. *Independent* (New York) 73: 769–773.

Films and Recordings

Taizumo, Y. 1912. *The Japanese South Polar Expedition*. M. Pathe film company, Japan. SAEMM.

Unpublished Sources

Telegram from T. W. E. David to N. Shirase. March 1912. SAEMM.

Japanese map, 'Present Antarctic Continent with South Polar Regions drawn to illustrate the probable topography as well as the effects of Messrs Amundsen's and Shirase's expedition to the Antarctic. By M. Ikeda "Nogakushi" (Chief Scientist to Mr. Shirase's Antarctic Expedition).' Received by the Royal Geographical Society 13 June 1913. RGS mr Antarctic S/G.10.

Letter from S. Keltie to Lord Curzon, 7 September 1912. RGS CB8 1911-20 2 of 7.

CHAPTER 6: LOCKED IN

Books

Filchner, W. 1922. *Zum Sechsten Erdteil*. Im Verlag Ullstein, Berlin.

Filchner, W. 1994. *To the Sixth Continent: The Second German South Pole Expedition*. Bluntisham Books and Erskine Press, Bluntisham (originally published in Berlin, 1922).

Filchner, W. 1903. *Ein Ritt über den Pamir*. E. S. Mittler u. Sohn, Berlin.

Hart, I. B. 2006. *Whaling in the Falkland Islands Dependencies 1904–1931: A History of Shore and Bay-Based Whaling in the Antarctic*. Pequena, Newton St Margarets.

Hasle, G. 2008. *Isens Menn: Under Fremmed Flagg* Vega Forlag, Oslo.

Lunde, S.-T. 2004. *Grytviken: Seen Through a Camera Lens.* Institut Minos.

Murphy, D. T. 2002. *German Exploration of the Polar World: A History, 1870–1940.* Universty of Nebraska Press, Lincoln.

Journal Articles and Reports

Anonymous. 1911. The Monthly Record. *Geographical Journal* 37: 312–323.

Anonymous. 1911. The German Antarctic Expedition. *The Times* 4 January: 5.

Anonymous. 1904. Gaussberg in the Antarctic. *Bulletin of the American Geographical Society* 36: 559–560.

Balch, E. S. 1912. Recent Antarctic discoveries. *Bulletin of the American Geographical Society* 44: 161–167.

Barkow, E. 1913. Vorläufiger bericht über die meteorologischen beobachtungen der Deutschen Antarktischen expedition 1911/12. *Veröffentlichungen des Königlich Preußischen Meteorologischen Instituts,* Berlin, Nr. 265, Abhandlungen Bd. IV. Nr. 11, 11.

Brennecke, W. 1921. Die ozeanographischen arbeiten der Deutschen Antarktischen Expedition 1911–1912 (Forschungsschiff 'Deutschland'). *Aus dem Arkhiv der Deutschen Seewarte und des Marine-Observatoriums* 39: 1–216.

Brennecke, W. 1914. Deutsche Antarktische Expedition. Die ozeanographischen arbeiten im Weddell-Meer. *Zeitschrift der Gesellschaft für Erdkunde zu Berlin* 2: 118–129.

Cunningham, S. A. 2005. Southern Ocean circulation. *Archives of Natural History* 32: 265–280.

Filchner, W., Przybyllok, E. 1913. The German Antarctic Expedition. *Bulletin of the American Geographical Society* 45: 423–430.

Filchner, W. 1911. *Denkschrift über die Deutsche Antarktische Expedition.* E. S. Mittler & Sohn, Berlin.

Hamilton, R. V. 1869–1870. On Morrell's Antarctic voyage in the year 1823, with remarks on the advantages steam will confer on future Antarctic explorers. *Proceedings of the Royal Geographical Society of London* 14: 145–156.

Holdich, T., Murray, J., Beaumont, L., Buchanan, J. Y., Markham, A. 1904. The German Antarctic Expedition: Discussion. *Geographical Journal* 24: 148–152.

Hornik, H., Lüdecke, C. 2007. Wilhelm Filchner and Antarctica. *In Steps of Foundation of Institutionalized Antarctic Research Proceedings of the 1st SCAR Workshop on the History of Antarctic Research Bavarian Academy of Sciences and Humanities, Munich (Germany), 2–3 June, 2005.* (C. Lüdecke, ed.) Berichte zur Polar- und Meeresforschung, 52–63.

Kirschmer, G. 1985. *Dokumentation über die Antarktisexpedition 1911/1912 von Wilhelm Filchner.* Deutsche Geodätische Kommission, München.

Mills, E. L. 2005. From Discovery to discovery: the hydrology of the Southern Ocean, 1885–1937. *Archives of Natural History* 32: 246–264.

Penck, A. 1914. Antarktische probleme. *Sitzungsberichte der Königlich Preussischen Akademie der Wissenchaften*: 50–69.

Przybyllok, E. 1913. Deutsche Antarcktische Expedition. Bericht über die tätigkeit nach verlassen von Südgeorgien. *Zeitschrift der Gesellschaft für Erdkunde zu Berlin* 5: 1–17.

Schott, W. 1987. *Early German Oceanographic Institutions, Expeditions and Oceanographers.* Deutsches Hydrographisches Institut, Hamburg.

Newspaper and Magazine Articles

Anonymous. 1912. The race to the South Pole: News possible at any moment. *Manchester Guardian* 29 February: 5.

Anonymous. 1911. The German Antarctic expedition. *The Times* 4 January: 5.

Anonymous. 1910. The Antarctic expeditions. *The Times* 15 July: 10.

Anonymous. 1910. The Antarctic expeditions: British and German co-operation. *Manchester Guardian* 13 July: 14.

Anonymous. 1910. The ethics of exploration. *Manchester Guardian* 10 March: 7.

Anonymous. 1910. German expedition to the South Pole: Ambitious plan. *Manchester Guardian* 7 March: 6.

Anonymous. 1909. The Scottish Antarctic expedition: Dr. Bruce's plans. *The Times* 2 April: 23.

Anonymous. 1899. The German Antarctic Expedition. *Geographical Journal* 13: 406–410.

Mossman, R. C. 1914. The Weddell Sea: Sir Ernest Shackleton's plans. *The Times* January 5: 9–10.

Unpublished Sources

Letter from W. Filchner to W. Bruce, 6 July 1911. SPRI MS 101/41/7.

Letter from W. Filchner to H. R. Mill, 13 January 1911. SPRI MS 100/35/2.

Letter from W. Filchner to W. Bruce, 29 October 1910. SPRI MS 101/41/2.

Letter from W. Filchner to H. R. Mill, 15 October 1910. SPRI MS 100/35/1.

CHAPTER 7: ICE-COLD IN DENISON

Books

Ayres, P. 2003. *Mawson: A Life*. Melbourne University Press, Melbourne.

Bickel, L. 2000. *Mawson's Will: The Greatest Polar Survival Story Ever Written*. Steerforth Press, Hanover.

Crossley, L. 1997. *Trial by Ice: The Antarctic Journals of John King Davis*. Bluntisham Books and Erskine Press, Bluntisham.

Davis, J. K. 2007. *With the 'Aurora' in the Antarctic 1911–1914*. Erskine Press and Bluntisham Books, Norwich (Originally published in 1919 by Andrew Melrose Ltd).

Davis, J. K. 1962. *High Latitude*. Melbourne University Press, Melbourne.

Flannery, N. R. 2005. *This Everlasting Silence: The Love Letters of Paquita Delprat and Douglas Mawson 1911–1914*. Melbourne University Press, Melbourne.

Haddelsey, S. 2005. *Born Adventurer: The Life of Frank Bickerton, Antarctic Pioneer*. Sutton Publishing, London.

Hayes, J. G. 1928. *Antarctica*. Richards Press, London.

Holmes, A. 1965. *Principles of Physical Geology*. Thomas Nelson and Sons Ltd, London.

Jacka, F., Jacka, E. 1988. *Mawson's Antarctic Diaries*. Allen and Unwin, London.

Laseron, C. F. 1957. *South With Mawson*. Angus & Robertson, Sydney.

Marr, J. E. 1903. *The Scientific Study of Scenery*. Methuen & Co., London.

Mawson, P. 1964. *Mawson of the Antarctic.* Longmans, Green and Co. Ltd, London.

Mawson, D. 1915. *The Home of the Blizzard: Being the Story of the Australasian Antarctic Expedition, 1911–1914.* William Heinemann, London.

Rossiter, H. 2011. *Mawson's Forgotten Men: The 1911–1913 Antarctic Diary of Charles Turnbull Harrisson.* Pier 9, Sydney.

Journal Articles and Reports

The scientific reports of the Australasian Antarctic Expedition are available as free PDF downloads at http://mawsonshuts.antarctica.gov.au/national-heritage/scientific-reports.

Bayly, P. G. W., Stillwell, F. L. 1923. Geology. Part 1: The Adelie Land meteorite. *Australasian Antarctic Expedition 1911–14 Scientific Report, Series A, Volume IV.* A. J. Kent, Sydney, 18.

Chree, C. 1909. Presidential address to the Physical Society of London, 12th February, 1909. *Proceedings of the Physical Society of London* XXI: xiii–xxxii.

Close, J. H. C. 1929. With Mawson on the Antarctic ice. *Australian Geographer* 1: 94–96.

Dana, J. D. 1873. On some results of the Earth's contraction from cooling, including a discussion of the origin of mountains, and the nature of the Earth's interior. *American Journal of Science (3rd Series)* 5 (30): 423–443.

Davis, J. K. 1913. The soundings of the Antarctic ship 'Aurora' between Tasmania and the Antarctic Continent (1912). *Geographical Journal* 42: 361–362.

Fisher, O. 1882. On the physical cause of the ocean basins. *Nature* 25: 243–244.

Kidson, E. 1946. Meteorology. Discussions of observations at Adelie Land, Queen Mary Land and Macquarie Island. *Australasian Antarctic Expedition 1911–14 Scientific Report, Series B, Volume VI.* T. H. Tennant, Sydney, 121.

Lucas, A., Henderson, C., Leane, E., Kriwoken, L. 2011. A flight of the imagination: Mawson's Antarctic aeroplane. *Polar Journal* 1: 63–75.

McLean, A. L. 1919. Bacteriological and other researches. *Australasian Antarctic Expedition 1911–14 Scientific Report, Series C, Volume VII. Part 4.* W. A. Gullick, Sydney, 141.

Madigan, C. T. 1929. Meteorology. Tabulated and reduced records of the Cape Denison Station, Adelie Land. *Australasian Antarctic Expedition 1911–14 Scientific Report, Series B, Volume IV.* A. J. Kent, Sydney, 304.

Mawson, D. 1940. Geology. Part 12. Record of minerals of King George Land, Adelie Land and Queen Mary Land. *Australasian Antarctic Expedition 1911–14 Scientific Report, Series A, Volume IV.* T. H. Tennant, Sydney, 36.

Mawson, D. 1929. Part 1. Narrative. Part 2. Cartography. *Australasian Antarctic Expedition 1911–14 Scientific Report, Series A, Volume I.* G. P. Office, Sydney, 492.

Mawson, D. 1925. Terrestrial magnetism and related observations. Part 1. Records of the Aurora Polaris. *Australasian Antarctic Expedition 1911–14 Scientific Report, Series B, Volume II.* A. J. West, Sydney, 199.

Mawson, D. 1914. Australasian Antarctic Expedition, 1911–1914. *Geographical Journal* 44: 257–284.

Mawson, D. 1911. The Australasian Antarctic Expedition. *Geographical Journal* 37: 609–617.

Shackleton, E. 1912. The future of exploration. *North American Review* 195: 414–424.

Shearman, D. J. C. 1978. Vitamin A and Sir Douglas Mawson. *British Medical Journal* 1: 283–285.

Simpson, G. C., Wright, C. S. 1911. Atmospheric electricity over the ocean. *Proceedings of the Royal Society of London. Series A, Containing Papers of a Mathematical and Physical* 85: 175–199.

Siple, P. A., Passell, C. F. 1945. Measurements of dry atmospheric cooling in subfreezing temperatures. *Proceedings of the American Philosophical Society* 89: 177–199.

Turnour, Q. 2007. 'A.K.A. Home of the Blizzard': Fact and artefact in the film on the Australasian Antarctic Expedition, 1911–1914. *NFSA Journal* 2: 1–12.

Webb, E. N. 1977. Location of the South Magnetic Pole. *Polar Record* 18: 610–611.

Webb, E. N., Chree, C. 1925. Terrestrial magnetism. *Australasian Antarctic Expedition 1911–14 Scientific Report, Series B, Volume I*. A. J. Kent, Sydney, 305.

Newspaper and Magazine Articles

Anonymous. 1915. Captain Scott's example. *Observer* 24 January.

Anonymous. 1913. Sir Ernest Shackleton's view: Mawson's position obscure. *Manchester Guardian* 26 February: 7.

Anonymous. 1911. The race to the South Pole: Dr. Mawson's expedition. *The Times* 21 November: 5.

Anonymous. 1911. Mawson expedition: No aeroplane flight. *Sydney Morning Herald* 31 October: 9.

Anonymous. 1911. Lieut. Watkins and the Vickers monoplane. *Flight* 5 August: 684.

Anonymous. 1911. Lectures: Australasian Association for the Advancement of Science Antarctic Committee. *Sydney Morning Herald* 22 June: 1.

Bruce, WS. 1914. Two years spent on the polar ice: Dr. Mawson's return. *Manchester Guardian* 27 February: 9.

Masson, O., David, T. W. E., Henderson, G. C. 1911. The Australasian Antarctic Expedition. *Sydney Morning Herald* 22 April: 9.

Masson, O., David, T. W.E., Henderson, G. C. 1911. Antarctic Expedition: An Australian project. *Advertiser* (Adelaide) 22 April: 23.

Mawson, D. 1911. Sir Ernest Shackleton's appeal. Dr. Mawson's thanks. *Daily Mail* 13 May: 8.

Shackleton, E. 1911. An appeal from Sir E. Shackleton. The Australasian Antarctic Expedition. *Daily Mail* 8 May: 9.

Films and Recordings

Hurley, F. 1913. *Home of the Blizzard*. NFSA 6465.

Hurley, F. 1911. *The Mawson Australasian Antarctic Expedition 1911–1913*. NFSA 1356.

Unpublished Sources

F. Bickerton. Western Sledging Diary, 1912–1913. SPRI MS 1775/1.

Letter from C. Chree to T. W. E. David, 13 April 1912. ML MSS. 3022/1 C73810.

Letter of introduction from T. W. E. David for J.K. Davis, 16 April 1913. SLV MS8311 3269/10.

Letter from T. W. E. David to C. C. Farr, 1 February 1912. ML MSS. 3022/1 C73810.

J. K. Davis. Private Journal of S. Y. Aurora, 14 August 1911 – 15 March 1913. SLV MS8311 3232/5.

Letter from J. K. Davis to W. S. Bruce, 21 December 1912. SPRI MS 101/35/10.

Letter from J. K. Davis to W. S. Bruce, 26 September 1911 SPRI MS 101/35/7.

Letter from J. K. Davis to T. W. E. David, 24 September 1913. ML MSS. 3022/1 C73810.

Letter from W. Filchner to A. Reid, 11 September 1911. MAC 159 AAE/1.

W. H. Hannam. Diary. ML MSS 384.

Letter from W. Heinemann to D. Mawson, 10 May 1918. MAC 151 AAE.

Letter left at cairn from A. Hodgeman, F. Hurley and A. McLean for D. Mawson, 29 January 1913. MAC 49 AAE.

F. Hurley. Southern Sledging Party Diary. ML MSS 389/1.

A. McLean. Diary 1911–1914. ML MSS 382 2 (2).

D. Mawson. Untitled appeal for funding to cover AAE debts, undated. ML MSS 3022/5 Item 4.

D. Maswon. Rough Draft of Meteorological Notes, Far East Journey. MAC 69 AAE.

Letter from D. Mawson to A. Geikie, Jan/Feb 1910. SPRI MS1517/1.

Letter from D. Mawson to H. R. Mill, 18 July 1922 SPRI MS 100/75/6;D.

Letter from D. Mawson to H. E. Scrope, 16 March 1956. MAC 23 DM.

Notes by D. Mawson on L. Whetter, AAE Main Base. MAC 43 AAE.

X. Mertz. Far Eastern Party Diary Island (in German). MAC 70 AAE.

A. J. Sawyer. Macquarie Island diary. ML MSS 383.

Letter from R. F. Scott to T. W. E. David, 11 May 1910. ML MSS. 3022/1 C73810.

Letter from R. Skelton to R. F. Scott, 8 October 1911. SPRI MS 342/14/9.

Tasmanian Government authority for AAE to establish a base and wireless station on Macquarie Island. MAC 42 AAE.

Correspondence between Vickers and D. Mawson, June–July 1914. MAC 137 AAE.

E. Webb. Sledging Diary 1912–1913. ML MSS 2895.

F. Wild. Memoirs, 1937. ML MSS 2198.

Letter from E. Wilson to T. W. E. David, 24 February 1910. ML MSS. 3022/1 C73810.

Worsley motorised sledge plans and photographs. MAC 135 AAE.

CHAPTER 8: MARTYRS TO GONDWANALAND

Books

Berkman, P. A., Lang, M. A., Walton, D. W. H., Young, O. R. 2011. *Science Diplomacy: Antarctica, Science and the Governance of International Spaces.* Smithsonian Institution Scholarly Press.

Caviedes, C. N. 2001. *El Niño in History: Storming Through the Ages.* University Press of Florida, Gainsville.

Ellis, A. R. 1969. *Under Scott's Command: Lashly's Antarctic Diaries.* Taplinger Publishing Company, New York.

Jones, M. 2003. *The Last Great Quest: Captain Scott's Antarctic Sacrifice.* Oxford University Press, Oxford.

Shackleton, E. 1914. *South: The Endurance Expedition.* Penguin Classics, London.

Solomon, S. 2001. *The Coldest March: Scott's Fatal Antarctic Expedition.* Yale University Press, New Haven.

Stroud, M. 2004. *Survival of the Fittest: Anatomy of Peak Physical Performance.* Vintage, London.

Wegener, A. 1924. *The Origin of Continents and Oceans.* Methuen & Co. Ltd., London.

Wheeler, S. 2002. *Cherry: A Life of Apsley Cherry-Garrard*. Vintage, London.

Journal Articles and Reports

Baker, A. J., Pereira, S. L., Haddrath, O. P., Edge, K.-A. 2006. Multiple gene evidence for expansion of extant penguins out of Antarctica due to global cooling. *Proceedings of the Royal Society B: Biological Sciences* 273: 11–17.

Balch, E. S. 1912. Antarctic names. *Bulletin of the American Geographical Society* 44: 561–581.

Barton, C. E., Hutchinson, R., Quilty, P., Seers, K., Stone, T. 1987. Quest for the magnetic poles: relocation of the South Magnetic Pole at sea, 1986. *Bureau of Mineral Resources, Geology and Geophysics Record*, 1987/3, 20.

Bertler, N. A. N., Barrett, P. J., Mayewski, P. A., Fogt, R. L., Kreutz, K. J., Shulmeister, J. 2004. El Niño suppresses Antarctic warming. *Geophysical Research Letters* 31: L15207.

Boger, S. D. 2011. Antarctica—Before and after Gondwana. *Gondwana Research* 19: 335–371.

Chapman, F., Parr, W. J. 1937. Zoology and Botany. Part 2. Foraminifera. *Australasian Antarctic Expedition 1911–14 Scientific Report, Series C, Volume I*. D. H. Paisley, Sydney, 196.

Cooper, A., Penny, D. 1997. Mass survival of birds across the Cretaceous–Tertiary boundary: Molecular evidence. *Science* 275: 1109–1113.

Dalziel, I. W. D. 1992. Antarctica: A tale of two supercontinents. *Annual Review of Earth and Planetary Sciences* 20: 501–526.

David, T. W. E. 1914. Antarctica and some of its problems. *Geographical Journal* 43: 605–627.

David, T. W. E. 1907. *The Geology of the Hunter River Coal Measures, New South Wales* W.A. Gullick, Sydney.

Deacon, G. E. R. 1975. The oceanographical observations of Scott's last expedition. *Polar Record* 17: 391–396.

Fogarty, E. 2011. *Antarctica: Assessing and Protecting Australia's National Interests*. Lowry Institute for International Policy, Sydney.

Irving, E. 2005. The role of latitude in mobilism debates. *Proceedings of the National Academy of Sciences* 102: 1821–1828.

Kidson, E. 1947. Meteorology. Daily weather charts. Extending from Australia and New Zealand to the Antarctic continent. *Australasian Antarctic Expedition 1911–14 Scientific Report, Series B, Volume VII.* T. H. Tennant, Sydney, 412.

Mawson, D. 1943. Macquarie Island: Its geography and geology. *Australasian Antarctic Expedition 1911–14 Scientific Report, Series A, Volume V.* G. P. Office, Sydney, 197.

Parish, T. R., Walker, R. 2006. A re-examination of the winds of Adelie Land, Antarctica. *Australian Meteorological Magazine* 55: 105–117.

Piwowar, J. M., Derksen, C. P. 2008. Spatial-temporal variability of Northern Hemisphere sea ice concentrations and concurrent atmospheric teleconnections. *Journal of Environmental Informatics* 11: 103–122.

Priestley, R. 1977. The Professor. *Polar Record* 18: 371–374.

Ross, N., Bingham, R. G., Corr, H. F. J., Ferraccioli, F., Jordan, T. A., Le Brocq, A., Rippin, D. M., Young, D., Blankenship, D. D., Siegert, M. J. 2012. Steep reverse bed slope at the grounding line of the Weddell Sea sector in West Antarctica. *Nature Geoscience* doi: 10.1038/ngeo1468.

Royer, D. L., Osborne, C. P., Beerling, D. J. 2003. Carbon loss by deciduous trees in a CO_2-rich ancient polar environment. *Nature* 424: 60–62.

Royer, D. L., Pagani, M., Beerling, D. J. 2011. Geologic constraints on earth system sensitivity to CO_2 during the Cretaceous and early Paleogene. *Earth System Dynamics Discussion* 2: 211–240.

Seward, A. C. 1914. Antarctic fossil plants. *British Antarctic ('Terra Nova') Expedition, 1910. Natural History Report*, London, 1 (1), 49.

Simpson, G. C. 1919. *Meteorology Vol. I: Discussion (British Antarctic Expedition 1910–1913)*. Thacker, Spink & Co., Calcutta.

Simpson, G. C. 1919. *Meteorology Vol. II: Weather Maps and Pressure Curves (British Antarctic Expedition 1910–1913)*. Thacker, Spink & Co., Calcutta.

Simpson, G. C. 1923. *Meteorology Vol. III: Tables (British Antarctic Expedition 1910–1913)*. Harrison and Sons, Ltd, London.

Slack, K. E., Jones, C. M., Ando, T., Harrison, G. L., Fordyce, R. E., Arnason, U., Penny, D. 2006. Early penguin fossils, plus mitochondrial genomes, calibrate avian evolution. *Molecular Biology and Evolution* 23: 1144–1155.

Solomon, S., Stearns, C. R. 1999. On the role of the weather in the deaths of R. F. Scott and his companions. *Proceedings of the National Academy of Sciences* 96: 13012–13016.

Thomson, M. R. A., Vaughan, A. P. M. 2005. The role of Antarctica in the development of plate tectonic theories: from Scott to the present. *Archives of Natural History* 32: 362–393.

Watson, C., Burgette, R., Tregoning, P., White, N., Hunter, J., Coleman, R., Handsworth, R., Brolsma, H. 2010. Twentieth century constraints on sea level change and earthquake deformation at Macquarie Island. *Geophysical Journal International* 182: 781–796.

Wegener, A. 1912. Die entstehung der koninente. *Geologische Rundschau* 3: 276–292.

Willis, B. 1910. Principles of palaeogeography. *Science* 31: 241–260.

Newspaper and Magazine Articles

Anonymous. 1913. To the South Pole with the cinematograph: Film records of Scott's ill-fated expedition. *Scientific American* 108: 560–569.

Anonymous. 1913. Antarctic exploration: Experiences on a moving glacier. *The Times* 2 June: 7.

Anonymous. 1913. Polar exploration: Lord Curzon on the Scott expedition. *The Times* 27 May: 5.

Anonymous. 1913. 'An explorer's death.': Lieut. Filchner's tribute. *Nottingham Evening Post* 13 February: 5.

Anonymous. 1913. Antarctic disaster: Loss of Captain Scott and his party. *The Times* 11 February: 8.

Anonymous. 1913. The polar disaster: Captain Scott's career. *The Times* 11 February: 10.

Anonymous. 1913. Death of Captain Scott. Lost with four comrades. *Daily Mail* 11 February: 5.

Anonymous. 1913. Terra Nova back. *Evening Post* (Wellington) 10 February: 8.

Brown, R. N. R. 1913. The difficulties of the journey: Why there was no return. *Manchester Guardian* 12 February.

Drummond, J. 1913. Mystery of Scott's fate: Why did the fuel give out? *Daily Chronicle* 13 February: 1.

Unpublished Sources

Letter from L. Beaumont to Lord Curzon, 17 April 1913. BL MSS EUR/ F112/51.

Letter from L. Beaumont to Lord Curzon, 19 April 1913. BL MSS EUR/ F112/51.

Letter from L. Beaumont to Lord Curzon, 24 April 1913. BL MSS EUR/ F112/51.

Letter from W. Lashly to R. Gibbings, 4 October 1938. URL MS 15.

Letter from L. Beaumont to K. Scott, 15 March 1913. SPRI MS 2.

Letter from L. Beaumont to K. Scott, 18 April 1913. SPRI MS 2.

Letter from L. Beaumont to K. Scott, 15 July 1913. SPRI MS 2.

Letter from L. Beaumont to K. Scott, 24 September 1913. SPRI MS 2.

A. Cherry-Garrard. Diary, 16 January to 15 March, 1913. SPRI MS 559/11.

Letter from J. F. Cunningham to Lord Curzon, 20 November 1912. BL MSS EUR/F112/41.

Lord Curzon. Notes, 16 April 1913. BL MSS EUR/F112/51.

Letter from T. W. E. David to E. Evans, 6 December 1912. ML MSS. 3022/1 C73810.

Telegram from King George V to Lord Curzon, 10 February 1913. BL MSS EUR/F112/51.

Letter from S. T. Goldie to Lord Curzon, 18 April 1913. BL MSS EUR/ F112/51.

Letter from H. A. Hunt to T. W. E. David, 28 May 1912. ML MSS. 3022/1 C73810.

Letter from S. Keltie to Lord Curzon, 10 February 1913. RGS CB8
   1911-20 3 of 7.

Lady Scott. Diary, 1913. CUL Kennet D/5.

Letter from C. Markham to F. Nansen, 22 July 1913. NB Brevs 48.

Letter from C. Markham to F. Nansen, 8 March 1913. NB Brevs 48.

Letter from F. Nansen to S. Keltie, 11 March 1912. RGS C8 1911-20.

Letter from F. Nansen to S. Keltie, 16 March 1912. RGS C8 1911-20.

Letter from F. Nansen to C. Markham, 4 April 1913. NB Brevs 48.

E. A. Wilson. Sledging Diary, 1 November 1911 to 27 February 1912.
   BL MS Add. 47459.

POSTSCRIPT

Journal Articles and Reports

Barnes, D. K. A., Kuklinski, P. Jackson, J. A., Keel, G. W., Morley,
   S. A., Winston, J. E. 2011. Scott's collections help reveal accel-
   erating marine life growth in Antarctica. *Current Biology: CB* 21:
   R147–R148.

Cook, A. J., Poncet, S., Cooper, A. P. R., Herbert, D. J., Christie, D. 2010.
   Glacier retreat on South Georgia and implications for the spread of
   rats. *Antarctic Science* 22: 255–263.

Sladen, W. J. L., Menzie, C. M., Reichel, W. L. 1966. DDT residues in
   Adelie penguins and a crabeater seal from Antarctica. *Nature* 210:
   670–673.

Newspaper and Magazine Articles

Anonymous. 1914. Sir E. Shackleton and his expedition: Plan may be
   'spectacular'. *Manchester Guardian* 10 February.

Anonymous. 1913. The Antarctic: Funds for the Shackleton Expedition.
   The Times 31 December: 61.

Websites

For a taste of what it's like in the field, follow me on twitter (@ProfChris-
Turney) and on YouTube (www.youtube.com/christurney). Details of
future expeditions will be posted at www.christurney.com.

Many wonderful groups are bringing science and the public together. Two standouts are Earthwatch Worldwide (www.earthwatch.org) and Raleigh International (www.raleighinternational.org).

Great work is also being done on South Georgia, where rats brought to the islands by whaling and sealing ships in the past are threatening native wildlife once again. As the glaciers retreat, overland routes are now opening up between peninsulas, allowing previously isolated rat populations to expand across the island into the few remaining areas that had been rodent-free.

The South Georgia Heritage Trust (www.sght.org) has instigated the largest rat-eradication program ever attempted, costing millions of dollars. Phase 1 is now complete and has been a success. If you would like to help finish the job by supporting Phase 2, find out more at the SGHT website.

INDEX

A

Adelie Land 225, 227, 236
Adelie penguins 91, 161–2
Admiralty Range 152
aerial photographs 32
aeroplanes 223
Ainsworth, George 224, 235
Aladdin's Cave 245
albatrosses 161
alcohol 123, 199, 248
Alexandra Mountains 165
American Amundsen–Scott South
    Pole Station 296
American expeditions 13, 19,
    69–70, 79, 226–7
American Geographical Society
    174, 205
Amundsen, Leon 109, 115, 121, 285
Amundsen, Roald 4, 84, 285
    on *Belgica* 27, 105–6
    and Campbell 86
    diary entries 123, 129–30
    early life 105–6
    and Edwards 112–13
    health of 131
    in Japan 173
    and Johansen 123–4
    as leader 123–4, 131–2
    lectures by 135–6
    and Markham 139, 262–3
    and Nansen 114–15, 139–40
    North Geographic Pole
        expedition 108–9, 140
    Northwest Passage expedition
        106–8
    and publicity 133–42

and RGS 98–9, 121, 137, 140–1
and Scott 97, 114–15, 135–6, 262
sketches 128
South Pole 117, 136–8, 299
and Wilson 103
Amundsen's Norwegian Antarctic
    expedition 84, 102–3, 218
    date reached 130
    dogs 110, 122, 124–5, 128,
        132, 141
    journey to pole 124–31
    King Edward VII Land
        work 124
    location measurements 125–7
    meets German Antarctic
        Expedition (Filchner) 186
    meets Shirase's Japanese
        expedition 162–3
    meets *Terra Nova* expedition 86,
        120–1
    newspaper rights 121, 132–3
    oceanography 115, 137
    preparations 110–17, 118–19
    publicity after 132–6
    return to Framheim 123–4, 131–2
    start out 122–3, 124–5
    weather observations 117–18,
        119–20, 129–30, 136
Antarctic Andes 179, 182, 191, 269,
    270, 274
Antarctic Circle 2–3, 22
Antarctic Circumpolar Current
    278
Antarctic Committee of Enquiry
    287
Antarctic Convergence 190–1

Antarctic Expedition Supporters'
    Association 147, 173
Antarctic Manual (Markham) 31, 44
Antarctic Surface Water 190–1
Antarctic Treaty 283
Antarctica 3, 27, 268–9
    land bridge 44–5, 232, 234–6,
        274–5
    place names 40–1, 270
    see also Terra Australis Incognita
Antarctica Research 170–1
Antarktikos 3–4
Arctowski, Henryk 37, 110
Armitage, Albert 31, 36–7, 52–3
Arrol-Johnston motorcar 55, 56–7
Auckland Islands 202
Aurora 217–18, 229, 245–6, 253
Aurora Australis 49, 251–3
Australasian Antarctic
    Expedition (AAE)
    dogs 241, 242
    Far Eastern Party 240–7
    Far Western Party 229-31,
        248, 267
    funding 215–16, 217–18,
        221–3, 253
    geological samples 241, 248
    Macquarie Island base
        224–6, 249
    magnetic observations 220,
        237–9, 248, 255–6
    oceanography 232, 235–6
    plans 218–21
    publicity after 253–8
    scientific observations 239, 295–6
    second winter 246–7
    Southern Party 247–8
    supplies 242, 244, 248
    team 217, 220, 241
    team relationships 239–40

voyage down 223–5, 227–8
    weather observations 236–7,
        244–5, 248, 255, 266–7
    Western Party 248
    Wild's base 229–30, 253
    Wild's team 246
    Winter Quarters 228–9,
        236–7, 253
Australasian Association for the
    Advancement of Science 35,
    214–15
Australian government 221
Australian National Antarctic
    Research Expeditions 282
Axel Heiberg Glacier 129, 171, 269

B
Bage, Robert 247–8, 284
Balloon Bight 32, 46–7, 86
balloons 89–90
Bay of Whales 47, 115, 117,
    169, 172
Beacon Sandstone 62, 88, 269
Beardmore Glacier 62, 65, 100,
    271, 272–3
Beardmore, William 38, 41, 55
Beattie, J. W. 135
Beaufoy 13
Beaumont, Lewis 288–9
Belgian Antarctic Expedition
    27, 249
Belgica expedition 27, 75, 105–6,
    187–8
Berlin Geographical Society 179
Bernacchi, Louis 28, 75–6
Bickerton, Frank 249, 251, 252
biological samples 48, 161, 219,
    296
Bjaaland, Olav 131, 134
Bjövik, Paul 196

Blijde Boodschap 9
boots 54–5, 164, 242
Borchgrevink, Carsten 27–8, 55, 77, 114, 236
Borchgrevink's expedition 27–8, 66, 68, 219
Bowers, Henry Robertson 94–5, 102, 260
Bransfield, Edward 12
Brennecke, Wilhelm 183, 200, 209–11
British Antarctic Expedition (BAE) 39–40, 45, 111
see also Nimrod expedition (BAE)
British Antarctic expeditions 4, 12, 25–6, 27–8, 38
see also Borchgrevink's expedition; *Discovery* expedition; National Antarctic Expedition; *Nimrod* expedition (BAE); *Terra Nova* expedition
British Association for the Advancement of Science in Australia 284
British, Australian and New Zealand Antarctic Research Expedition (BANZARE) 286
British government 22, 41, 42, 68, 108, 221
British Scott Polar Research Institute 282
Brown, Rudmose 263
Bruce, Wilfrid 148
Bruce, William Speirs 30, 142, 178, 182, 232, 234–5
Buckley Island 271, 273
Burberry 54, 107
Butcher's Shop 128
Byrd, Richard 174

C
Campbell, John 2
Campbell, Victor 85–6, 117, 121
Canadian coastline 21–2
Cape Adare 28, 76–7, 218–19
Cape Crozier 32, 94–5
Cape Denison 228, 240, 248–9
Cape Disappointment 189
Cape Evans 85, 100
Cape Royds 47
carbon dioxide 277
Carmen Land 137–8, 142, 207–8, 269
Carnegie Institute of Washington 112–13, 220
Challenger, HMS 22, 187, 188
Cherry-Garrard, Apsley 78–9, 91, 94–5, 100, 125, 261, 287, 292, 298
Chishima Islands 145–6
Chree, Charles 74, 220
Christiania Geographical Society 50
chronometers 101–2, 126, 127
Clarence and Richmond Examiner 154
climate 74–6, 265–7
clothing 53–5, 96, 107, 164
Clyde 224
coal 62, 65, 271–2
Coats Land 137, 178, 207
Commonwealth Bay 228, 245, 246, 254
Company Islands 268
compasses 14–16, 18, 20, 58–9, 81, 127
Cook, Frederick 27, 69–70, 109–10, 138–9
Cook, James 10–11, 189
cookers 53, 119

Crean, Tom 101
Curzon, Lord 24, 140, 141, 174,
    262, 287–9, 291

D
Daily Chronicle 121, 133, 136, 291–3
Daily Mail 64, 216, 259
Daily Telegraph 155, 157
Daini Hoko-maru 149
Dana, James Dwight 233
Darwin, Charles 43–4, 167–8
Darwin, Leonard 64, 71, 121
Dash Patrol 164, 172
David, Edgeworth 217
    and AAE 215, 247, 253
    and Amundsen 135
    on Antarctic research 42
    on coal 271–2
    and funding expeditions 42,
        43, 215, 253
    and geological samples 77
    health of 60
    lectures by 66–7
    letters home 46
    and Mawson 66
    and *Nimrod* expedition (BAE)
        40, 45
    and Penck 284
    and RGS 267–70
    on science 35–6, 299, 301
    and scientific observations 48
    and Shirase's Japanese expedi-
        tion 153, 155, 157–8, 169–70
    South Magnetic Pole
        expedition 56–61
Davis, John King 61, 121, 202,
    214, 298–9
    and *Aurora* 229–32, 245–6, 253
    Macquarie Island base 224–5
    and Mawson 253

oceanography 232, 235–6, 248
de Gerlache, Adrien 27
Debenham, Frank 78, 82, 83–4,
    87–8, 272, 282
Deception Island 191
dehydration 129
Delprat, Paquita 227, 249, 286
Denison, Sir Hugh 228
Deutschland 182, 184, 193, 206
    see also German Antarctic
        Expedition (Filchner)
Devil's Ballroom 128
Discovery 31, 80
Discovery expedition 31–3, 38, 116
    comments on 73–4
    dogs 82–3
    funding 29, 31
    leader 29
    magnetic observations 32, 48–9
    preparations 28–30
    weather observations 32, 73–6,
        119–20
    see also Scott, Robert Falcon
dogs
    Amundsen's Norwegian
        Antarctic expedition 110,
        122, 124–5, 128, 132, 141
    Australasian Antarctic
        Expedition (AAE) 241, 242
    Discovery expedition 82–3
    German Antarctic Expedition
        (Filchner) 205
    Nimrod expedition (BAE) 52–3
    Shirase's Japanese expedition
        149–50, 164, 169
    Terra Nova expedition 100, 263
Drake Passage 189, 278
D'Urville, Jules Sébastien César
    Dumont 19, 225–6
Dutch East India Company 9

E

earthquakes 234, 276

Edmonds, Harry 112–13, 137

El Niño 265–6

Elephant Island 285

Ellisworth Mountains 3

emperor penguins 32, 93–5, 166–7

Enderby, Captain 201

Endurance 285

Engelstad, Ole 113–14

equipment *see* supplies

Erebus, HMS 19–20, 21

Evans, Edgar 260

Evans, Edward 'Teddy' 37, 79, 80, 101, 274, 288–93

Expedition World 147

exploration and science mix 14, 30, 293, 297–9, 300–302

F

Farr, C C. 255

fauna 44, 161–2, 190, 192, 278

see also penguins

Ferrar, Arthur 287

Ferrar, Hartley 62

Filchner Ice Shelf 207

Filchner, Wilhelm 4, 175, 177–9, 286

Exposé 195, 210

on future trips 206–7

at Grytviken 193

preparations for expedition 181–6

and Scott 183, 263

search for land 202–3

To the Sixth Continent 195, 199

and Vahsel 195–6, 200

weather observations 208–9

see also German Antarctic Expedition (Filchner)

film rights 165–6

films 165–7, 170, 237, 254, 283, 297

Finsås, Ronny 114

Fisher, Andrew 215

Fisher, Osmond 232–3

Fishery Protection Vessel 189–90

flights 221–3

Flinders, Matthew 20

flora 43–4

food 27, 53

see also meat

Forster, Johann Reinhold 93

fossils 43–4, 62, 65, 274, 275, 276–7, 279

see also Glossopteris

Fox Dip Circle 20

Fram 51, 110, 114, 132, 137, 149, 285

see also Amundsen's Norwegian Antarctic expedition

Fram Museum, Oslo 106

Framheim 115, 116, 117

Franklin, Sir John 21, 25, 29, 41, 105, 106, 108, 144

Franz Josef Land 51–2

French expeditions 19, 225–6

Freshfield, Douglas 254–5

funding 296–8, 299

Australasian Antarctic Expedition (AAE) 215–16, 217–18, 221–3, 253

British Antarctic expeditions 26

Discovery expedition 29, 31

Nimrod expedition (BAE) 40–3, 55, 68–9

fur clothing 54, 96

G

Galton, Francis 201

Gauss 180

Gauss, Carl Friedrich 18

Gaussberg 219
geographical exploration 25
Geographical Society of London
    see Royal Geographical Society
    (RGS)
geological samples 31, 57–8, 76–7
    Australasian Antarctic
        Expedition (AAE) 241, 248
    French expeditions 270–1
    Nimrod expedition (BAE) 48,
        56, 298
    Shirase's Japanese expedition
        167–8, 171–2
    Terra Nova expedition 101, 260,
        261, 271–3
geology 43–4, 62, 65, 101
geomagnetic poles 17
German Antarctic Expedition
    (Filchner) 4, 175, 205
    base 196–8
    dogs 205
    at Grytviken 192–3, 204–5
    meets Amundsen's Norwegian
        Antarctic expedition 186
    oceanography 185–6, 209–10
    post-voyage 204–7
    preparations 181–6
    scientific observations 179, 180,
        198, 206, 207–11, 296
    search for land 202–3
    team relationships 198–200,
        203–7
    voyage down 186, 188–9, 193–6
    weather observations 208–9
    see also Deutschland; Filchner,
        Wilhelm
Gerritsz, Dirk 9
Gilbert, William 15–16
Ginkgo biloba 277
Gjøa 106–8

Glossopteris 43, 80, 274, 276–7
gloves 54
Gondwanaland 44, 275–6, 278–9
Graham, George 18
Graham Land 137
Gran, Tryggve 82, 83
Great Ice Barrier 21, 28, 32, 46,
    115, 172, 270–1
Gregory, John Walter 30, 73–4
Grytviken 191, 192–3
Gunji, Naritada 145–6, 173

H
Haakon, King 131
Halley, Edmund 17–18
Hamilton, Sir Richard 29
Hamre, Ivar 166, 174–5
Hann, Julius von 119–20
Hanssen, Helmer 132
Hassel, Sverre 131–2
Hayes, Gordon 257–8
health of explorers 60, 129,
    131, 244, 245, 246–7
    see also scurvy
Heiberg, Axel 128
Heinemann, William 136
Helland-Hansen, Bjørn 115
Heroic Age of Antarctic
    Exploration 4, 26
Hilary, Sir Edmund 247
Hinks, Arthur 125
Hints to Travellers (RGS) 23–4,
    88, 101, 111, 201
Hooker, Joseph 19, 24, 43
horses 52–3, 82, 87, 100, 182,
    205, 263
Hurley, Frank 220–1, 237, 247,
    254, 258, 285
Huxley, Thomas 47–8, 298
hypsometers 111, 128–9

I
IceCube 296
Ikeda, Masakichi 156, 158, 173–4
Imperial Trans-Antarctic
    Expedition 284–5, 299–300
Indo-Australian Pacific Plate 276
International Geographical
    Congress, Sixth 25–6
International Polar Year 186–7

J
Jackson, Frederick George 52,
    53, 107
Jackson–Harmsworth Expedition
    52
Jane 13
Japan Times 155
Japanese expeditions 4
    see also Shirase's Japanese
    expedition
Japanese government 173, 175
Japanese Polar Research
    Institute 175
Jeffryes, Sydney 250–1, 252
Johansen, Hjalmar 51–2, 108,
    123, 140

K
Kainan Bay 162, 174
Kainan-maru 149, 151, 169, 173
Kaiser Wilhelm Ice Barrier 195
Kaiser Wilhelm II Land 180, 248
Keedick, Lee 135
Keltie, John Scott 109, 139, 141, 174
Kerguelen Land 202
Kidson, Edward 266–7
King Edward Point 191
King Edward VII Land 28–9,
    32, 165–9, 171, 174, 269,
    270, 274–5

king penguins 92
Kishiichi, Kokubo 148
kites, man-bearing 113–14
Kling, Albert 186, 198, 202
Kohl, Ludwig 193
König, Felix 183, 199, 200,
    202, 206
Kuril Islands 145–6, 173

L
land bridge 44–5, 232, 234–6,
    274–5
Larsen, Carl Anton 192–3, 205
Laseron, Charles 229, 240
Lashly, William 101, 292–3
latitude measurements 125, 136,
    202
Le Maire, Jacob 9
Lindstrom, Henrik 118, 122, 123
Lloyd-Creak dipping circle 58, 81
location measurements 23, 125–7
longitude measurements 102, 125,
    202
Longstaff, Llewellyn 29, 36
Lorenzen, Wilhelm 200, 203, 205
Lucas sounding machine 234–5
Luitpold Land 194, 195, 269–70
Lyttleton, New Zealand 45, 151
Lyttleton Times 151

M
Mackay, Alistair 56–61
McLean, Archibald 245, 250
McMurdo Sound 20, 31, 47
Macquarie Island 224–6
Madame Tussauds 64
Madigan, Cecil 250
Magellan, Ferdinand 7–8
Magnetic Crusade 18
magnetic fields 15–16, 18–19

magnetic observations 18–19, 20, 31
  Australasian Antarctic
    Expedition (AAE) 220,
    237–9, 248, 255–6
  Discovery expedition 32, 48–9
  Nimrod expedition (BAE) 65–6
  Terra Nova expedition 255–6
magnetic poles 16–18
see also North Magnetic Pole;
  South Magnetic Pole
Magnetic Union 18
Magnetograph House 237–8
Manchester Guardian 133
maps 2, 3, 8–9, 173–4, 268–9
Markham, Sir Clements 24–5, 64,
  121, 286
  and Amundsen 139, 262–3
  Antarctic Manual 31, 44
  on Australasian Antarctic
    Expedition (AAE) 216
  on geological samples 273
  and German Antarctic
    Expedition (Filchner) 208
  Lands of Silence 67, 174, 268
  and National Antarctic
    Expedition 28–9, 30
  and RGS 25, 71
  and Scott 261–2
  and Shackleton 67–8
Mawson, David 4, 43, 286
  and Australasian Association for
    the Advancement of Science
    214–15
  Australian National Antarctic
    Research Expeditions 282
  calls home 249
  and David 66
  and Davis 253
  Far Eastern Party 240–7
  funds 256–7

  future expeditions 76–8
  health of 244, 245, 246–7
  Home of the Blizzard 253–4,
    256, 298
  and Jeffryes 250–1
  letters home 227
  magnetic observations 65–6
  and *Nimrod* expedition (BAE) 45
  plans to return 213–16
  publicity after 253–5
  and RGS 234, 254–5
  and Scott 77, 218
  and Shackleton 213–14
  and Shirase's Japanese
    expedition 157
  South Magnetic Pole
    expedition 56–61
  and Wilson 77
  see also Australasian Antarctic
    Expedition (AAE)
Meares, Cecil 82, 83, 100, 148, 289
meat 27, 60, 91, 100, 182, 242–3
Meiji Restoration 144–5
Meinardus, Wilhelm 210
Mertz Glacier 228, 243
Mertz, Xavier 241, 242–3, 247
Meteorological Office 73–4
Miisho, Seizo 158
Mill Rise 236, 274
Mitsuhara, Tsuchiya 148
mittens 54
Moluccas 7
Morrell, Benjamin 201–2
Morrell Land 201, 268
Mossman, Robert 208
motorcars 55, 56–7
Mount Betty 171
Mount Buckley 273
Mount Erebus 20, 48, 56, 75, 89–90
Mount Nobu 174

Mount Okuma 174
M. Pathe film company 165–6, 170
Murakami Inlet 174
Murray, John 26, 28–9, 74–5

N
Nansen, Eva 51
Nansen, Fridtjof 49–52, 54, 81–2
  and Amundsen 114–15, 139–40
  on equipment 106–7
  and Scott 262–3
National Antarctic Expedition 28–33
  see also Discovery expedition
Natural History Museum,
  London 273
Nautical Almanac 126, 127
New South Greenland 201
New South Shetland 12
New York Times 133
New Zealand government 42,
  45, 221
New Zealand Times 151
Newnes, Sir George 28
newspaper rights 121, 132–3, 297
Nimrod 39–40, 80
Nimrod expedition (BAE) 52–5
  base 47
  biological samples 48
  collects men 60–1, 64
  conditions 47–8
  dogs 52–3
  funding 40–3, 55, 68–9
  geological samples 48, 56, 298
  horses 52–3
  magnetic observations 65–6
  preparations 49, 52–5
  and RGS 39–40
  South Geographic Pole 61–4, 68
  supplies 53–5, 58–9, 63–4
  team 45

trip to pole 53–5
voyage down 45–7
weather observations 48–9
  see also Shackleton, Ernest
Ninnis, Belgrave 241–2, 247
Nomura, Nackichi 153–4, 156, 158
Nordenskjöld, Baron Adolf 41
Norman, Robert 15, 16
North Geographic Pole expedi-
  tions 50–1, 69–70, 108–9, 140
North Magnetic Pole 19, 50, 106–7
Northcliffe, Lord 216
Northwest Passage 21, 106–8
Norwegian expedition
  see Amundsen's Norwegian
  Antarctic expedition

O
Oates, Lawrence 'Titus' 79, 87,
  260, 261
Observer 137, 153, 254
ocean properties 187–8
oceanography 182, 187, 232–6, 248
  Amundsen's Norwegian
    Antarctic expedition 115, 137
  Challenger 22
  German Antarctic Expedition
    (Filchner) 185–6, 209–10
  Terra Nova expedition 274–5
Okuma Bay 167, 174
Okuma, Shigenobu 147, 155–6,
  157, 262
One Ton Depot 87, 99–100

P
Palmer Archipelago 274–5
Palmer Land 27
Palmer, Nathaniel 13
Paramore, HMS 17–18
Parsley Bay 154

Peary, Robert 69–70, 109, 111–12, 121–2
pemmican 53, 291
Penck, Friedrich Albert 179, 183–4, 206, 284
penguins 32, 91–5, 278–9, 296
   Shirase's Japanese expedition 151–2, 161–2, 166–7, 168–9
   see also Adelie penguins; emperor penguins; king penguins
Pharos 190
photography 66–7, 78, 134–5, 141, 220–1, 254
Physical Society of London 74
place names 40–1, 270
plants 43–4
Pointe Géologie 225
Polar Front 190–1
poles 14, 16–17
Polheim 130–1, 134, 135, 292–3
ponies 52–3, 62, 82, 87, 100, 205, 263
Ponting, Herbert 78, 91, 100, 283
Prester John 8–9, 190
Prestrud, Kristian 123, 124
Priestley, Raymond 40, 65, 78, 282
Prinz Luitpold Land 269
Prinzregent Luitpold Land 194
Przybyllok, Erich 183, 199, 206
psychological effects 249–51

Q
Queen Maud Range 127–8

R
Raymond 55
Relief Inlet 60
Resolution, HMS 10
Richards, Sir George 50
Roosevelt Island 117, 172
Ross Ice Shelf 21, 270–1

   see also Great Ice Barrier
Ross Island 20, 32, 47, 175
   as base 31, 37, 38–9
Ross Sea 172, 174, 208, 269, 270
Ross, Sir James Clark 19–21, 202
Royal Company's Islands 235
Royal Geographical Society (RGS) 297
   and Amundsen 108–9, 121, 137, 140–1
   and British Antarctic expeditions 25–6, 38
   and Cape Adare 218
   and David 267–70
   female fellows 24
   formation 22–3
   Hints to Travellers 23–4, 88, 101, 111, 201
   and Mawson 234, 254–5
   and National Antarctic Expedition 29–30
   and *Nimrod* expedition (BAE) 39–40
   and Peary 121–2
   and Royal Society 29–30
   and Scott 71–2, 263–4
   and Shackleton 39, 64–5
   and Shirase's Japanese expedition 173–4
   and *Terra Nova* expedition 98–9, 288–9, 291
Royal Meteorological Society 73
Royal Navy (British) 14, 17, 19, 29
Royal Society in London 10, 17, 18, 29–30
Royal Society of New South Wales 157
Royal Society of Victoria 26, 41, 41–2
Royds, Charles 73, 119

S
Sawyer, Arthur 234
science
  and exploration mix 14, 30, 293,
    297–9, 300–302
  global endeavours 186–7
  and sport 35–6, 299
scientific equipment 14, 43, 48,
  76, 106–7
  see also compasses
scientific expeditions 25, 30
scientific observations 29, 32, 39,
  48–9, 84, 87–8, 89
  Australasian Antarctic
    Expedition (AAE) 239, 295–6
  comments on 73–4
  German Antarctic Expedition
    (Filchner) 179, 180, 198, 206,
    207–11, 296
  Terra Nova expedition 101–2
  by Weddell 13–14
  see also magnetic observations;
    weather observations
Scotia Arc 193
Scotia Sea 278
Scott, Lady Kathleen 216, 219,
  222, 264, 287–9
Scott, Robert Falcon 4
  and Amundsen 97, 114–15,
    135–6, 262
  and Cape Adare 218
  death 259–62, 291
  diary entries 288, 292–3
  experiences 99–100
  and Filchner 177, 183, 263
  future expeditions 70–3, 111
  and horses 87
  as leader 87
  leaves London 177
  and Markham 261–2

  and Mawson 77, 218
  and Nansen 262–3
  and National Antarctic
    Expedition 29, 32–3
  on penguins 92
  remembered 259, 261–2, 263
  and RGS 71–2, 263–4
  and Shackleton 36–7, 38, 67, 177
  and summer 249–50
  and supplies 288, 290
  on Victoria Land 115
  weather observations 75
  see also Discovery expedition;
    Terra Nova expedition
Scottish National Antarctic
  Expedition 30, 79
Scott's Last Expedition 272
Scouten, Willem 9
scurvy 27, 32, 63, 91, 101, 146, 288
Sea of George the Fourth 13–14
sealers 11–12
seals 27, 161, 191–2, 224
Seasonal Affective Disorder 48
sennegrass 54–5
Seward, Albert 273–4
Shackleton, Ernest 33, 36
  and Amundsen's Norwegian
    Antarctic expedition 121
  and Arctowski 37–8
  and funding expeditions 40–1,
    42, 214, 215–16
  and German Antarctic
    Expedition (Filchner) 182
  Heart of Antarctica 46
  Imperial Trans-Antarctic
    Expedition 284–5, 299–300
  lectures by 66
  letters home 64
  and Markham 67–8
  and Mawson 213–14

and National Antarctic
    Expedition 32
and *Nimrod* expedition (BAE)
    45, 49, 52–5, 61–4, 64–5
as poet 45–6
and RGS 39
and Scott 36–7, 38, 68, 177
South 283
see also Nimrod expedition (BAE)
Shackleton Ice Shelf 270
ships and ice 50–1
Shirase, Nobu 4, 143–4, 158,
    285–6
    and Amundsen 173
    on Chishima Islands 145–6, 173
    and Japanese government 173,
        175
    monument to 175
    in New Zealand 151
    and Tada 160
Shirase's Japanese expedition
    in Australia 153–9
    dogs 149–50, 164, 169
    films 165–7
    geological samples 167–8, 171–2
    King Edward VII Land 165–9
    letter to David 157–8
    meets Amundsen's Norwegian
        Antarctic expedition 162–3
    in New Zealand 150–1
    penguins 151–2, 161–2, 166–7,
        168–9
    to pole 163–5
    preparations 146–50
    publicity after 169–72
    Record of Antarctica 170
    voyage down 151–3, 159–63
Simpson, George 76, 88–90, 187,
    252, 264–5
Skelton, Reginald 40, 81–2, 222

skis 50, 55, 82, 164, 242
sledges 50, 52–3, 99–100, 122,
    124–5
    motorised 81–2, 99, 121
sleeping bags 96, 164
Smith, William 12
snow blindness 54
snow predictions 74–5
Solomon, Susan 266
South Geographic Pole 38, 296
    Amundsen's Norwegian
        Antarctic expedition 110–17
    Borchgrevink's expedition 28
    Discovery expedition 32
    Nimrod expedition (BAE) 39,
        61–4, 68
    ocean access 13
    Terra Nova expedition 96–8, 116
South Georgia 188–92
South Magnetic Pole 31, 32
    expeditions to 19–21, 27, 59–61,
        247–8
    location of 57, 58–9, 256
South Shetlands 275
South with Scott 91
Southern Ocean 22, 44, 172
    research in 173, 175, 219, 232,
        248, 274
    rock in icebergs 167–8
    weather conditions 84, 159
    wild life in 190, 192, 278
Southwest Passage 9
sport and science 35–6, 299
Sprent, Chas 42
Staten Land 9–10
Stopes, Marie 80, 274
Strait of Magellan 8
Suess, Edward 44, 233–4
sun movement 102
Sun (Sydney) 154–5

supplies 118–19
  Australasian Antarctic
    Expedition (AAE) 242, 244,
    248
  Nimrod expedition (BAE) 53–5,
    58–9, 63–4
  Terra Nova expedition 95–6,
    260, 288–91
  see also clothing; food; meat;
    scientific equipment
swords 158–9
Sydney Morning Herald 223

T
Tacoma Times 153–4
Tada, Keiichi 160
Tafel, Albert 183–4
Takeda, Terutaro 148, 158
Tasman, Abel 10
Tasman Rise 236
Tasmanian state government 224
Taylor, Frank Bursley 233
Taylor, Griffith 78, 88, 272
telegraphy 120–1
Terra Australis Incognita 8, 9, 11,
    12, 13, 17, 33
Terra Nova 80–1, 98, 149
Terra Nova expedition 252, 291
  comments on 98–9, 263–4
  dogs 100, 263
  geological samples 101, 260,
    261, 271–3
  lectures 90–1
  magnetic observations 255–6
  meets Amundsen's Norwegian
    Antarctic expedition 86, 120–1
  oceanography 274–5
  preparations 80–3
  scientific observations 101–2
  scientific reports 264

supplies 95–6, 260, 288–91
  team 76–80, 83–4
  trip to Cape Crozier 94–6
  voyage down 84
  weather observations 88–90,
    101, 264–7
  see also Scott, Robert Falcon
Terror, HMS 19–20, 21
Tierra del Fuego 8–9, 21, 27, 110
The Times 68, 69, 72, 109, 115, 259,
    267, 282
Tokyo Geographical Society 147,
    148
Transantarctic Mountains 270, 278
Travellers Club in Pall Mall 22
Trinity Land 12–13, 27
Turney, Chris
  research by 286–8, 290
  trips to Antarctica 1–2, 302

U
Union Steamship Company 45
University College, Christchurch
    255
University of Cambridge 273–4

V
Vahsel Bay 195
Vahsel, Richard 184, 186, 195–6,
    199, 200, 203
Vickers 222, 257
Victoria Land 20, 28, 32, 171
  mountain range 61, 65, 115, 269
Victorian state government 41–2
Victory, HMS 19
vitamin A levels 243, 244, 247
vitamin C levels 27
von Bellingshausen, Fabian
    Gottlieb 12, 191
von Drygalski, Eric 180

von Goeldel, Wilhelm 199, 200, 204, 206
von Neumayer, Georg 107

W
Walk in the Snow festival 175
Watkins, Hugh Evelyn 222–3
weather observations
  Amundsen's Norwegian Antarctic expedition 117–18, 119–20, 129–30, 136
  Australasian Antarctic Expedition (AAE) 236–7, 244–5, 248, 255, 266–7
  Discovery expedition 32, 73–6, 119–20
  German Antarctic Expedition (Filchner) 208–9
  Nimrod expedition (BAE) 48–9
  Terra Nova expedition 88–90, 101, 264–7
Webb, Eric 220, 238–9, 247–8, 249, 255
Weddell, James 13–14, 178, 191
Weddell Sea 14, 178, 185, 204, 207–8, 269
  as base 70
Wegener, Alfred 275–6, 278

whales 21, 32, 47, 161
whaling stations 191, 192
Whetter, Leslie 239–40
Wild, Frank 65, 217, 222–3, 229–30, 246, 253, 267, 285
Wilkes, Charles 19, 180, 226–7
Williams 12
Wilse, Anders Beer 134
Wilson, Edward 74, 88, 260, 292–3
  and Amundsen 103
  and base locations 28–9
  and biological work 92–5
  diary entries 289–91, 292
  geological samples 272–3
  and Mawson 77–8
  and National Antarctic Expedition 32, 36–7
Wilson, Oriana 289, 292
wireless telegraphy 120–1, 224, 240, 248–9, 251–2
woollen clothing 54, 96
World War I 283–5
Wright Brothers 222–3
Wright, C. S. 252

Y
Yamato Yukihara 165
Yasunao, Taizumi 166